PUNCH
& JUDY
POLITICS

PUNCH & JUDY POLITICS

AN INSIDERS' GUIDE TO
PRIME MINISTER'S
QUESTIONS

AYESHA HAZARIKA & TOM HAMILTON

Biteback Publishing

First published in Great Britain in 2018 by
Biteback Publishing Ltd
Westminster Tower
3 Albert Embankment
London SE1 7SP

ISBN 978-1-78590-184-3

10 9 8 7 6 5 4 3 2 1

A CIP catalogue record for this book is available from the British Library.

Set in Adobe Caslon by Adrian McLaughlin

Printed and bound in Great Britain by
CPI Group (UK) Ltd, Croydon CR0 4YY

MIX
Paper from
responsible sources
FSC
www.fsc.org   FSC® C020471

CONTENTS

ACKNOWLEDGEMENTS

This book could not have been written without Ed Miliband and Harriet Harman, who gave both of us roles behind the scenes preparing for PMQs and learning its secrets. It's a huge privilege to have had this unique and very special experience. If we'd been better at our jobs, we might still be helping them prepare for PMQs even now, in government – the non-existence of this book would be one of the least notable features of that alternative political timeline. The book would also not exist without Iain Dale, Olivia Beattie and the rest of the team at Biteback Publishing, who saw the project's potential and stuck with it, and us, through a series of missed deadlines, stand-up tours and an unexpected general election.

We are still astonished at how many leading figures, including several who were on the opposite side to us during our time working on PMQs, generously agreed to give us their time and their insights: former Prime Ministers and Leaders of the Opposition who have taken part in the leaders' joust; MPs who have asked questions, heckled from the back benches or even stood in for their leaders;

advisers who have helped prepare both sides; journalists who have watched from the press gallery and given their instant verdicts; and the Speaker of the House of Commons, who runs the whole show. Several of the people we spoke to for this book have performed more than one of these roles at different stages of their careers; perhaps some will go on to perform more of them in future.

Our thanks go to John Bercow, Gabby Bertin, Theo Bertram, Tony Blair, Kevin Brennan, Vince Cable, David Cameron, Alastair Campbell, Jo Coburn, John Crace, Angela Eagle, Danny Finkelstein, Miranda Green, Bruce Grocott, William Hague, Harriet Harman, Paddy Hennessy, Rob Hutton, Sean Kemp, Neil Kinnock, Ian Lavery, Alison McGovern, Ed Miliband, Joe Murphy, George Osborne, Bob Roberts, Tim Shipman, Dennis Skinner, Anna Soubry, Ann Treneman and John Whittingdale. We're grateful to all of them, and to their staff members who helped arrange interviews, as well as to the current and former politicians and advisers who spoke to us on condition of anonymity: they know who they are, and they know how grateful we are. Throughout the book, for ease of reference it should be assumed that unless otherwise attributed all quotations, including anonymous quotations, are taken from our interviews.

We are grateful, too, to those who kindly agreed to read the manuscript at different points in its gestation. Sarah Coombes, James Hamilton, Rob Hutton, Catherine MacLeod, Dominic Murphy (a former custodian of the David Cameron quotes catalogue, as well as regular compiler of the 'bucket of shit' – see Chapter 3), James Robinson, Jonathan Simons and Josh Simons read drafts of some or all of the book and made invaluable comments. Any errors that remain are, of course, entirely our responsibility.

Ayesha Hazarika would like to thank Iain Dale for being such a good friend since she left politics (even though he's wrong on most things) and Tom for being a great person to work with. Again!

Tom Hamilton would like to thank Sarah Hamilton, for her constant love, support and encouragement in this project as in everything, as well as for her constructive comments on the manuscript; and William, who made no constructive comments at all, on any of it.

INTRODUCTION

It's Wednesday morning. You're the Leader of the Opposition. It's your job to choose one of this week's top political news stories and write six questions to the Prime Minister about it. Not exam questions, not questions that you might ask an expert, but awkward, hostile questions that will put the Prime Minister on the back foot, make her embarrassed and defensive and make you look good. If she can answer them easily, then they're not good questions. If you don't know the answers yourself, then they're almost certainly terrible questions, unless you're absolutely certain that she doesn't know the answers either.

Six different questions. Six interesting questions. Six difficult questions. Think about the relationship between them, so that each one flows logically from the previous one. What does the answer to the first question tell you, and what should you ask next? What is the cumulative effect of the correct answers? Keep them tight: a forensic approach is almost certainly more effective than non-specific bluster.

Do some proper research: if your questions turn out to contain factual errors then you will look ridiculous.

Now, look at the questions again. What are they leading up to? It has to be more than just a demonstration that the Prime Minister doesn't know as much as she ought to about the thing you're asking about. Try to make a bigger political argument at the same time: the government is incompetent, the government's whole ideological approach is wrong, the Prime Minister is out of touch, the Prime Minister is a bad person, the minister responsible for the area you're asking about should resign, whatever you like. Make each question support the argument. You can build the argument a sentence or two at a time, but you need to keep coming back to a question. Keep each one brief.

This is still much too easy. Let's make it more complicated. The Prime Minister isn't just going to answer the questions factually and leave it at that. She wants to attack you, too. So don't just think about what the correct answer to each question is. Think about what else the Prime Minister wants to say, and try to block her. If you're asking about an issue where the opposition has no policies, she will point that out. If you're asking about an issue where the previous government's record was not perfect, she will talk about that. And don't just think about the issue your questions are focused on. Read the papers. What are your own best-known failings as a politician and as a person? What do people, fairly or unfairly, think about you? What is the worst thing people can say about you? What is your party being attacked for at the moment? If your party is divided, if an opposition politician has praised the government or criticised current opposition policy, the Prime Minister will remind everyone. If there is a big political story at the moment which makes the government look good and the opposition look bad, she will mention it – even if it has nothing to do with your line of questioning.

Anticipate the form those attacks on you will take, and think of a couple of responses to each one. Try to make them as funny and cutting as possible. You want to shut these new subjects down, not allow yourself to be side-tracked. Don't look flustered. Get back to the issue you started with. Write another question.

You'll have to ask these questions to the Prime Minister's face, in a room that's too small for the crowd packed into it, with hundreds of people shouting at you so loudly you can barely hear your own voice. These people are all adults, they're your colleagues, and many of them are respected and famous and influential – at other times, you have perfectly civilised meetings and work conversations with them – but right now they're yelling in your face, and neither you nor they think this is odd, or rude. Behind you, hundreds more people will be cheering everything you say and jeering at the Prime Minister – but not all of them like you, some of them want your job and if you do badly they may find it easier to remove you from it.

Above your head, rows of journalists are watching, looking out not just for mistakes but for your tics, your mannerisms, your accent – gathering material for articles whose main purpose is to mock you. The whole thing is being broadcast on live TV and dissected on Twitter. When it's over, TV journalists will read out a balanced selection of tweets from viewers, half of which will say you were great and half of which will say you were useless.

Let's approach the same exercise from the other side. You're the Prime Minister. It's an important and demanding job, and you're pretty busy, but you have to spend half an hour each week answering questions from MPs on anything that's the government's responsibility. You don't know most of the questions in advance. It's your job to know the answers, and if you get any of your facts wrong then you are, by definition, bad at your job. You can't pass and say, 'I don't know.' Some of the questions will be very easy, but a lot of them will be impossible to answer truthfully without either admitting that you are failing in your job or dumping on a colleague. You are absolutely not allowed to lie.

The government is responsible for a lot of things. Some of them are going well and some of them are going badly. Some of them you know about and a lot of them you don't. There are well over 100 ministers, and all of them have specialist and often quite technical areas of policy to deal with, any of which you could be asked about. You are ultimately responsible for all of them, and it is your job to know about all of them, even though you don't and nobody does.

Despite this, you need to be confident and fluent, demonstrating your mastery of detail and your command of the House of Commons Chamber, not only answering the questions but dropping in personal touches about each questioner and their constituency, as well as attacks on your opponents and topical jokes.

Again, you'll be answering them in the same crowded room, in the face of a wall of noise from your opponents, with many of the people behind you who are cheering you on actually willing you to fail, and on live TV. As Prime Minister, you're supposed to be the most powerful person in the country. But you're not in charge here. Perform badly, and your authority will slip.

Prime Minister's Questions is complex, and doing it well on either side takes skill and preparation. As a joust between the Prime Minister and the Leader of the Opposition, with each trying to outwit the other, it carries a special element of risk that's not present in most other political set pieces. Stage-managed events can go wrong – an intruder can disrupt your speech, you can have a coughing fit, or letters can fall off your backdrop, to take just three recent examples – but in general they go the way the political parties want them to. PMQs is dangerous, and it carries a potential for success or failure that few other moments in a political leader's week can match.

PMQs is important to us. We worked together on it in Labour's PMQs prep team for several years. One of us – Ayesha – was a special adviser to Harriet Harman in government until 2010, helping her when she stood in at PMQs for Gordon Brown. She then worked for both Harriet and Ed Miliband, preparing them for PMQs until the end of Harriet's second spell as Labour leader in September 2015. The other – Tom – became the Labour Party's head of research in 2010 and worked on PMQs throughout Ed Miliband's leadership, and continued in the same role under Jeremy Corbyn for his first few months as Labour leader, until February 2016.

Many people loathe PMQs. So, sometimes, did we. It occupied too many of our thoughts and too many of our working hours for too long – writing more questions than the Leader of the Opposition could ever ask, predicting the Prime Minister's answers with varying degrees of accuracy, suggesting jokes that were never delivered, jokes that landed perfectly and jokes that bombed, watching our bosses win and watching our bosses get crushed – for us to think about it with unqualified pleasure. And of course, while we may have played a part in some PMQs victories along the way, we were ultimately on the losing side, and losing hurts. But for all the time we spent on it, and for all the frustration it caused, when we were working on it we would not have wanted to be doing anything else. It is easy to deride PMQs as 'Punch and Judy politics' – the title of this book, and the phrase David Cameron used to describe a style of politics he said he disliked, but found it difficult to escape. But PMQs is still the point of contact between the main party leaders, where their arguments clash and their skills and the skills of the teams beneath them are tested. It matters.

It can be difficult to defend some of what goes on at PMQs – indeed, some of what goes on at PMQs can put people off politics in general. Answers that seem to have little to do with the questions; leaders who are more interested in scoring petty political points than in grappling with difficult policy issues that affect real people's lives; MPs shouting across the Chamber at each other. We won't defend all of it. But part of the point of this book is to argue that PMQs is more interesting than it looks, and that the more you understand about what's going on in it, the more you see. PMQs is more than just a weekly question-and-answer session: when used properly, it is a vital tool of internal management for both government and opposition, helping to identify problems and weaknesses and to find solutions to them. It forces both sides to think hard about where they are about to be attacked, and to make sure that they have the right defences in place.

Parliamentary oral questions, of which PMQs is the most prominent example, sit in their own unique category of political communication. The questions and answers at PMQs are not speeches, although they require some of the rhetorical skills and techniques that speech-making employs: each speaker can only use a maximum of a few sentences at a time, and any attempt to build an argument is inevitably interrupted by the other speaker trying to throw it off course. PMQs is not a debate, although it involves two sides making – usually – opposing arguments. It is not a courtroom cross-examination: while the questioner may try to be as forensic as possible in order to force an embarrassing admission, the Prime Minister in the House of Commons Chamber, unlike a witness in a courtroom, can avoid the question, change the subject or even attack the questioner over an unrelated issue. It is not an interview, despite the question-and-answer format: the two participants in the leaders' exchanges both want the same job, and neither is trying to give the other the opportunity to make themselves look good. It is not a quiz: there are few definitively correct or incorrect answers, and the scores, allocated by watching MPs, journalists and the public, will be subjective, contested and dependent on performance and party political loyalty as much as on facts.

Even though PMQs has been a significant part of the lives of Prime Ministers and Leaders of the Opposition since the 1960s, it's noticeable that most political histories, biographies and memoirs mention it only in passing, if at all. As Tony Blair told us, 'If you describe your premiership in policy terms it can be a footnote, but if you describe it in personal terms it's quite a big part of your time as Prime Minister' (Blair's own memoirs, more personal and less policy-focused than most senior politicians' autobiographies, are an exception, giving PMQs nearly five pages). This book is partly an attempt to fill the gap, and to do justice to an event which, love it or hate it, dominates the working lives of our most senior politicians.

Margaret Thatcher, who devoted around eight hours a week to preparing for PMQs and for whom the PMQs process was, as we

were told by one of her close advisers, an essential part of running
her government, hardly mentioned it at all in her own memoirs. But
on one of the few occasions on which she did, she made clear how
important she thought it was:

> It is Questions to the Prime Minister every Tuesday and Thurs-
> day which are the real test of your authority in the House, your
> standing with your party, your grip of policy and of the facts
> to justify it. No head of government anywhere in the world
> has to face this sort of regular pressure and many go to great
> lengths to avoid it; no head of government, as I would some-
> times remind those at summits, is as accountable as the British
> Prime Minister.[1]

It is not at all difficult to imagine her making this point to her fellow
world leaders.

In fact, PMQs has often been a source of great fascination abroad:
it is broadcast regularly on the American channel C-SPAN, and has
been watched by several US Presidents. George H. W. Bush said
in 1991, 'I count my blessings for the fact I don't have to go into
that pit that John Major stands in, nose to nose with the opposition
all yelling at each other.'[2] Tony Blair says, 'I used to have this
conversation with American Presidents about what's it like doing
PMQs, they were always fascinated by it, and would it be a good
idea to try and introduce it here, and I used to say, "Absolutely not,
if you don't have to do it, don't do it."' Bill Clinton, Blair told us,
'used to watch it all, and he could have done it, by the way, because
he's very quick'.

In writing this book we have drawn on our own experience of working on, and what sometimes felt like living for, PMQs, as well as the insights of many other participants and professional observers. We want to use those insights to take you through PMQs. What goes into thinking about what questions to ask and how to ask them? What is happening in the Leader of the Opposition's office and in 10 Downing Street in the run-up to 12 noon on a Wednesday? How can the Prime Minister really be expected to answer questions on everything? We will look at how the joust works, how both sides work out their best attacks and best defences – and best jokes – and predict when and where to use them. We will try to show you how it feels to be in a packed House of Commons Chamber while PMQs is going on. We will look at the supporting cast and what they are doing: the backbenchers asking their own questions and contributing to the cacophony; the Speaker trying to keep order; the journalists looking on. And we will assess the point of the whole exercise: what is it good for, does it tell us anything useful about those who lead us or seek to lead us, and is it really worth having at all?

But first, we want to look at the history of PMQs: where it comes from, how it has changed, and how it came to occupy the central place in British political and parliamentary life that it now has.

I

EVOLUTION

Prime Minister's Questions was not created out of nothing: the weekly event we know today has gradually faded into existence. Depending on how you measure it and which features you think are most important, PMQs dates back to 1997, or 1993, or 1989, or 1979, or 1975, or 1961. Each of these years saw the introduction of a feature of PMQs which was revolutionary – or, at least, noticeably evolutionary – at the time but now seems natural and indispensable. And each of these new elements made a big difference to what PMQs was and, unintentionally, enabled what it has become.

In 1961 Prime Minister's Questions was formalised as a regular scheduled parliamentary event. In 1975, MPs started tabling open questions, enabling them to ask supplementary questions on whatever they wanted, introducing a new element of both surprise and topicality. In 1979, the new Prime Minister, Margaret Thatcher, announced that she would answer all the questions at PMQs herself, instead of transferring some questions on given issues to the Cabinet ministers responsible for those issues. In 1989, Parliament was tele-vised for the first time, increasing the audience for parliamentary debates in general and, given its profile and bite-sized length, PMQs in particular. This development built on the introduction in 1978 of radio broadcasts from the House of Commons – both innovations strongly resisted by traditionalists. In 1993, Labour leader John Smith decided that, unlike his predecessors, he would consistently take his full allocation of questions – three per fifteen-minute session, or six per week – creating a precedent that subsequent Leaders of the Opposition have generally followed. And in 1997, the incoming Prime Minister, Tony Blair, reconfigured PMQs from twice-weekly fifteen-minute sessions at 3.15 p.m. on Tuesdays and Thursdays to a single weekly thirty-minute session at 3 p.m. on Wednesdays; the half-hour slot was moved to 12 noon at the beginning of 2003.

Although the fiftieth anniversary of PMQs was marked in 2011, Prime Ministers have answered questions in the House of Commons for far longer than that. The key 1961 development, commemorated fifty years later, was to give questions to the Prime Minister their own permanent, timetabled slot. Before 1881, all ministers including the Prime Minister answered questions in whatever order they were asked on any day when they were present. Then, as a concession to the 72-year-old Prime Minister William Gladstone, it was agreed that questions to him should come last on the day's list so that he could come in late.[3] The effect on his fitness was evidently profound, given that the last of his four spells as Prime Minister did not end until 1894, when he was eighty-four years old.

Even with efforts to accommodate their needs, Prime Ministers could not be forced to prioritise the House of Commons: David Lloyd George, preoccupied with European statesmanship immediately after the First World War, did not answer questions for a whole year.[4] Asking questions of the Prime Minister was not always the priority of MPs anyway: 'few saw much point in eliciting monosyllabic replies from Mr Attlee'.[5] It was the health of another relatively elderly and infirm Prime Minister, Winston Churchill, which prompted the next significant timetable change in 1953, with an agreement that he should answer questions only on Tuesdays and Thursdays. Churchill's successors Anthony Eden and Harold Macmillan may have been much younger and fitter, but they both stuck with this convention, and who can blame them?[6]

Despite reforms to increase the length of time spent on questions, and to ensure that questions to the Prime Minister began no later than number fifty-one, then forty-five, then forty on the list for the day, it was common for the question session to run out of time before the Prime Minister had answered them all. Sometimes, he did not have time to answer any. This caused understandable irritation among MPs. On 6 December 1960 Harold Macmillan wrote in his diary:

> PQs [he never refers to them as 'PMQs' in his diary] were scarcely reached – another protest and demand that my questions shd start at 3.15. I hope still to avoid having to agree. In some ways it would suit me; but I think it will only lead to fewer and fewer questions being got through and longer and longer supplementaries.[7]

In July 1961 the House of Commons accepted a recommendation by the Procedure Committee to experiment with a fixed fifteen-minute slot for the Prime Minister to answer questions on Tuesdays and Thursdays. Macmillan may have recorded his misgivings in his diary, but he told the House that 'this arrangement suits me much better because I know when to come here'.[8] Three months later the Speaker announced that the experiment had been a success, and that 'in these circumstances the Prime Minister is willing that it should be continued'.[9]

The first ever question to the Prime Minister in PMQs' newly permanent slot, on 24 October 1961, looks at first glance to be a quite exceptionally dull one, and it received what looks like an equally dull answer. Hansard records it as follows:

> Mr Shinwell asked the Prime Minister whether the statement
> by the Minister of Transport during his visit to the Scandinavian
> countries, about government policy concerning subsidies to help
> the shipbuilding industry and shipping, represents the policy of
> Her Majesty's Government.
> The Prime Minister (Mr Harold Macmillan): Yes, Sir.[10]

We'll come back to this first question later – there's more going on here than you think. At this first PMQs the Leader of the Opposition, Hugh Gaitskell, did not ask a question at all. It has got more interesting since then.

Once PMQs had been given a permanent, fixed, timetabled slot, there was no going back. MPs would never again accept a situation in which they could not be sure there would be time to question the

Prime Minister in any given week. In its fifteen-minute Tuesday and Thursday slots and now the thirty-minute Wednesday slot, PMQs was and is a regular beat in the rhythm of the parliamentary week. But it took time for it to be seen as the opportunity it is today for *any* MP to hold the Prime Minister to account. Labour MP Dennis Skinner told us that when he first entered the Commons in 1970, most MPs never even tried to ask questions at PMQs: 'They had a little coterie of people who used to do Prime Minister's Questions, and people on both sides used to say, "Don't, this is a minefield, it's difficult." You invaded territory that was occupied by about twenty, thirty people on both sides, like a club. There weren't many people put in.' Skinner says that the competition to table a question was so low that on one occasion 'Eric Heffer had two in one day, and it was only a quarter of an hour'.

The next big change in how PMQs worked made it much more interesting and much less predictable. In 1975 Labour MP John Golding asked what looked on the face of it like a very boring question to the Prime Minister: 'if he would state his engagements for April 29th'. As Tam Dalyell later wrote,

> By asking a purely formal question, acceptable to the Table Office and the stringent rules of parliamentary order, John Golding had outflanked the vetting system on questions of the Prime Minister and gained the opportunity to put a supplementary question on almost any aspect of policy which might be on his mind. The genie was out of the bottle. Pandora's Box was opened. From now on MPs could ask the Prime Minister about virtually anything under the political sun.[11]

In fact, it isn't entirely clear that Golding was the first to do this, or that it was his idea rather than that of the parliamentary clerks – and as it happened the particular question Dalyell cites ended up being answered in writing, not at PMQs, anyway.[12] But we like the idea of ascribing it to Golding, author of *Hammer of the Left*, the classic account of Labour's battles against Militant in the 1980s, and the holder of the record for the longest ever Commons speech, with an eleven-hour effort on the Telecommunications Bill in 1983; since it was a standing committee debate, and not in the Chamber, he was able to take breaks for lunch and dinner.[13]

Golding's innovation – if it was his – was probably the most significant of all the changes to PMQs discussed in this chapter. Before the development of the open 'engagements question', all questions to the Prime Minister, like all questions to all ministers, had to be closed questions on specific topics. So for example, here are the first few questions tabled to Harold Wilson on 13 February 1968, a fairly ordinary PMQs session for the time:

Q1. Mr Ridley asked the Prime Minister what proposals he has for celebrating Human Rights Year.

Q2. Mr Ridley asked the Prime Minister if he will appoint a minister to coordinate the work of the Department of Economic Affairs and the Ministry of Labour with regard to the pay norm for incomes policy.

Q3. Sir Knox Cunningham asked the Prime Minister if he will make a statement about his visits to the President of the United States of America and the Prime Minister of Canada.

Q4. Mr Longden asked the Prime Minister if he will give instructions to ministers in the Cabinet to refuse to appear on television programmes whose primary object is entertainment; and if he will seek to confine ministerial appearances on television to occasions when they wish to explain government policy to the nation.

Q5. Mr Blaker asked the Prime Minister if he will make a statement on his recent consultations in the United States of America.

Q6. Mr Onslow asked the Prime Minister if he will instruct all members of the government that any legislation introduced by them must in future include in the explanatory memorandum an estimate of the effect of such legislation upon the size of the civil service.

Q7. Mr Bruce-Gardyne asked the Prime Minister whether the public speech of the Chancellor of the Exchequer on television, on Tuesday, 16 January, on the economic situation, represents the policy of Her Majesty's Government.[14]

Each of these questions is closed. Each one has a relatively narrow focus, and deals with an issue the Prime Minister was personally responsible for. After the Prime Minister's answer to each one, the original questioner had the opportunity to ask a relevant supplementary question. Any other MP who also wished to ask a supplementary, which must again be relevant to the topic of the original question, was then called by the Speaker. Each of the questions on the order paper, then, led to an exchange involving four or five different MPs (except question four on stopping ministers appearing on TV, which appears to have been a personal bugbear of the Conservative MP Gilbert Longden – nobody else bothered to ask a supplementary on that). Harold Wilson didn't know exactly what supplementaries were coming, but he knew roughly what he was up against, and could make sure he was briefed accordingly.

The 'engagements question' has several key advantages to MPs – and disadvantages to the Prime Minister. It can be tabled long in advance, before MPs have given any thought to what they would actually like to ask about. This is particularly important for a popular event like PMQs where there are far more MPs who want to ask questions than the length of the session will allow, so that any time spent devising a substantive question has a good chance of being wasted. It is impossible for the Prime Minister to transfer to another minister, since it is self-evidently a question about the Prime Minister's personal responsibilities and nobody else's, and so any supplementary question, whatever the subject, will have to be answered by the Prime Minister too. It provides a new element of surprise, because the Prime Minister can have no idea what the supplementary will be about, unless the MP decides to tell her in advance. And it enables PMQs to be topical, because supplementaries can cover breaking news stories right up to the moment MPs stand up to ask them.

There are other ways of devising questions which the Prime Minister cannot transfer, such as an MP asking whether the Prime Minister has any plans to visit his constituency: the MP can then ask a supplementary question about whatever local issue he likes, without risking it being transferred to the relevant minister. This is not as good as the engagements question, because the supplementary will still have to be about something to do with the constituency, so lots of possible topics will be out of bounds. In 1971, Dennis Skinner found an ingenious variant on the constituency question when he wanted to highlight the amount of time Edward Heath, a keen sailor, spent on his yacht. He tabled a question asking the Prime Minister 'if he will pay an official visit to Cowes'[15] – not in Skinner's own constituency. He told us: 'There was a big argument as to whether it was ironic, in the Table Office, because they said, "It's irony." I said, "Well, if I said pay an official visit to somewhere else in Britain, you'd agree to it." And it got a laugh before I even opened my mouth.'

The apparently dull question to Harold Macmillan about shipping policy quoted above, the first one ever to be asked in the new permanent timetabled PMQs slot, was itself designed to be untransferable. By asking the Prime Minister whether a statement by the Transport Secretary represented government policy – that is, whether Macmillan was prepared to endorse a statement by one of his ministers – Emanuel Shinwell was able to avoid having it transferred back to the Transport Secretary, and therefore to attempt to embarrass Macmillan with a supplementary question about a possible contradiction over subsidies to the shipping and shipbuilding industries. It's a convoluted way of going about it, though.

Even after the engagements question became widespread, and the most common question tabled in every PMQs session, the Prime Minister still had to answer it every time. The standard formula at the start of PMQs, even now, is 'This morning I had meetings with ministerial colleagues and others, and in addition to my duties in this House I shall have further such meetings later today.' This is a notably uninformative answer to a question nobody really cares about in the first place. Subsequently, MPs would stand up and say the number of their question, and the Prime Minister would respond, 'I refer the honourable gentleman/lady to the answer I gave some moments ago.' When we first started paying attention to PMQs in the 1990s, we heard these words so often that we started to think of them as John Major's catchphrase. Only then would the supplementary, the real point of the exercise, be asked. In a fifteen-minute session, these formulaic responses would take up a significant amount of time, cutting into the space available for actual questions. As Matthew Parris wrote in a parliamentary sketch in November 1996, 'Along with the pauses and the getting up and sitting down, it consumes some eleven seconds. The initial diary recitation consumes some fifteen seconds. Simple arithmetic suggests that Major has now spent nearly six hours of his life in bland recitations of his day's diary, or referring his Hon Friends to the reply he gave some moments ago.'[16]

It was only in 1997, as part of Tony Blair's wider overhaul of PMQs, that this was rationalised so that after the very first question MPs could just stand up and put their supplementary question as soon as they were called.[17] Today, submitting an engagements question has been simplified to the extent that MPs now merely have to sign a form containing the letter 'E'. The whips on both sides hand these forms out to try to make sure that as many of their party's own MPs as possible are in the draw. Labour MP Kevin Brennan describes Labour whip Jessica Morden as 'the principal purveyor of "E"s'.

The unpredictability of PMQs is a big part of what makes it so daunting to Prime Ministers, and the reason it needs so much preparation: when you don't know what's coming, you have to prepare for everything. It is the open questions that make it so unpredictable. But closed questions on a particular, defined subject, now almost

unheard of at PMQs, have their perils too. With closed questions –
still the main type of question at departmental question times in the
Commons – the minister has to keep taking supplementary questions
on the same topic, from all sides, until the Speaker decides to move on.

The sustained pressure this can lead to is almost impossible to
replicate in the modern PMQs. Aside from the leaders' exchanges,
questions do not come in sequences of two or more. The fact
that questions have no set topic means that after a difficult question
from an opposition MP, the Speaker will always call a government
MP next, on whom the Prime Minister can rely to change the subject.
Before open questions became the norm, this release valve did not
exist. Indeed, throughout the 1960s and early 1970s Prime Ministers
frequently had to deal with supplementary after supplementary on
the same issue, often with the Leader of the Opposition coming in
towards the end if it appeared they were struggling.

In his diary for 5 July 1960 – before the creation of the dedicated
fifteen-minute PMQs slot – Harold Macmillan records:

> PQs went very badly for me. There was a sudden storm about U2
> [a US spy plane which allegedly flew reconnaissance missions
> from British bases], arising from a supplementary, and I allowed
> myself to be taken by surprise and rattled by Brown, Healey,
> Silverman, Warbey, like a lot of hounds. When he saw it was a
> good run, Gaitskell joined in. I did _not_ manage it at all well.[18]

Hansard shows that Macmillan was asked a total of nine increasingly
hostile supplementaries on the same topic, without a break, an ordeal
for the Prime Minister that simply could not happen today.[19]

The growth of the open question made the next significant development in PMQs almost inevitable. The number of topics that are unavoidably the responsibility of the Prime Minister alone is relatively small, so Prime Ministers could justifiably transfer questions to other ministers, leaving PMQs to focus on a fairly narrow set of subjects. Before the 1960s, most questions to the Prime Minister were on foreign affairs.[20] Once open questions, with their unpredictable supplementaries, were on the table, the number of questions the Prime Minister could choose to transfer went down, and the number of subjects the Prime Minister had to be briefed on went up. Eventually, transferring questions became pointless.

At the same time, it also transformed the role of the Leader of the Opposition at PMQs. When questions were closed, and invariably tabled by others, the Leader of the Opposition had a small number of known topics to choose from when deciding when or whether to ask a supplementary question or questions, and had only a limited opportunity to introduce up-to-the-minute new information. In fact, PMQs could only sometimes, by coincidence, cover what we would now think of as 'the issue of the day'. With open questions, and with no restrictions at all on the topic of supplementaries, the element of surprise expanded hugely, as did the ability of the Leader of the Opposition to set the PMQs agenda rather than following a backbencher's lead. The ability of PMQs to include a self-contained duel between the main party leaders, on an issue of the Leader of the Opposition's choosing, is a direct result of the 'engagements question' becoming the dominant question tabled to the Prime Minister by backbenchers.

In July 1979 Margaret Thatcher announced that although she retained the right to transfer questions to her departmental ministers where they related to 'detailed constituency matters', in general she expected 'to answer substantive questions that raise issues of general significance and national interest, if Honourable Members wish to ask them',[21] whatever the subject. Her predecessor, James Callaghan, had only rarely transferred questions, making Thatcher's announcement less of a watershed than some have implied it was. But Thatcher boasted, accurately, that she was going further than Callaghan by transferring none,[22] and she stuck to her commitment. Neil Kinnock, Leader of the Opposition for most of Thatcher's premiership, thinks that 'Thatcher decided to take Prime Minister's Questions seriously, because having flagged badly behind Jim as leader of her party and potential leader of the country this must have been seen by her advisers as a way of demonstrating capability and strength.'

Thatcher's decision not to transfer questions to the relevant departmental minister was not as brave as it looks, and given the increase in open questions she was bowing to the inevitable: continuing a trend rather than making a new departure. By the end of the 1970s no Prime Minister was ever going to get away with the approach taken by Sir Alec Douglas-Home, who, when Harold Wilson asked him about the UK's trade figures in March 1964, simply refused to answer on the grounds that he had not been given notice of the question.[23] Refusing to answer questions makes the Prime Minister look weak; being willing to take all of them doesn't just make her *look* stronger; it really *does* strengthen her, at the expense of her departmental ministers. As early as 1972, we find complaints that 'The increasing use of "peg" questions to the Prime Minister, on to which are hung supplementaries about anything the MP cares to raise, blurs the concept of individual ministerial responsibility. The Prime Minister is made to appear responsible for all the actions of the government.'[24] This process reached its logical conclusion under Margaret Thatcher, and has stayed there ever since.

The real impact of making PMQs cover any and every possible topic was the consolidation of the power and reach of the Prime Minister's office. If the Prime Minister is prepared to answer questions about anything and everything, then the Prime Minister must be briefed about anything and everything. If the Prime Minister is accountable to Parliament for the performance of every department, then every department must make sure the Prime Minister is aware of how well it is performing. You can't keep secrets from a Prime Minister who is about to be asked in public about all your secrets.

This is the hidden power of PMQs: it doesn't just make the Prime Minister accountable to Parliament, it also makes every minister and every department accountable to the Prime Minister. It extends Downing Street's tentacles across Whitehall, giving it a legitimate pretext to know about everything that might be going wrong. It even functions as a form of ministerial performance management. This is why Thatcher resisted attempts by Bernard Weatherill, elected as Speaker in 1983, to 'restore the former practice whereby questions of detail were deflected to the departmental minister concerned, leaving the Prime Minister to answer for broad strategy … Mrs Thatcher liked open questions precisely because they enabled her to display her command of detail: the fact that she might be asked about anything gave her the excuse she needed to keep tabs on every department.'[25] As Peter Hennessy put it, 'It was an irony that an increase in prime ministerial accountability to Parliament after 1961 strengthened the possibility of an overmighty premiership.'[26]

In 1965, Tam Dalyell visited Harold Wilson in No. 10. 'Apart from the "Garden Girl" typists,' he wrote, 'the Prime Minister's staff appeared to be his personal secretary Lady Falkender, his press secretary Sir Trevor Lloyd-Hughes, and the cat. Twenty years later [*sic*] I witnessed Tony Blair's Downing Street, bustling with special advisers – a veritable parallel government to the great departments of state.'[27] Dalyell ascribed the growth of this parallel government, a wholly negative development as he saw it, directly to the new requirement for accountability arising from a changed PMQs. Thatcher wrote in her memoirs that 'each department was, naturally, expected to provide the facts and a possible reply on points that might arise. It was a good test of the alertness and efficiency of the Cabinet minister in charge of the department whether information arrived late – or arrived at all; whether it was accurate or wrong, comprehensible or riddled with jargon.'[28]

A prize like this for a Prime Minister can make the ordeal worthwhile, as David Cameron recognised. Answering a question *about* PMQs *at* PMQs in July 2015, he said: 'For all its faults, and there are many, I would say that it has two important points: it puts the Prime Minister on the spot to the public, but it also puts the government on the spot to the Prime Minister – needing to know issues right across every department before coming to the House at twelve o'clock on a Wednesday is an important mechanism of accountability.'[29]

Theo Bertram, an adviser on PMQs to Tony Blair and Gordon Brown, has written about the scene in the Cabinet Room on a Tuesday evening or Wednesday morning where 'briefing documents from every department are coldly laid out like dead bodies on a slab in a mortuary. Each stack of papers contains the evidence of some government or political failure that might be raised in the Chamber.' The No. 10 advisers go through emails from government departments on Wednesday mornings, trying to spot 'the cryptically casual comment in a sub-clause from a special adviser, the "just-wanted-to-let-you-know-about-one-small-thing" from a principal private secretary, or the matter-of-fact group email from some cheery researcher in the Whips Office who is just doing what his boss tells him: all calculated to ensure the sender can later say truthfully that the Prime Minister had been *informed* of this problem *before* PMQs'. There are politely threatening calls to officials who haven't provided the information the PMQs briefing team needs from them: 'Look at the clock: in thirty minutes we will talk to the Prime Minister. Shall we tell her that there is a problem and that you are withholding the solution from her?'[30]

The possibility of being asked questions on everything led Margaret Thatcher, and her successors, to ensure that her briefing book had everything covered. As Neil Kinnock remembers, 'She developed the technique of turning up to Prime Minister's Questions with this massive compendium to answers on everything. I mean, previous leaders maybe starting with Heath had brought in files, but what she brought in with her was at least twice or three times as thick as anything anybody had ever taken in before.'

The next important development in the evolution of PMQs was to allow it to be seen by a larger audience than the one in the Chamber itself. The idea of broadcasting Parliament was under discussion almost as soon as the technology was available, but it was a long time before anything could actually be agreed upon. Most MPs were hostile, for reasons ranging from the technical problems created by putting cameras and TV lighting in the House of Commons Chamber, to fears that some members might try to communicate with the public outside rather than their fellow MPs or, as Sir Godfrey Nicholson put it in 1962, that it might 'encourage the exhibitionism and vanity which are occupational hazards of politics'.[31]

Radio broadcasting of Parliament, including PMQs, began in April 1978, although live coverage of PMQs stopped again in 1980. It was not universally regarded as a positive development. According to Charles Moore's biography of Margaret Thatcher, her advisers were concerned that the broadcasts 'had made life even more difficult for a woman leader because the public could hear her shrieking to make herself audible over the hubbub'. Labour, meanwhile, found Thatcher's first broadcast PMQs very encouraging, with James Callaghan's head of policy, Bernard Donoughue, writing in his diary that 'she looked very pale and tense and sounded harsh. This was in some ways a trial run for the election, and we came away feeling very confident.'[32]

The Conservative MP John Stokes, arguing in 1985 against the televising of Parliament, said that 'the [radio] broadcasting of Prime Minister's Question Time has harmed the occasion and damaged the institution of Parliament. Why? Because of the gladiatorial nature of that quarter of an hour twice a week, which is by no means typical of how we spend most of our time.'[33] Much, in fact most, parliamentary business is indeed less raucous, less crowded, more technical and, frankly, duller than PMQs, and so PMQs does give a misleading picture of what MPs get up to most of the time.

Parliament continued to reject being televised throughout almost the whole of the 1980s, with Conservative MPs taking a lead from the Prime Minister herself. Margaret Thatcher 'thought it would do her personally no good. Gordon Reece and Bernard Ingham both tried to persuade her that she would only gain from being seen trouncing Kinnock at the dispatch box twice a week; but she was afraid she would come over as strident (as well as being seen wearing glasses to read her brief) and feared that the BBC would edit the exchanges to her disadvantage.'[34] MPs voted narrowly against a motion to televise Parliament in November 1985, after a debate in which the Labour MP Joe Ashton warned that 'politicians will ultimately end up as the nation's clowns, portrayed as they are in *Spitting Image*', and that

> Every Tuesday and Thursday we shall have 'The Maggie and Neil Show – Scrap of the Day' – an everyday story of people having a bash at each other. Prime Minister's Question Time would become another soap opera, like the 'Buckingham Dallas' with Prince Charles and Princess Diana. It used to be said that religion was the opium of the people. We now have the 'soapium' of the people, and the House will become yet another soap opera.[35]

Thatcher made her opposition clear, telling the BBC, 'I've thought about it very deeply. The Commons is a small, intimate chamber; those heavy lights, the heat, I think it would be dreadful.'[36] In contrast Kinnock supported the idea equally strongly: 'I thought you couldn't have democracy and technology and not put the two together, just ludicrous.' In 1988 MPs voted to televise the House of Commons, and in November 1989 proceedings were shown for the first time.

The Conservative MP Roger Gale wrote a letter to the Prime Minister before the first televised session to give her advice on how to change her performance to make sure she came across well on television, with tips including 'Ministers should speak only at microphone level and never seek to "top" heckling from the opposition: this may sometimes work in the Chamber but will sound – and look – strident on television' and 'To give the impression of looking the opponent – Leader of the Opposition or spokesman – in the eye, it may be necessary to "cheat" the eyeline over the head to Camera 2.' A note from Thatcher's private secretary Dominic Morris suggested that MPs should be encouraged to be animated in their support, so that the viewing public could tell they were impressed: 'It looks much better if, rather than sitting solemn, they show obvious approval (as did Mr [Kenneth] Baker on one occasion) when telling points are made. That clearly applies generally to the support which colleagues give to any frontbench spokesmen.'[37]

Kinnock was less well prepared: 'What I didn't do is even think about mastering the technique of leaning into the microphone and recognising that my voice would carry whatever the noise in the place, and that was a serious mistake on my part. Thatcher got it a long time before I understood it. She had a lot of coaching in any case, but I should have realised that if you leaned in and spoke firmly into the microphone then your voice would carry.'

Nick Robinson writes that Thatcher's preparation was thorough, with a rehearsal in the Chamber, new TV-friendly make-up and notes in larger type which she could read without her glasses. But 'though she produced a confident performance she was seen shuffling through her papers, destroying the impression given to radio listeners that she carried all the relevant facts in her head. Despite the bigger type she still had to reach for her glasses to read out key quotes.'[38]

Television changed Parliament, and PMQs, for ever. For a start, it gave both sides the ability to have their best lines shown on the evening news and seen by millions; which meant that for both sides it was worthwhile – even more so than before – to have some good lines. For the leaders, PMQs was now a high-profile public-facing event. They had to look the part, sound the part and, most importantly, deliver pithy, witty, powerful political messages. You don't need soundbites if nobody is listening; you don't need to make sure your best line will work properly in a TV package if nobody is there to clip it. As Kinnock says, 'To the extent that we spent time on preparing for Prime Minister's Questions, a fraction of the time that Thatcher spent on it, we were acknowledging the importance of the fact that the words were being broadcast.'

The need to make sure PMQs would work on TV could, at worst, lead to a focus on the scripted clip at the expense of the argument. John Whittingdale, who was working for Thatcher when the cameras first came in, remembers that especially in the days before 24-hour news, 'On Tuesdays and Thursdays the chances were that the six o'clock and ten o'clock [news bulletins] would carry the clip from Prime Minister's Questions, and there wouldn't be any other opportunity for them, that would be the only time in the entire day when they had got the Prime Minister on record, so inevitably they used to carry it.' Alastair Campbell, Tony Blair's press secretary in both opposition and government, told us, 'There definitely did come a point where we had a sense that both the Leader of the Opposition and the Prime Minister were delivering the clip in the last question. It got a bit tedious.'

Television adds to the pressure on modern leaders to look the part. Jeremy Corbyn's unconventional dress sense was part of his

appeal during his leadership campaigns, but it was highlighted by
David Cameron during a PMQs exchange in February 2016. When a
Labour MP heckled 'Ask your mother' (Cameron's mother had been
revealed to have signed an anti-cuts petition), Cameron responded,
'I know what my mother would say. She would look across the dispatch box and say, "Put on a proper suit, do up your tie and sing the
national anthem."'[39] Corbyn's Twitter account responded later in the
day with a quote it attributed, not necessarily accurately, to Einstein:
'If most of us are ashamed of shabby clothes & shoddy furniture
let us be more ashamed of shabby ideas & shoddy philosophies.'[40]
But it wasn't long before Corbyn was taking Cameron's advice and
wearing smarter suits. During the 2017 election campaign *The Sun*
quoted a senior Labour source as saying, 'Jeremy looks good in a blue
suit, and we're pleased with how he's coming across. Presentation is
important.'[41] By the end of the year, he was on the cover of *GQ*.

Politicians of both sexes are used to getting the full works at the
TV studios: being made up by the miracle-worker Brenda before *The
Andrew Marr Show* is a rite of passage. And since the Chamber is,
among other things, a well-lit TV studio it makes sense for leaders to
get made up before big appearances – even if it is just a light dusting
of face powder. Tony Blair was one of the first male politicians to
realise this, and Gyles Brandreth, then a Conservative MP, told his
diary in March 1997 how his party attempted to exploit it:

> When I told the PM a few weeks back that I was sure Blair
> wore make-up at PMQs he seemed genuinely surprised. 'We
> need to give that greater currency, don't you think?' So we're
> going to have a go tomorrow, either with a planted question,

'Can my Right Honourable Friend take this opportunity to salute the cosmetics industry in the United Kingdom etc...' or by having someone shout out as Blair rises: 'He's wearing make-up!' Yes, it's come to this.[42]

The following day, at John Major's last ever PMQs as Prime Minister, 'our absurd cries of "He's wearing make-up" bounced off Blair unheeded'.[43]

For Ed Miliband – who faced a huge amount of comment about his looks, much of it rather mean-spirited – getting his make-up done was an important part of the PMQs ritual. This normally happened at about 11 a.m., just when the pressure was ratcheting up, and always by one of his female staff. By this time Ed was often losing confidence in the entire set of questions and political strategy that we had all slaved over for the last three hours, and the poor make-up woman would have to carry on delicately applying under-eye concealer or dabbing powder on his nose, while Ed was frantically asking the rest of the team for more information, statistics or detail. Sometimes he would suddenly ask the staffer applying his make-up what she thought of the whole thing. There would be an expectant pause before – sympathetic to the hours everyone else had put in – she would invariably reply, 'I think you're in great shape, Ed.' We would breathe a sigh of relief until the next 'new' person entered the room and was asked whether we should start again from scratch. Sometimes there would be a discussion about the quality of Ed's make-up – mainly from the male media advisers – that it was too light or too heavy or that the circles under Ed's eyes looked too dark. However, none of them ever offered to have a go themselves. The same process was going on on the other side, it turns out, with the same expectation about who was responsible: Gabby Bertin, David Cameron's press secretary, told us that she would occasionally apply make-up to the Prime Minister's face just before PMQs, but 'the thing is the research hasn't been done into it, so he hasn't gone down to the Clinique counter and had a match, so on the rare occasions we put make-up on I would generally be there with my own compact. It wasn't ideal.' In this case, there were definitely girls' jobs and boys' jobs.

The use of make-up by the main party leaders is one reflection of the fact that PMQs is now an important showcase for both of them. This has not always been the case. In 2000 Tam Dalyell, as part of a hell-in-a-handcart polemic about centralisation and the shift in power from Parliament to the government and political party machines, wrote a line about PMQs which, from any modern observer of British politics, will induce an amazed double-take:

> Harold Macmillan, in his retirement at Birch Grove, testified
> that he had often felt physically sick at lunch time on Tuesdays
> and Thursdays preparing for the ordeal of twice-weekly Prime
> Minister's Questions. Prime Minister's Questions were a serious
> matter. How he answered was a genuine measure of the govern-
> ment's stock, and when, once every three weeks or so, Hugh
> Gaitskell, as Leader of the Opposition, asked a question, it was
> an event.[44]

Every three weeks or so! The idea that the Leader of the Opposition might stand up at PMQs to ask the Prime Minister a question so infrequently seems hilarious, so central are the leaders' exchanges to

PMQs now. But there has never been a requirement that the Leader of the Opposition asks any questions at all: it is an entitlement, not a duty. Not all were as relaxed as Gaitskell; Harold Wilson was highly energetic at PMQs in his first spell as Leader of the Opposition. For example, he spent PMQs on Tuesday 12 May 1964 bouncing up and down in a state of hyperactivity, asking one supplementary question to the Prime Minister, Sir Alec Douglas-Home, on a question about trade with Cuba,[45] another on United Nations peacekeeping operations,[46] and another on the European Economic Community.[47] Given Douglas-Home's weakness at the dispatch box, it's no surprise that Wilson wanted to ask him as many questions as he could.

The fact that the PMQs duel between the main party leaders was not yet formalised into the expectation that it would fill the Leader of the Opposition's allocation of questions does not mean that it did not matter, or that the two leaders did not take it seriously. Norman Shrapnel, *The Guardian*'s parliamentary correspondent in the 1960s and 1970s, wrote that 'when Heath and Wilson got up each Tuesday and Thursday for their question-time bout, the parliamentary spectators were excited but also rather disconcerted to find that they meant it. Here for once were two statesmen who were not pretending to loathe each other. They really did.'[48] In January 1972 Wilson took it too far, with Labour MPs orchestrating a riotous demonstration over the fact that unemployment had passed the million mark, which caused the Speaker to suspend the sitting and cancel PMQs entirely. '"You ought to be ashamed of yourself," shouted Dennis Skinner as he shook his fist in Heath's face. "You're better fitted to cross the channel and suck President Pompidou's backside."'[49] According to Shrapnel,

Ted Heath was unruffled, handing his portfolio to the parliamentary private secretary sitting behind him and walking out
past the Speaker's chair with his small, calm, emergency smile.
Later – it was the sort of telling gesture he was good at – he put
out an unruffled statement regretting that the angry charade and
its consequences should have prevented him from answering
questions on all sorts of urgent matters, like unemployment.[50]

Even though Leaders of the Opposition could ask up to three
questions twice a week if they wished, this often did not happen
in practice. John Bercow, Speaker of the House of Commons since
2009, noted in a speech to the Centre for Parliamentary Studies in
2010 that

> Margaret Thatcher, when Leader of the Opposition, averaged
> only 1.6 interventions a session. This was partly because if she
> was due to speak in a parliamentary debate on a Tuesday or
> Thursday she frequently would not participate in PMQs at
> all but also because her team came to the view that if she had
> not drawn parliamentary blood in the first two questions then
> it would be counterproductive to strain the patience of the
> House with a third one.[51]

Nobody thinks like this any more, but it seems a perfectly sensible
approach. According to Neil Kinnock, Thatcher 'didn't offer any
serious challenge to Jim [Callaghan], partly because Jim spoke from
a great height, and generally with a very avuncular tone, and she
couldn't find her feet in any case. She was also of course both within

and without the Conservative Party very unpopular, everybody forgets that. And Prime Minister's Questions, although more important than in the '50s and early '60s, was still not regarded to be the gladiatorial contest worthy of airtime.' As for Callaghan, 'At the first PLP [Parliamentary Labour Party meeting] after the '79 election, he said that he hoped the PLP understood that he wasn't going to try and get up in every Prime Minister's Questions, only when the situation warranted it or there were issues that needed to be pressed, and I don't recall anybody being upset about that. As it turned out, of course, that isn't what happened. He got up every time.'

Kinnock himself, although often using his full allocation, was aware of the disadvantages of doing so: 'By the time I became leader it was not usual but certainly not unknown for the Leader of the Opposition to ask three questions. But certainly in the early years I wondered about the efficacy of three questions, and the appropriateness, because you always remember that the more questions you ask the less are available to the backbenchers, including, at times of Tory division, their backbenchers.'

This is not a consideration subsequent opposition leaders have appeared to take seriously although, as Speaker, John Bercow has made a point of extending the session when the leaders' exchanges have gone on for a long time, to make sure that backbenchers have the opportunity to take part. Bercow has claimed that Kinnock 'came to office as a relatively unknown figure and felt obliged to employ PMQs as a device for enhancing his profile'[52] – something Kinnock himself didn't think was quite true when we put it to him. But Kinnock did ask more questions at PMQs than his predecessors: an average of 2.5 per session.

It was John Smith who, as Bercow puts it, 'established the precedent that he would always take his full allocation of three questions per session',[53] although he did not do so straight away. He became Labour leader in 1992 and for the first four months of his leadership, he asked three questions in only about half of his PMQs appearances. On one occasion in November 1992 he even agreed to ask a couple of questions given to him by Downing Street, to enable John Major to announce that the Queen had decided to pay tax,[54] something we can't imagine an opposition leader colluding with today. But from February 1993 onwards, as Major's government continued its slow descent into a national laughing stock – as Smith put it in a debate that June, referring to recent events which were hardly the government's fault but somehow summed up the mood, 'It is no wonder that we live in a country where the Grand National does not start and hotels fall into the sea'[55] – he asked the maximum three questions at very nearly every PMQs. The only exceptions were when he wanted to ask about foreign affairs, when he would sometimes leave it at two, and one occasion following the Shankill Road bombing carried out by the IRA in October 1993, when he asked just one, to express cross-party support for the democratic process.[56]

John Smith's time as Labour leader was cut short. Even now, when you know what's coming, reading through the Tuesday and Thursday Hansards for Smith's PMQs, there's a sudden jolt when you get to Thursday 12 May 1994 and the opening words of the day are from the Speaker: 'I regret to have to report to the House the death of the Right Honourable John Smith QC, member for Monklands East.'[57]

The precedent Smith set of asking all three questions was not immediately taken up by his successor. Tony Blair, in his first PMQs session as Labour leader in October 1994, asked two questions, confidently speaking without notes ('I don't think I really used notes very often as Leader of the Opposition,' he told us), one hand laid on the dispatch box. In the pause after he stood up but before he spoke, his new deputy, John Prescott, pointed at the Tory front bench, grinned and said, 'Petrified.' In fact, Alastair Campbell told us, Blair was petrified too: 'I've very rarely seen him as nervous as he was before the first one. I think he knew it was a moment, he knew he had to do it well.'

At his next PMQs Blair asked just one question; at the one after that, no questions at all. That third PMQs session, in which Blair did not ask anything, was immediately followed by a statement by John Major on standards in public life, to which Blair did respond – meaning that broadcasters seeking a clip of Blair speaking in the Commons for their bulletins would have no choice over which one to use. For several weeks Blair asked fewer questions than Smith had: on one occasion in December 1994 when he did ask three, Tony Newton, standing in for John Major, replied to the third one with a dismissive 'The right honourable gentleman would have done better to stick to his recent practice of asking rather fewer questions.'[58]

As Blair grew into the role of Leader of the Opposition, he asked three questions at more and more of his PMQs sessions, although never as consistently as Smith had or his successors would: 'Sometimes what I'd notice is that by the time they got to the third answer they'd kind of worked out how to whack you back, so if you left it at the second they'd go, "Hang on a minute, I was just about to give you my best line!"'

As Leader of the Opposition from 1997 to 2001, William Hague often stopped one short of his full allocation (which had now become six questions, rather than three – see below), with his team reasoning that 'One of the few things that you've got is that they don't know when to shoot off their "The Tories are useless" rhetoric, and so you've got control of when to do that.' Ed Miliband asked his full allocation of questions absolutely without exception, even when asking about consensual topics, and Jeremy Corbyn has done the same. We occasionally discussed whether Ed should take fewer than six questions. The tactical case for doing it from time to time was strong: there would have been no sixth question for David Cameron to give his scripted final answer to; it would have created a precedent whereby Cameron could no longer be certain how many questions Ed would ask each week, and therefore would not know how best to structure his replies; and we would have avoided the need to 'burn' questions, stretching out a tightly constructed set of four or five questions with a question or two that fills space but does nothing to build the argument. But we never followed through on the idea. Fundamentally, Ed feared that it would have looked weak, deliberately ducking Cameron's attacks. In retrospect, this was probably a mistake – Danny Finkelstein, who helped several Conservative leaders prepare for PMQs and is now a Conservative peer, says that when Hague asked fewer than six questions, 'we never got slagged off for it, people didn't care' – but the fact that stopping before six felt impossible to Ed is also a sign of how far the role of the leaders' exchanges at PMQs has changed since the 1960s. John Bercow says that 'the proportion of all questions asked by party leaders rose from 10 per cent in 1967/8 to 25 per cent in 1987/8 to 33.4 per cent by 2007/8'.[59]

The expectation that the Leader of the Opposition will use all his questions is the development that has formalised what is now the main point of PMQs as a public spectacle: a duel between the two main party leaders, backwards and forwards, trying to catch each other out and deliver the best jokes and rhetorical flourishes. It takes time from the backbenchers, and even when it doesn't it drains attention from them. And the current length and structure of the leaders' duel is a direct, if not entirely foreseen or intended, result of reforms introduced by Tony Blair.

Labour's 1997 manifesto contained the entirely opaque commitment: 'Prime Minister's Questions will be made more effective.'[60] While this told voters nothing at all of any interest, Tony Blair had already decided what he wanted to do, and his landslide victory gave him the mandate to do it: he shifted the thirty minutes of PMQs from two fifteen-minute slots twice a week, on Tuesdays and Thursdays, to one thirty-minute slot once a week, on Wednesdays. Blair wrote:

> I could see from watching John Major that the physical and mental effort of each of the twice-weekly fifteen-minute slots absorbed the whole day: the morning and early afternoon were spent in preparation; meetings, if held at all, did not receive full concentration; the late afternoon and early evening were spent reflecting on what had happened. Two PMQs equalled two days. That's a lot of time.[61]

As John Whittingdale, who worked with Margaret Thatcher on PMQs, told us, it would take her four hours to prepare for each session, twice a week; each session 'only lasted fifteen minutes but of course preparation for fifteen minutes is as long as preparation for half an hour because she doesn't know what's coming'.

The very first question Blair fielded at PMQs as Prime Minister, from the Conservative backbencher Ian Taylor, opened with a sarcastic barb at the reform: 'I warmly welcome the Prime Minister to his role of answering questions and I am grateful to him for finding the time in his diary to do so. At some point he might consult the House about these changes.'[62] Within weeks, the new Leader of the Commons, Ann Taylor, revealed that she had had letters from American fans of PMQs complaining that 'there isn't the same entertainment value' in the thirty-minute sessions as in the twice-weekly fifteen-minute clashes.[63] This may have had as much to do with the new political reality as with the timetable itself, with a subdued and beaten Conservative opposition challenging a newly elected Labour government with a huge majority.

Some of the negative reaction to the reform was predicated on the idea that Blair had changed things to make his life easier. On Blair's own account quoted above, this was not an unfair suggestion, although you might think that making the Prime Minister's life easier – and in particular, allowing him or her to spend less time preparing for PMQs and more time doing the various other important things a Prime Minister has to do – is not a wholly pernicious idea. As Blair put it, 'It may have seemed a small reform, but for the personal well-being of the Prime Minister, it was vital.'[64] He told us, 'It really did free up an enormous amount of time, and once we'd moved it to midday, it meant you had the night before, and then the four hours, five hours before PMQs, and that's it and then it's finished.'

Margaret Thatcher clearly thought that the change made Blair less accountable than she had been. During the 2001 general election campaign, the *Daily Telegraph* reported that she rebutted suggestions that her 144 majority in 1983 had turned her into a 'dictator with a handbag', a one-woman Cabinet. 'Young man,' she said, turning towards a middle-aged reporter who had plucked up courage to make the parallel, 'I went down to the House of Commons twice a week, answering all sorts of questions. I was answerable to the people. Tony Blair only goes once a week. Didn't you know that? Well if you knew it, you should have reflected that in your question.'[65]

The move from twice a week to once a week had diary implications for the Prime Minister and the Leader of the Opposition, but its consequences for the wider rhythm of politics were more far-reaching, and almost certainly neither foreseen nor particularly intended. While the fifteen-minute sessions on Tuesdays and Thursdays presented as much opportunity for the leading protagonists to succeed or fail as any other potential timeslot, they also acted as pressure valves in the parliamentary week. A problem emerging over the weekend could be put to the Prime Minister and dealt with, satisfactorily or not, by Tuesday afternoon; a bad set of Tuesday answers could be returned to two days later; a new political story developing midweek could be asked about on Thursday. The single Wednesday slot allows pressure to build, so that any serious story developing from Wednesday afternoon onwards cannot be put to the Prime Minister until the following Wednesday. And of course, if you lose, you have to wait a whole week, stewing, before you can have another go.

At the same time – and somewhat to mix our metaphorical cooking techniques – the lack of opportunities to scrutinise the Prime Minister until Wednesday lunchtime allows important issues to go off the boil. As William Hague says, 'it reduced the topicality of issues: if something big happened on a Thursday, by the following Wednesday it seemed out of date to ask about it. If there were two sets of Prime Minister's Questions a week, the Leader of the Opposition could really get the Prime Minister on the ropes on nearly successive days.' Issues that arise as a direct result of PMQs – such as evidence that the government has no satisfactory answer to a particular line of questioning – have nowhere to go for a week. If there's no mechanism to seize on an issue in Parliament, then an issue won't be seized there. George Osborne says that 'there's no doubt it cut down the exposure of the Leader of the Opposition in half and was generally a pro-Prime Minister move'. The Conservative criticism in 1997 that a single weekly session would allow the Prime Minister to 'hide from events'[66] has to an extent been borne out. The current Wednesday lunchtime slot makes PMQs quite literally the centrepiece of the political and parliamentary week, with the build-up and aftermath covered almost like a sporting event – a level of coverage which, as with many sports fixtures, the event itself sometimes struggles to live up to.

At least as significant was the shift for the Leader of the Opposition from having up to three questions in two separate sessions to having up to six questions in one session. The then Speaker, Betty Boothroyd, has said that this was her decision, having not been consulted on the timetable shift and not being particularly happy about it: 'The only leverage I had, I said to Major, "Well, how many questions do you have on Tuesdays and Wednesdays [*sic*]?" He said, "I've got three questions on Tuesdays and three on Wednesdays." I say, "OK, double up, let's make it six, and the Liberal Democrats can have two."'[67]

On the face of it, this is an obviously equitable solution: the Leader of the Opposition has exactly the same number of questions as before, over exactly the same length of time. The outcry if Tony Blair or any subsequent Prime Minister had sought to cut the entitlement would be easy to predict, and so far as we know nobody ever has sought to cut it (although in June 1997 the Conservative MP Sir Peter Emery protested, quite wrongly as it turned out, that the new timetable meant that there was no chance that the Leader of the Opposition would be called six times in the same session, and that Blair 'has now made six equal three').[68] But the new right to ask as many as six questions is one of the most important features of contemporary PMQs, with huge impact on the behaviour of both main party leaders. Osborne points out that the move 'did actually open up a new line of attack, which was six questions on one subject, which was much, much tougher than three questions on one subject. It has created, for a good Leader of the Opposition and a Prime Minister on the ropes, a really effective way of exposing the Prime Minister.' William Hague told us, 'It set it up as more of a debate. Once you had six questions which you could use all in a row or could parcel them up into a couple of sets, it created more of a set-piece than it was before.'

Having six questions is not always an advantage. When the Prime Minister is having a good week, the need to ask six questions can be daunting. As Neil Kinnock, who never had the opportunity to ask as many as six questions at PMQs himself, told us, 'It suits Prime Ministers to have a Leader of the Opposition who can ask up to six questions, which means of course they have to.'

There are various different ways of using the six. You can of course do a single block on one topic. But Hague discovered that this was not the only option and sometimes, as Osborne recalls, asked his questions in two blocks of three, 'once we'd established we could do that, which again was not known, until one week we just asked, "Well, could we split it into two blocks?" to the Speaker. And we didn't tell Blair, so he was absolutely astonished when Hague got up for a second time.' Danny Finkelstein remembers the scene in which Blair 'looks completely startled, he shoots the Speaker a look, are you going to stop this or allow it, and the Speaker says nothing so he has to answer it. And that's it, then we knew we'd done it for good.'

If you do break the questions into blocks of unrelated topics – a 'three and three' or a 'four and two' – you can either ask them all at once or sit down after the first set of questions and return for another go later in the session. You can do 'two and four', or 'one and five', in both of which you 'burn' the first questions by asking about something relatively consensual before moving into something more partisan. Ed Miliband used the 'one and five' in his first ever PMQs, opening with a question about Linda Norgrove, a British hostage killed in Afghanistan in an attempted rescue attempt, and then moving on to a series of much more political questions about the government's proposed changes to child benefit. You can do 'two, two and two', as Jeremy Corbyn did in his first PMQs. You can adopt the relatively unusual 'three, two, one' strategy, which we hesitate to describe as the 'Christmas tree formation'. This tactic was used by Corbyn in an early PMQs, in which he cleverly ended on a single consensual question on a brand new topic, in order to block David Cameron's ability to answer the final question with an unanswerable political attack sound-bite. Occasionally, 'six ones', or what William Hague calls the 'multiple moving strike', is an option: flitting from subject to subject over six questions, but usually with an overarching political theme – perhaps broken promises, or U-turns, or sleaze, or incompetence – which links the otherwise disparate topics.

If you break the set up into a number of topics, realistically you are only going to get significant media coverage and attention for one of them. Ed Miliband, who tried various different combinations at different times but most often stuck with a straightforward 'six' on one topic, felt that moving on let Cameron off the hook, and in particular that using his right to break up the set by sitting down halfway through, only to stand up again on a different topic later, looked like an inadvertent admission of defeat on whatever the first topic was. Bruce Grocott, who took part in Ed's prep sessions having advised a succession of Labour leaders on PMQs in both opposition and government, was always a strong advocate of the 'three and three' strategy, usually to no avail.

It seems unlikely that Parliament will ever return to the old system of two fifteen-minute PMQs sessions a week. Although the Conservative Party opposed the change when it was made, many of their MPs recognised that if it benefited the current Labour Prime Minister, then it might one day benefit a Conservative Prime Minister. Cameron told us, 'I thought Blair was right to go to one. I didn't say so at the time, no one did, all the Conservatives said, "Bring back two Prime Minister's Questions a week." In fact, there was a famous moment when Michael Howard said, "I think I'm going to announce today that we will return to two Prime Minister's Questions a week," and George [Osborne] and I both said, "Well, if you do that we're resigning from your briefing team."'

John Bercow has a different reform proposal: 'Personally I would quite favour it being for an hour,' he told us. He is doing his bit to make that happen. As Speaker, he has regularly allowed PMQs to go on long beyond the thirty-minute allocation anyway. He gives three reasons for this: 'First, there is some loss of time when the Prime Minister, and I'm not complaining about this or criticising the holder of the office, refers to lives lost in a theatre of conflict or to some other tragedy, or even commemoratively in a favourable way to something, but which takes time. So I've always felt, well, that shouldn't come out of the half-hour. If the Prime Minister wants to do that because he or she regards it as a duty of the Prime Minister so be it, but it shouldn't detract from the opportunities for backbench members. Secondly, there is a good deal of heckling and interruption; admittedly sometimes my interruptions take a little bit of time. Thirdly, and you will inevitably think that this is critical but it isn't intended in a personally discourteous way, the time now taken up by the frontbench exchanges is greater than ever.'

Bercow rightly points out that if the leaders' exchanges go on until 12.18 or 12.20 p.m., it is completely impossible for him to get through all the backbenchers on the order paper without allowing the session to overrun. If PMQs is overrunning more often, and yet no more questions are being asked overall, says Bercow, 'I don't think it's because backbenchers are asking longer questions, I think it's because the exchanges between the leaders are longer and Prime Ministerial replies are longer.' A longer PMQs slot may never end up being formally codified, but it is gradually becoming the norm thanks to the behaviour of the Prime Minister, the Leader of the Opposition and the Speaker.

PMQs as it now exists is a product of evolution, not intelligent design. And we can still see traces of more primitive forms, like vestigial organs, in the event that now takes place every Wednesday lunchtime. But without each of the developments traced here, PMQs would be a very different beast. The permanent, fixed slot ensures time is carved out in the schedule for the Prime Minister to be held to account. The open questions give it its element of surprise and unpredictability. The willingness of the Prime Minister to answer any question, no matter what the subject, gives PMQs its powerful role in extending 10 Downing Street's reach across Whitehall. The television cameras give PMQs, and its protagonists, an audience unparalleled by any other regular parliamentary occasion anywhere in the world. The primacy of the leaders' duel gives the Leader of the Opposition a unique platform to make the case against the Prime Minister and advance an alternative vision – or to be exposed as inadequate. The extended run of six questions and answers for the two main contenders allows maximum opportunity for each to put their case in gladiatorial combat. If you were starting from scratch, this isn't the way you'd build it. But this is what it is. We think it works.

2

THE QUESTIONS

Prime Minister's Questions is asymmetric warfare. Both sides are aiming to win, but they have to perform very different tasks in order to do so. One side is – at least at first glance – defending, and the other attacking. One side is heavily armed, with a vast array of information at its disposal and the full weight of the government machine behind it. The other is attempting to be nimble, to catch its adversary off guard: its most important weapon is the element of surprise.

The Prime Minister has to deal with each question as it comes; she doesn't get to choose the subject of the main line of attack. For the Leader of the Opposition, the choice of topic is both a luxury and a burden, as William Hague explains: 'You've got the choice of the subject, and that means you've got to be more reactive to the news agenda, how the media will regard it, and you've got to balance what is a really *good* line of attack, or what's an *important* line of attack, and they may not be the same thing. Are you going for part of a strategic pattern or are you going for just a spectacular attack? You've got all these things to weigh up as well as making them effective questions, so there was more to weigh up really, there was more doubt as Leader of the Opposition about should it be this, should it be that, which as Prime Minister you don't really have to think about.'

Ed Miliband says: 'I think for all opposition leaders there is a kind of tug-of-war between the strategic imperative and the strategic case you're wanting to prosecute, and the day-to-day, week-to-week policy issues that arise – minimum alcohol pricing, you know, there's a list of hundreds of them – that you can easily get sucked into, and I think that is really hard because the other thing is you're constantly aware of the presence of the lobby [parliamentary journalists – see Chapter 9], which is the filter for all of this stuff. And so therefore, you might have a strategic imperative which is to be landing vested interests or energy prices or the NHS, but they'll be saying, "Well, you've got to do x because it's on the front pages of lots of newspapers," even though x is a slightly here-today, gone-tomorrow issue.'

Part of the strategic case the Leader of the Opposition is trying to make is about policy, pushing the political debate onto the opposition's territory in the choice of topics and arguments, but at least as big is the personal case: using PMQs to show that the Leader of the Opposition is the kind of person the public can imagine being Prime Minister. Alastair Campbell says that with Tony Blair between 1994 and 1997, 'What we were trying to do, I think, was to show that Tony was competent, on top of a brief, rigorous, fair, not over the top.'

The bigger the news story, the more difficult it is to justify not asking about it. If Wednesday morning's news is dominated by a particular political issue, then asking about it at PMQs is a good way to ensure that it continues to lead the bulletins and has a chance of carrying on into the next day's papers. If it's a news story that is on the face of it bad for the government, then failing to ask about it looks like negligence, or weakness, or an admission that the government's position is stronger than it appears. So, all things being equal, the biggest story is the best topic. And, of course, if you ask about the issue that is strategically important for you but not considered a big news story today, then there's a good chance you won't get it into the news bulletins or the papers anyway.

Often, however, there is no single dominant story on a Wednesday morning, so the Leader of the Opposition has a relatively wide choice, aiming to be as topical as possible, to ask about areas where the opposition is in a strong position and the government is in a weak position, and to preserve the element of surprise. William Hague says, 'When there might be eight different things you could ask about, then you're looking to sneak up with this little tactic where you're going to take him by surprise on something. Or get into a level of detail that he's not comfortable with.' Not all of the candidate topics will work, as Danny Finkelstein recalls of his time helping to prepare Hague: 'Very typically you'd get a story that had appeared in Tuesday's *Daily Mail* that said the governor of the Bank of England really disagrees with the Prime Minister, but when you worked it through you found it was not true. It was true enough to create a *Daily Mail* headline, but it had an easy response which was not in the article. It was never *not* true actually, interestingly, that was not what they did, it was always true, but what you were looking for was something that was true, but didn't have a very good response.'

Over time, the Leader of the Opposition will ask questions across a broad spread of policy while trying to avoid being, as Ed Miliband would put it, 'Roger Irrelevant'. In his 135 PMQs sessions between 2010 and 2015, Ed asked about the economy – including not just the overall state of the economy, but unemployment, wages, living standards and tax, among other things – more than any other topic. The next most common PMQs subjects were the NHS and foreign policy, and a huge range of other issues got at least one outing; but, as Ed told us, 'I don't think the public are looking at your PMQs and thinking, "How much health has he done, how much crime has he done, how much education has he done?"'

The wider ups and downs of the political cycle mean that for each side PMQs fluctuates between being something they dread and something they look forward to – and also dread. As a general rule of thumb, when the opposition is on top, the Leader of the Opposition is in a position to pick the big arguments as PMQs topics; when the government is on top, smaller issues tend to dominate PMQs. A confident opposition will also feel emboldened to challenge on the government's core territory, where the governing party generally trusts it has public opinion on its side: when the Conservatives are in government, crime or immigration; when Labour is in government, the NHS and other public services. As opposition leader, and despite plenty of work to position the Conservatives as a party that could be trusted on public services, culminating in the infamous airbrushed 'I'll cut the deficit, not the NHS' posters, David Cameron only devoted two PMQs sessions to asking Gordon Brown about the NHS – three if you count a couple of non-political questions seeking information about the swine flu epidemic in 2009.[69]

The economy is always core territory for the government, which-ever party is in power, and the opposition's willingness to focus on it at PMQs is a good test of how confident it feels about its argument. Again, Cameron's behaviour is instructive. He never asked Tony Blair about it at PMQs, and only asked Brown about it from 2008 onwards, after the start of the financial crisis – after which he felt able to return to it again and again.

The reason for this is that political arguments are a bit like giant parades of North Korean military hardware: they may look impressive, but the key question is how well they will perform in combat. However good your party's narrative on a given topic sounds, and however well it polls, and however central it is to your argument to the electorate, if it disintegrates on contact with the Prime Minister at PMQs then it's better to prosecute it elsewhere and use PMQs to do other, smaller things. Cameron did tease Blair at one PMQs in March 2007 that the Conservative Party was ahead of Labour on the economy in the polls – which it was at the time – but he notably did not feel con-fident enough to ask any substantive questions on the issue.[70] This was perfectly sensible of him. A good opposition will know what the Prime Minister's arguments are, and will be able to make an informed judgement about whether a particular topic is worth pursuing.

Ed Miliband made a conscious decision to use PMQs to make the 'big argument' on the economy – not every week, but regularly throughout his time as leader – not because he expected to win on it every time but because he thought it was important to have the clash of arguments and show confidence in the Labour position. William Hague told us something similar: 'Sometimes you are thinking about, do you actually want to win or do you just want to have a big row? Your objective is not to win, it is just to have a big exchange of views. Of course you want to make it as advantageous as possible, but subjects that are very high profile in the news, the Prime Minister can see them coming, and almost guess what the Leader of the Opposition will ask about, will have lots of defences ready, but you still do it because you want the big argument.' Even if you don't win, you raise the salience of the issue you have chosen, and give it another day in the news bulletins. As Hague says, 'You want the nine, ten o'clock news to say, "The Prime Minister and Leader of the Opposition had a furious argument today," and then if they say that, that's a success, so whether you've won the argument is less important than it's a big argument.'

There are better ways of finding out facts than asking the Prime Minister for them in the House of Commons Chamber; in fact, there aren't many worse ways. Ultimately, both leaders at PMQs are trying to get a message across, through the medium of a question-and-answer session. For the Leader of the Opposition, the best way of getting this message across will usually be through tight, focused, forensic questioning. The Prime Minister is trying to move away from that onto a wider argument. As Tony Blair says, 'As Leader of the Opposition it's got to be really inquisitive and really sharp; when you're Prime Minister you've got to work out, because you don't know where they're going to come at you from, where do you want to guide the debate?' Ed Miliband found that you need to be 'specific, not windy and blustery. I think if you're Prime Minister then windy and blustery is where you want to be. Never ask two questions when you can ask one. Never ask an open question.' Harold Macmillan said that Hugh Gaitskell never grasped this lesson:

He made the mistake, which Lloyd George warned me about, of making too many points ... he would ask ten, or fourteen, questions – one of which was unanswerable, without telling him a direct lie ... I soon learned that you only answered the easy ones ... If he had asked one question which he knew I couldn't give the answer to truthfully, it would have been much more effective. But he asked so many questions, it was like one of those exams where you know that the candidate need not attempt more than any four! So you attempted the four easy ones. Poor man. I did it over and over again to him; he never spotted it.[71]

William Hague, who was the first opposition leader to have six questions to work with at PMQs, developed new tactics and techniques, and even gave them names. He and his former team recalled some of them to us: 'We had the poisoned pincers: that was the "Yes or no?" they can't get off, when you're demanding the "Yes or no?" answer and both are politically impossible to say.' This required thinking through which way the questions should go depending on the answer, and George Osborne remembers Hague setting it out visually on the piece of paper he took into the Chamber: 'William Hague was very forensic about it, he would have a kind of spidergram of, if Blair answers this then do this, if Blair answers no then do this, he would write it out as a kind of upside-down tree.' Here are Hague's poisoned pincers in action, in October 1998:

WILLIAM HAGUE: The Prime Minister committed himself at the election to a referendum on the voting system in this Parliament. Is he still committed to it?

TONY BLAIR: We have made it clear that we will state our position when the Jenkins commission reports tomorrow.

WILLIAM HAGUE: What is wrong with answering a question in this House yes or no? Does not the Prime Minister's answer reveal that he has got himself into something that he does not know how to get out of? He now has the Foreign Secretary, wherever he is, passionately in favour of proportional representation, the Leader of the House passionately against it, and himself passionately concerned to avoid answering the question, not knowing whether to betray the Liberal Party or the Labour Party ... The Prime Minister has become as indecisive as the late Lord Wilson, who also had a faithful dog called Paddy, although not on this particular subject. On 11 February 1997, he said in the *Financial Times*: 'We have made it clear all the way through that we are committed to a referendum and we are committed to it as part of our programme for the next Parliament.' Does that apply – yes or no?

TONY BLAIR: As indeed I said a few days ago, we have always envisaged holding a referendum this parliament, but we have also said that we shall wait for the Jenkins commission, to see what precise system of voting change it proposes. I should have thought that it was sensible to wait for the Jenkins commission to report before stating a view on it.

WILLIAM HAGUE: How is it that a commitment in the Labour Party manifesto depends on the writings of the former leader of the Social Democratic Party; and that the Prime Minister now envisages keeping a promise, but will wait to see whether he is going to do so? Even he is laughing at the silliness of his own answers.[72]

There were more. 'There's the one which is the rolling brief,' says Osborne, 'where you go, "How many people are waiting on hospital waiting lists?" and then the next question is "Well, the real number is x, but on class sizes, how many people are in classes?" and then the Prime Minister goes, "Well, let me just pick up on the health thing," and he goes, "No, no, we're asking you about education." It doesn't always work because sometimes, if you've been beaten, it looks like you're changing topic.' There was what Hague told us he called the 'deep minefield, that's asking a question for much later that explodes much later. That is, asking something about the ministerial code of conduct when nobody thinks it's relevant really, and then six months later it *is* relevant, and you've got it on the record, that is the one that gets them.'

Hague even realised that he could exploit the structure of Tony Blair's briefing folder: 'I did actually get down to the level of thinking about how his briefing was organised, and how I could take advantage of that, I got down to that level of tactical detail. While his briefing was in two files – I think he changed this later – I would try to ask him something that would be in one file, and then the next in the other one. And that is really nerdy. So yes, in that sense alphabetical order was a weakness.' Inevitably, this tactic also had a name: 'We used to have the multiple moving strike, this I particularly got into, this was asking a series of questions that were thematically related, putting it as it were horizontally not vertically, so instead of saying, I'm going to ask about whatever, taxation, all the questions about tax, it was all things that have got worse or all things that have increased, I would go through six different areas of policy.' Hague says that this approach 'is actually quite effective for opposition leaders, because Prime Ministers when they have read their briefs are reading them in silos, housing policy, health policy, environmental policy, and the Leader of the Opposition has the freedom to turn this into "we're going to go across all of these policies", and it doesn't fit in with the way the briefing of the PM is structured. The first time I did that I know it really caught Tony Blair, that we were going from one subject to another.'

Simply finding ways to delay Blair's ability to turn to the right page in his folder was worthwhile, Hague thought – for example, by holding back the key word which revealed the policy area the question was about until the end of the sentence. If the Leader of the Opposition says, 'Can the Prime Minister explain the recent increase in…' the Prime Minister has to wait for the sentence to be completed before even starting to think about the answer. Is it a recent increase in business taxes? Immigration? Benefit claimants? Unemployment? NHS waiting lists? 'Sometimes a split-second advantage is worth having at PMQs,' says Hague.

Hague was particularly effective at PMQs on the Wednesdays after Gordon Brown's Budgets on a Tuesday. The Leader of the Opposition has to respond to the Budget immediately after the Chancellor's speech – one of the most difficult tasks faced by any politician – but twenty-four hours later, taking advantage of the preparation he had already done along with the time to analyse the Budget properly, Hague could go to PMQs and put the results to Blair. 'There would always be, after all these tax cuts, there would be a line there in the appendix that showed you got three billion more tax out of this measure that was never much talked about in the Budget,' he told us. After the 1998 Budget it gave him one of his best gags, revealing a hidden tax rise with the line 'That is in the Red Book – or, apparently, in the Prime Minister's case, the unread book.'[73]

After a few years of this, the Labour government moved Budget day from Tuesday to Wednesday, straight after PMQs – so it could no longer be the topic of PMQs until a week later. The Conservatives have shown no inclination to move it back. Now, Budget-day PMQs are usually innocuous affairs, with the Leader of the Opposition asking about small or consensual topics – or sometimes, topics which he may not be all that interested in, but which it is worth being able to say he has covered at PMQs – in the full knowledge that it has no chance of getting on the news anyway, and with the time that is usually given over to PMQs prep largely occupied with writing a Budget response speech instead.

Rather than discovering new facts by asking questions you don't know the answers to, PMQs is a good forum for highlighting facts that are already known. As Neil Kinnock told us, 'I was much more interested in getting a figure across, you know, the kind of thing that was publicly available but not acknowledged by the government, you know, the reality of the length of youth unemployment, try and get that across, the reality of bed shortages, try and get that across, the reality of public investment in Germany in comparison to the United Kingdom.' By asking the Prime Minister for an embarrassing figure, or asking her to confirm one, the Leader of the Opposition is trying to force an admission from her or else make her evasiveness – and implicit concession of the uncomfortable truth – obvious to the audience. It was the latter that David Cameron achieved in 2009 by asking Gordon Brown whether Labour's plans involved a public spending cut after 2011:

> DAVID CAMERON: Does the Prime Minister accept that his
> own figures show that once the Treasury's forecast for inflation
> is taken into account, total spending will be cut after 2011?
> GORDON BROWN: No, total spending will continue to rise, and
> it will be a 0 per cent rise in 2013/14. In 2011/12 and 2012/13, it
> will continue to rise.[74]

Brown's insistence that there would not be a cut, and his desire to preserve the dividing line between a Labour government that would continue to increase public spending and a Conservative government that would cut it, led him to claim there would be a '0 per cent rise'. The Tories hung it round his neck until the general election: it was both easy to ridicule as ludicrous on its face, and easy to portray as revealing something of his character.

With a sequence of questions, you can set your opponent up: asking a question to which you already know the answer, and then following up. Here is a classic sucker punch from 1990 by Labour's deputy leader, Roy Hattersley, standing in for Neil Kinnock, against Lord President of the Council and Leader of the House of Commons Sir Geoffrey Howe, standing in for Margaret Thatcher:

> ROY HATTERSLEY: Will the Lord President tell the House
> what the standard rate of income tax will be after the next
> Budget?

SIR GEOFFREY HOWE: In all the questions asked by shadow spokesmen over many years that one beats all records for stupidity. One matter that Chancellors of the Exchequer like, properly, to reserve to their Budget statement is the level at which income tax will be fixed for the year ahead. The nation can take great comfort from the fact that for the past eleven years a succession of Chancellors have progressively introduced lower and lower rates of income tax.

ROY HATTERSLEY: My only criticism of that answer is that I think that the question is even more stupid than the right honourable and learned gentleman made out. As there is unanimous agreement that he cannot predict the level of taxes under this government in six months' time, will he ask the chairman of the Tory Party to stop asking for predictions about the level of taxation under the next Labour government?[75]

Howe's second answer is irrelevant: the point has already been made. If the Tories think it's stupid to predict what level taxes will be at under their own plans, they must concede it's at least as stupid for them to predict what level taxes would be at under Labour. (Effective though the question is in the moment, it hasn't stopped both parties continuing to make predictions about their opponents' tax plans over and over again throughout the subsequent decades, so let's not get carried away.)

Most weeks, PMQs is the opposition's highest-profile opportunity to attack the government and to set the agenda, given that generally it's the government, with its control of departmental announcements and inevitably more hold over the attentions of political journalists, that's in a position to decide the main political stories of the day. When the opposition feels it's on to something, it can be worth asking about the same issue again and again – what Neil Kinnock calls 'shoving the stick in and jiggling it around'. John Smith relentlessly pursued John Major over the Tories' decision to raise taxes after the 1992 election, in breach of an election promise. Tony Blair repeatedly asked Major about excessive pay for executives at the privatised utilities.

With only one session a week, running a sustained campaign at PMQs is more difficult now, but Ed Miliband did so in the autumn of 2013 to keep up momentum after his pledge in his conference speech to freeze energy bills. As Ed says, 'It's one of the odd things in politics, not particularly a PMQs point, if you're ahead of the curve on an issue at the start you're always going to remain there, and if you're behind the curve on the issue at the beginning you're never going to be able to get back, there's such a first-mover advantage. And David Cameron was basically just on the back foot.' The Conservatives had initially denounced Labour's energy announcement as dangerous Marxism, but then very quickly announced their own alternative plan to keep energy prices down, enabling Ed to ask the straightforward question, 'Is freezing energy prices a good idea or a communist plot?'[76] He stuck to the same topic for the whole of October, four sessions in succession. This helped to keep it in the news, which in turn provoked new developments – in particular, emerging divisions on the issue within the Conservative Party – for him to ask about.

Similarly, earlier in his leadership, he used PMQs to keep up the pressure on David Cameron over his NHS reorganisation. 'Fundamentally,' he told us, 'I wanted to use PMQs to augment, supplement big strategic arguments we were making. So that's also when it succeeded, actually. You know, you're making an argument about vested interests, so you make a big energy company argument, there was four in a row. It clearly augmented the strategic argument I was making about energy prices. The cost of living crisis and squeezed wages, I think that's an example of where strategically we were very strong and it was reflected in PMQs in the Chamber, because whenever Cameron would go on and say, "Actually people are doing really well," I would think people would be watching that and thinking, "The guy is just completely out of touch, he's telling us we're doing well," and in a way it shows some of the challenge of being the Prime Minister is that you end up trying to defend what you're doing. The NHS, similarly. Clearly the NHS was a big plank of our argument and we did over a series of months take them apart on the Lansley reforms and he had quite a sticky time of it.'

Cameron announced a pause on his NHS reforms in 2011, and the fact that he was under such sustained pressure at PMQs over the issue was part of the reason, but Ed pointed out to us that pressure on the Prime Minister at PMQs doesn't come out of a clear blue sky; it reflects real political and policy problems. 'It was all just terribly tricky for him. But remember, that was because the reforms were a dog of a set of reforms, it wasn't because I was being particularly skilful. Maybe there were some good ones in there, but I think the fundamentals are what matter. On energy prices he was fundamentally in trouble. The deficit stuff was difficult for us because of reasons that we know about. The fundamentals are what form the backdrop.'

Sometimes, when the fundamentals really are against you, discretion is the better part of valour and you have to be defensive.

There are two main options here: pick a subject on which you can't be attacked, or pick something obscure and unexpected. When the Prime Minister just has too much attack material and there's no way the Leader of the Opposition can win on any of the most high-profile topics even if he's confident that he's right on the substance, or when the main issue in the news causes his party as much angst as it does the government, he just has to duck. Jeremy Corbyn has rarely asked Theresa May about her Brexit strategy and the divisions over the issue in the Conservative Party, even though it has been overwhelmingly the dominant issue in British politics since she became Prime Minister. Neil Kinnock found it difficult to raise the miners' strike at PMQs in the summer of 1984, even though it was clearly the biggest political story at the time, and even though Margaret Thatcher's government was under huge pressure over it, because it caused enormous internal tension for the Labour Party. He told us, 'I was certainly not going to be in any sense opposed to the miners and their cause but I was absolutely certain that I wasn't going to provide an alibi for Scargill. Now that meant riding two horses uphill in a thunderstorm. So I did that for a year.' In July 1984, as Thatcher's biographer, Charles Moore, notes, Kinnock avoided asking about the strike at PMQs: 'His preferred subjects were merchant shipping, the bid by an American company, Standard Telephones, for ICL, and mortgage-capping.'[77]

The best defensive subjects are areas where there is political consensus. It's one of politics' dirty little secrets that when both sides are being statesmanlike and agreeing on a major issue, it's often because one side has made a conscious decision not to be beaten up, and the other side is frustratedly realising it would be inappropriate to throw a punch. When MPs came back from the Christmas recess for the first PMQs of 2012, Ed Miliband was in a particularly weak position, with the Tories having taken the lead in the opinion polls and several senior Labour figures publicly expressing their disquiet about his leadership in quotes which we knew were now sitting in David Cameron's briefing file waiting to be deployed. Ed's questions about the importance of Scotland staying part of the United Kingdom were not just asked because he thought it was important that Scotland stay part of the United Kingdom – although he did, sincerely. They were there to make any personal attacks by Cameron, who agreed with him on the issue, look completely inappropriate. Cameron duly agreed with him, the session fizzled out, and Ed was safe for another week.[78]

Cameron and Ed collectively ducked out of the last PMQs session before the Scottish independence referendum in September 2014 for a different kind of defensive reason. Both knew that with the historic vote taking place in eight days' time and some polls showing a lead for independence, the referendum was the only possible topic for the session. Both knew that the optics of the two main Westminster party leaders furiously agreeing with each other on TV, hundreds of miles from the action, would be terrible for the No campaign. They agreed to travel to Scotland to make separate campaigning visits, leaving William Hague and Harriet Harman to deputise, quietly and without making enough news to trouble the bulletins.

Consensual questions aren't always a mark of weakness: they can be used in a more subtle way, to pace the overall set of six questions, and to manipulate the mood and noise levels of the House. When Angela Eagle stood in at PMQs for Jeremy Corbyn against George

Osborne for the first time the meat of her performance was focused on Conservative divisions over Europe. But she started her set with two questions on a completely different subject: 'We decided to start on flooding. It's an obvious thing to do because that quietens the House, because nobody's going to shout and bawl when people's properties are being flooded and people are being ruined and businesses are being ruined, so I knew I could get into it and the House would be quite quiet, and then he was trying to be prime ministerial and answer me properly, and so that was quite a good way in before we got onto the main political thing.'

When there is a major international crisis, natural disaster or terrorist attack dominating the news, the Leader of the Opposition will often ask about it at PMQs, for at least three reasons. It's the main news of the moment, and so it's perfectly reasonable to ask the government about its response even if that isn't particularly controversial. It's an opportunity for the opposition to get lines about the issue into news broadcasts, and to demonstrate its sensible position on a newsworthy topic on which it's important that the public knows where the opposition stands. And when everyone is talking about an issue of huge importance that isn't party political, ignoring it and attempting political knockabout at PMQs would look weird anyway. Questions on big consensual topics have the added advantage for the Leader of the Opposition that they are easy to write and take little time to rehearse, because he doesn't need to worry about the Prime Minister attacking him in response.

The alternative defensive strategy to the big consensual lovefest is to go small, picking an issue which may not be dominating today's front pages, and probably won't dominate tomorrow's either, but where there's a case to be made against the government and a good chance that the Prime Minister's team won't have predicted the opposition's choice, maximising the element of surprise. This has the further advantage that the Leader of the Opposition can later point to the broad spread of policy topics he has covered over the course of any given timeframe.

Going small isn't always a defensive tactic – it can simply reflect something the Leader of the Opposition is interested in. Early on in his leadership Ed Miliband was genuinely outraged at the coalition government's decision to abolish the Agricultural Wages Board, and was keen to focus on it at PMQs. He was persuaded that the work he would have to do in his questions, and the work his press team would have to do afterwards, to explain what the Agricultural Wages Board actually *was* – let alone why its abolition was important – would outweigh any possible impact his questions could have. As Ed says now, 'The Agricultural Wages Board never quite took off, it's very hard to land a new argument that comes out of a clear blue sky at PMQs unless it's devastatingly obvious.' It became an in-joke. For years afterwards, when a draft set of questions was failing to come together and we were wondering whether to change topic, Ed or one of us would look up and ask 'Agricultural Wages Board?'

Another way of using the element of surprise is the ambush: a set of questions on an unexpected subject, using information which is revealed for the very first time at PMQs. Jeremy Corbyn did this very effectively in February 2017 with a series of leaked text messages from David Hodge, Conservative leader of Surrey County Council, implying that a 'sweetheart deal' was being done between the council and the government to avoid the need for a 15 per cent increase in council tax. Strictly speaking, the texts had not been leaked so much as sent to the wrong person – Nick Forbes, leader of the Labour group on the Local Government Association, rather than another Nick at the Department for Communities and Local Government. Theresa May was unable to answer convincingly – she had not, after all, seen the texts – and the result was not only a clear Corbyn win, but the high-profile launch of a new and unexpected news story highlighting social care underfunding to Labour's advantage.[79] It combined possible collusion to favour a Conservative council, intrigue about secret messages, comically incompetent phone address book management and, of course, the fun of a Prime Minister taken by surprise.

Ed Miliband had a similarly effective ambush of David Cameron in October 2014 with a 'secret tape' – that staple artefact of contemporary political folklore – of welfare minister Lord Freud, recorded by a Labour press officer at the Conservative Party conference. The main parties have a long-standing mutual agreement to send observers to each other's conferences, where they provide opposition briefing and rebuttal to journalists, wander around the exhibition collecting amusing memorabilia, and sit quietly in fringe meetings with recording devices hoping that a politician will say something silly. Usually they don't, but this time Labour's official observer, John Stolliday, struck gold. Freud had said that some disabled people were 'not worth the full wage' and that he was prepared to consider whether a disabled person should be able to 'work for £2 an hour' if they wanted to. Ed saved the questions for the second half of his six-question set, and then hit Cameron with the quote: 'In response to a question at the Conservative party conference, Lord Freud, the welfare reform minister, said: "You make a really good point about the disabled …

There is a group ... where actually as you say they're not worth the full wage." Is that the Prime Minister's view?'[80]

This is a nightmare question for any Prime Minister: being asked to comment on a quote that sounds terrible on the face of it but where you don't know the full story; having to defend a minister over something that may not be defensible for all you know; knowing, suddenly, that a damaging story has rocketed to the top of the news agenda and that nothing else you can say at PMQs will top it. Cameron did his best, but the day was lost.

Ambushes can backfire. It's all very well taking the Prime Minister by surprise, but if your information is wrong then the embarrassment is all yours. This happened to David Cameron in November 2009, when he asked Gordon Brown, ominously, whether the extremist group Hizb ut-Tahrir had received any public money. Brown, pinned, replied that he was not aware of any. Cameron triumphantly identified two schools established by a Hizb ut-Tahrir front organisation which had been awarded £113,000 of government money, 'some of which was from the Pathfinder scheme, whose objective is meant to be preventing violent extremism'. Brown had nowhere to go other than to promise that the allegation would be looked into.[81]

It was a triumph for Cameron and a disaster for Brown – until it turned out that Cameron's facts were wrong. The money the schools had received was not in fact from a scheme aimed at preventing violent extremism, and Cameron had to apologise in the House of Commons the following week.[82] It emerged that the person responsible for the incorrect information was Michael Gove, then the shadow Education Secretary. As Iain Martin wrote in the *Wall Street Journal*,

Gove is very good at impressions, and sometimes has to 'play' the part of Gordon Brown to help his leader get ready for a clash in the Commons. I wonder if for his next impression he can do a key member of the shadow cabinet, with a hitherto blemish-free record, apologizing to his leader for having dropped him in the soup by mistakenly briefing a load of old cobblers?[83]

An even more damaging self-ambush nearly happened to us too, when on one occasion a shadow Cabinet minister excitedly handed the PMQs team a leaked government document – a secret Tory plan to U-turn on a failing policy – for Ed to unveil at PMQs. It was dynamite. It would be a humiliation for the government. David Cameron would be forced to choose between defending a policy that he knew he was about to dump, or admitting that he had made a massive mistake – if we played it right, he might even do both. We redrafted Ed's set of questions and the BBC's chief political correspondent Nick Robinson was briefed so that he could explain the bombshell to viewers immediately after PMQs. We were tense, stomachs knotted with nervous anticipation. This was a big, big moment. And then, just minutes before Ed was due to enter the Chamber, the shadow Cabinet minister made an awful discovery: the leaked government document he had found in his office was not a leaked government document at all, but an internal paper produced by his own staff looking at how Tory policy might, hypothetically, change. He sheepishly explained the misunderstanding and Ed, somehow, got away with it, going back to an earlier set of questions and doing well enough against Cameron that nobody spotted the last-minute change of course – a performance that may have saved several careers.

Sometimes the Leader of the Opposition can be the victim of an ambush, too. In 1998 William Hague asked Tony Blair about his plans for House of Lords reform when, as Blair told us, 'He hadn't realised that we'd actually cut a deal with his Leader of the Lords. So he got up and asked me how I could possibly do this terrible thing, and I said, well, we're doing it because we've got the agreement of his leader in the House of Lords, that was pretty much a knockout blow.' Miranda Green, who was working for Liberal Democrat leader Paddy Ashdown at the time and witnessed it from the press gallery, remembers it as 'one of the most electrifying parliamentary moments of the whole time I worked in politics or journalism. You could see the blood drain from his face, he just didn't know what had happened. And there was just total uproar.' 'Oh yeah, he definitely had an advantage over me on that, he got me on that one,' says Hague. 'You don't win them all.'

Most questions aren't funny, and aren't trying to be, so most of the humour at PMQs will come in the rejoinders and supporting material. There are exceptions to this: there are certain kinds of mocking or dismissive questions which are barely questions and can be played for laughs, very effectively. One of Ed Miliband's best PMQs was won by a joke on the first question, which so disorientated David Cameron that the rest of the set didn't matter. The question was about a relatively low-key and not very party-political story about whether the government would introduce minimum alcohol pricing, but it played into a wider narrative about competence:

ED MILIBAND: In the light of his U-turn on alcohol pricing, is there anything the Prime Minister could organise in a brewery? DAVID CAMERON: I would like to organise a party in the brewery in my constituency, to which the right honourable gentleman would be very welcome, to celebrate that the shadow Chancellor should stay for a very long time on the front bench.[84]

Cameron was already lost for words in this first answer, an attempted joke about Ed Balls which didn't work at all; he came back to it in his second answer: 'Just returning to the right honourable gentleman's earlier question, the interesting thing ... about British politics right now is that I have the top team that I want and he has the top team that I want too. Long may they continue.'[85] If you're trying to explain a joke, you're losing. By this time Ed had already changed the subject to the economy anyway – we weren't actually all that interested in a forensic examination of alcohol pricing policy, and to be honest we weren't all that interested in the rest of the set: we knew when we came up with the joke that it was a one-punch PMQs. The joke helped to carry the alcohol pricing U-turn story into the evening news bulletins, and we were gratified to see that it also featured, among other things, in a cartoon in *Private Eye* and a song on BBC Radio 4's topical comedy programme *The Now Show* – the kind of crossover parliamentary gags rarely achieve.

The joke question is one way of having what William Hague calls 'a first strike that really knocks them off balance'. Another is to come at a predictable subject from an unpredictable angle. Here's Hague in 2000, asking about a recent policy announcement:

WILLIAM HAGUE: Let me ask the Prime Minister a straight-forward question. Does he remember announcing a new government policy last Friday, to a chorus of derision – something that he must be getting used to these days? In what was billed as a major announcement, he said that drunken and violent thugs would be picked up by the police, taken to a cashpoint and asked to pay an on-the-spot fine. Can he tell the House which person in the government came up with that brilliant idea?

TONY BLAIR: The essence of the proposal of course is that— [*Interruption*] The essence of the proposal is that there should be summary justice for disorderly conduct and that there should be— [*Interruption*] I am sorry to disappoint the right honourable gentleman; he should just listen. There should be on-the-spot fines for those people who engage in disorderly conduct. It is correct that it may be better to do that by fixed penalty notice, but summary justice, on the spot, is the essence of the proposal. Perhaps when the right honourable gentleman gets to his feet, he will say whether, if we introduce the proposal for summary fixed penalty notices, he will support it.

HON. MEMBERS: Answer!

WILLIAM HAGUE: If there were a fixed penalty notice for evading the question, the right honourable gentleman would be bankrupt by now. The shadow Home Secretary has said that we are happy to look at the principle of using more fixed penalty notices, but what we want to know about is last Friday's announcement, copiously leaked to the press as usual, of 'Blair's shock proposal to stop street violence' – which was all about people being taken to a cashpoint and given an on-the-spot fine. Whose idea was this? It could not have been the Home Office civil servants', because they said that they knew nothing about it. It could not have been the Home Office ministers', because they called it an 'ill-judged metaphor'. It could not have been the police's idea, because they said it was 'ludicrous' and 'unworkable'. Could it have been anyone in the Labour Party? Hands up anyone who thought of it. [*Interruption*] The Prime Minister is on his own, again. Who in the government came up with the obviously fatuous idea of getting drunken criminals to form orderly queues at cashpoints around the country?

TONY BLAIR: On-the-spot fines— [*Interruption*] Let us get the right honourable gentleman off what he likes to talk about, and get him on to the substance.[86]

Blair's discomfort here is obvious; Hague's trick is that instead of trying to engage with the substance of the policy and treating it as debatable on its merits, he makes the ridiculousness of the idea the premise of his question, and simply asks what idiot came up with it. It's very difficult for Blair to pivot away from an implicit consensus that it is a terrible policy, and to regain the initiative.

Other question strategies are less successful. Iain Duncan Smith developed a habit of asking Tony Blair for a statistic that he definitely would not know. How many teachers left schools in the latest year for which figures are available?[87] Can the Prime Minister tell us by how much council tax has increased since he came to office?[88] How many incidents of violent crime were recorded last year?[89] Can he tell us how many more crimes there are each day than there were a year ago?[90] Since he took office, what proportion of care homes for the elderly have closed?[91] Four years ago, the government said that all third-time burglars would get mandatory sentences of at least three years: how many such sentences have actually been given?[92]

Blair did not know the answers to any of these, or many others like them. That might make them look like good questions. But they weren't. The problem is that they were too specific. No reasonable person would have expected Blair to know the exact answer off the top of his head, or even to have the exact answer in his briefing book. And that means that when Blair failed to give a precise answer, and acknowledged that he didn't know the precise answer by saying, 'I do not have those figures,' before giving a more general answer on the same topic, no reasonable person thought that that was unreasonable. The 'Aha!' moment Duncan Smith was trying to set up never came, because Blair's ignorance was not humiliating. The overall impression this PMQs strategy creates is of a Prime Minister in command, and an irritating but ultimately trivial Leader of the Opposition trying to catch him out on detail because he knows he can't win on the big picture. Duncan Smith became so predictable that in July 2002 Labour's Kevin Brennan was able to humiliate him with a perfectly placed heckle which did nothing more sophisticated than predict the next two words he was going to say. As Osborne says, 'Suddenly one day he [Duncan Smith] stood up with his "how many" question and a Labour backbencher shouted out "How many?" just before he started, and that was the end of that.'

That doesn't mean that asking about specific detail is always a bad idea – done well, it can be highly effective. Here's Tony Blair in

December 1996 asking John Major about a story in that day's news about war pensions. His first question is a set-up, to introduce the topic: is it true that changes to war pensions which were supposed to be 'to simplify policy and procedures' actually mean £50 million of cuts? Major responds that Blair is 'just plain wrong', and tells him, 'I shall take the Labour leader through it gently, so that he understands.'[93] It's Blair's second question that kills, and it does it with detail:

> Let me deal with each part in turn, so that the Prime Minister can answer each part. The first involves hearing disability. The Prime Minister says that the changes were made on independent medical advice. If the reason for the changes was independent medical advice, why were all his social security ministers opposed to them, which they were, and why did not the Budget press release mention the fact that the changes reduced expenditure by £35 million? The second part involves the other changes that the Prime Minister mentioned. He says that they are merely a simplification. Are they on the basis of medical advice? Is that why widows' rent allowances are to be abolished for new cases? The Prime Minister shakes his head. Is that happening or not? Not issuing reminders to return claim forms – is that happening or not? Ceasing to issue copies of decisions to third parties – is that happening or not? Is the instruction 'Do not direct appellant to Royal British Legion as their representative' correct or not? Instead of patronising comments about how we do not understand, will the Prime Minister deal, first, with the matter of medical advice and his

social security ministers and, secondly, with each of the points
that I have made?[94]

This is an unusually long question – in fact, it has eight questions in
it – and its power is not about policy but about theatre, in a way that's
easy to see decades later, when the relevant policy questions have all
been forgotten. Blair is demonstrating, by introducing new technical
question after new technical question, without waiting for Major's
reply to each one, a mastery of the detail which he has been accused
of lacking and which, all things being equal, one would want a Prime
Minister to have. And he is using that detail, specific allegation
after specific allegation, to refute the Prime Minister's complacent
insistence that there is nothing to see here. The audience doesn't need
to understand any of the substance to get the impression that this is
a man who knows what he's talking about, and whose moral outrage
is well founded. And the foundation set by the detailed question two
sets up the *coup de grâce* in question three: 'They know that they have
been caught doing something shabby and mean-minded. If he cannot
be trusted with British war pensioners, why should he be trusted at
all?'[95] The difference between this and Iain Duncan Smith's detailed
questions is that this is the story of the day: the specifics are things
that both leaders are supposed to know, and Blair's presentation is
more convincing than Major's ('TB was terrific at PMQs, best ever,'
wrote Alastair Campbell in his diary afterwards).[96]

A few months before the 2015 election, Ed Miliband announced
that if he became Prime Minister he would introduce a new 'public
question time where regularly the Prime Minister submits himself
or herself to questioning from members of the public in the Palace

of Westminster on Wednesdays'.[97] This would have taken into government the public Q&A format Ed had been doing regularly, and which David Cameron had also previously done when he was Leader of the Opposition under the banner 'Cameron Direct'. As Ed told us, 'Once every two weeks you'd have a thing in Westminster Hall or somewhere, it was basically to take the attention away from PMQs, because PMQs was such a bad advert for politics, you'd have a different way of doing it. I think it would have been draining, but quite good. And I reckon what you'd have found, a bit like with the youth parliament, is that it would have been a much more civilised exchange.' That was the idea, but it gave at least some members of his PMQs prep team the willies. The potential for disaster on the one hand, or for legitimate accusations of stage management on the other, was immense. Labour's defeat meant that it was one of very many problems we never had to face. But Ed's successor found a way of involving the public in PMQs that was much lower-risk, much more controlled and, on occasion, highly effective.

A few hours after the announcement of Jeremy Corbyn's victory in the Labour leadership election on Saturday 12 September 2015, the Labour Party sent an email from him to members and supporters. After a tribute to the defeated leadership candidates, Corbyn asked the email's recipients to 'help me be your representative. When I stand at the dispatch box for Prime Minister's Questions on Wednesday, I want to be your voice. What do you want to ask David Cameron? Tell me now and I will put your questions to him in Parliament. My questions will be your questions.'[98]

Corbyn and some of his close advisers on his leadership campaign had come up with the idea of crowdsourcing questions a few weeks earlier, after it had started to dawn on them that he might actually win. The idea of letting members of the public ask questions to the Prime Minister fitted in well with the themes of his campaign, with its focus on building a mass movement and taking back control from 'a closed elite circle'. It was an early statement of intent and a tangible demonstration of change – immediately seeking to involve Labour's members and supporters in shaping a significant political event.

By the middle of Monday, two days later, over 33,000 questions had been submitted – just under a third of them from Labour Party members. By Wednesday lunchtime, Corbyn told MPs that he had received 40,000 questions and noted, 'There is not time to ask 40,000 questions today – our rules limit us to six.'[99] Obviously, there hadn't been time to read 40,000 questions either – and nobody had.

How do you pick the six best questions out of tens of thousands? Well, you don't. It can't be done – at least, not without significantly more time and resources than the Labour Party had at its disposal. In fact, even picking six remotely usable questions isn't all that easy. Most of the questions submitted by the public were badly worded, overlong, not topical, based on false information or a misunderstanding, too specific, too easy for the Prime Minister to answer, not questions at all but expressions of support for Jeremy Corbyn, blank, or simply obscene. Months after Lord Ashcroft and Isabel Oakeshott's biography claimed that David Cameron had put 'a private part of his anatomy' into a dead pig's mouth as part of a student initiation ceremony, members of the public were still emailing Jeremy Corbyn suggesting that he ask the Prime Minister why he did it.

In that first week, as in subsequent weeks, rather than using the crowdsourcing to direct his questioning, Corbyn and his team chose the topics he wanted to cover and then searched the database of submitted questions for appropriate keywords. For his first PMQs, Corbyn chose to cover housing, tax credits and mental health – three good and obvious topics which any Labour leader might well have chosen at that point in the political cycle, but which could be portrayed as a response to public demand.

That first PMQs was in fact the first time Corbyn had ever spoken from the front bench in his whole 32-year parliamentary career – a lack of frontline political experience which was in some ways a disadvantage, but also of course a big part of why he won the Labour leadership. As one Labour MP said to us, 'I don't think he's been ever that bothered about performing in Parliament, I don't think that it's been his focus at all in his entire parliamentary career. He was a backbencher who did a lot outside, who would come in and make speeches about particular things or ask particular questions but he never used to sit in the House for the sake of it or be a House of Commons-focused politician at all. And so it's not surprising that since his first outing from the front bench at all was as Leader, he was going to do it very differently.'

It was widely regarded as a success. Corbyn was wordy and took his time – for comparison, at his first PMQs he spoke 1,076 words, more than double the 503 words spoken by Ed Miliband at his final PMQs six months earlier. His first question took one minute and fifty-three seconds to read out, but it included an extended preamble. The question itself, from 'Marie', took up just twelve seconds:

I want to thank all those who took part in an enormous democratic exercise in this country, which concluded with me being elected as leader of the Labour Party and Leader of the Opposition. We can be very proud of the numbers of people who engaged and took part in all those debates. I have taken part in many events around the country and had conversations with many people about what they thought of this place, our Parliament, our democracy and our conduct within this place. Many told me that they thought Prime Minister's Question Time was too theatrical, that Parliament was out of touch and too theatrical, and that they wanted things done differently, but above all they wanted their voice to be heard in Parliament. So I thought, in my first Prime Minister's Question Time, I would do it in a slightly different way. I am sure the Prime Minister will absolutely welcome this, as he welcomed the idea in 2005, but something seems to have happened to his memory during that period. So I sent out an email to thousands of people and asked them what questions they would like to put to the Prime Minister and I received 40,000 replies. There is not time to ask 40,000 questions today – our rules limit us to six – so I would like to start with the first one, which is about housing. Two and a half thousand people emailed me about the housing crisis in this country. I ask one from a woman called Marie, who says, 'What does the government intend to do about the chronic lack of affordable housing and the extortionate rents charged by some private sector landlords in this country?'[100]

Corbyn's long-windedness – one of his characteristics as a public speaker in general – remained a feature of his PMQs performances as he settled into the job, and stayed after his second leadership election

victory and his unexpectedly narrow defeat at the 2017 general
election. This increased the amount of time taken up by the leaders'
exchanges: for example, at the first PMQs after the 2017 election
Theresa May did not finish answering Jeremy Corbyn's block of six
questions until more than eighteen minutes into the session. The
Speaker extended PMQs for an additional twenty minutes to make
sure that backbenchers had their fair share of time.[101]

At the start of his leadership, Corbyn had obvious weaknesses
as a parliamentary performer. He didn't deliver jokes effectively. He
didn't do detail and found it difficult to make a forensic argument.
After decades as a campaigning backbencher whose main disputes
were with other parts of the left, he had little knowledge of or experience of spending time engaging with the Conservative Party's main
political arguments. He wasn't good at thinking on his feet and
responding quickly to an opponent's attacks. All of these weaknesses
were to an extent mitigated by the crowdsourcing approach at PMQs.
A failure to do jokes could be portrayed as seriousness. A lack of
detailed knowledge could be hidden by reading out a question from
a member of the public – someone who might not be well informed
on policy, but had lived experience of the problem they were talking
about. And an inability to compete in the cut and thrust of debate
could be overcome by rising above it all, projecting a serious, school-
teacherly impatience with the theatricality of PMQs while acting as
a channel for the voices of those who could not otherwise be heard
in Parliament.

In fact, crowdsourcing proved to be an effective defensive tactic.
Channelling the voice of an ordinary member of the public makes
it harder for the Prime Minister to respond with abuse or a topical

attack. When Corbyn was faced with unfavourable headlines, he could hide behind a crowdsourced question to make it look as if an attack from the Prime Minister was an attack on a blameless member of the public, or a refusal to answer a question from a blameless member of the public, or both. It inhibited the wall of noise from the benches opposite too, as Conservative MP Anna Soubry told us: 'Using the emails, you will notice we're very, very careful with that. So we don't shout out too much, because if it is a real person, you do not attack a real person. And that's why it's quite a clever device.'

Crowdsourcing was very good at stopping the Prime Minister's usual unanswered assault on the Leader of the Opposition after question six. When the Leader of the Opposition is aiming to distil the theme of the session into an attack on the government, the Prime Minister can do the same. When the Leader of the Opposition is asking a serious question – sometimes on a topic that has not been covered in previous questions – on behalf of a concerned member of the public, the exchange is less likely to make the evening news, but it is harder for the Prime Minister to get a big attack in. In one PMQs in October 2015, just a few weeks into his leadership, Corbyn blocked David Cameron's space to attack on the sixth answer by not only using a crowdsourced question, from 'Louis', but by changing the subject entirely, from his initial questions on the steel industry and then tax credits, to the human rights of disabled people.[102] The switch of topic and the use of Louis's question meant that Corbyn came out of this exchange unscathed – but so did Cameron, whose answer was solid. In fact, George Osborne told us, Corbyn's tactics initially confused the Prime Minister's team: 'It took us a while with

Corbyn to work out he's not going to ask the obvious question. He would often ask completely offbeat questions.'

Other than the occasional unpredictability of the topic selection, Cameron did not find the questions challenging in the early months of Corbyn's leadership: indeed, they gave him an opportunity few other opponents had given him. He says: 'Jeremy Corbyn was terrible. Reading out those letters was fantastic, because it was just like, "Brilliant, I can now answer Janine from Brixton's question and take as much time as I want to," and actually I enjoyed it in a way because it gave me a platform to try and explain in as simple terms as I could exactly what we're trying to do on *x y z*.' The downside of asking the questions the public wants you to ask is that sometimes those questions aren't particularly difficult. Of course, even though Cameron found Corbyn easy to deal with, Corbyn still outlasted him – although the only people who would argue that Corbyn had anything to do with this are those who think he bears some responsibility for the result of the EU referendum.

As Corbyn's confidence grew, and especially after Cameron was replaced by the much less self-assured Theresa May, the use of crowdsourced questions declined and in many weeks there were none at all. There's no doubt that his performances and his question strategy have got much better over the course of his leadership, and in particular since the 2017 general election. As *The Guardian*'s sketchwriter John Crace puts it, 'He's definitely got better, he's gone from rank amateur to a sort of League One professional. You know, he's still two tiers down from the Premiership. You can rely on him not to fuck it up, but he's unlikely ever to dazzle.' Corbyn has developed some more conventional PMQs skills: he has become more confident at responding to May's answers with his own rejoinders – something he was noticeably reluctant to do early on – and at quoting Conservative politicians against the Prime Minister.

Corbyn's gradual improvement at PMQs did not cause Labour's unexpected election success, but as with so many external political events, the change in political fortunes led to a change in atmosphere in the House of Commons Chamber which everyone present could feel. Harriet Harman says: 'I think the change-over was with the general election, because leading up to the general election they were like an absolute pack of hounds. There was a hue and cry going on on the other side, and we were shrinking down in our seats expecting to be, as the *Daily Mail* so helpfully said, crushed. And so when we came back in and we had sitting amongst us the MP for Canterbury, the MP for Kensington & Chelsea, the very startled MP for Stroud re-elected, they did as much cheering as they could but we knew it was hollow because they came back with fewer. So that was the moment at which it looked suddenly like Jeremy was a world statesman at PMQs and Theresa May looked like an empty vessel. So the context can sometimes recast you.' There is more to PMQs – much more – than asking questions.

3

NORMAN SHAW
SOUTH

In the hours before noon on a Wednesday, the Prime Minister and the Leader of the Opposition are working a few hundred yards apart. The Prime Minister is in her offices in 10 Downing Street or her parliamentary office, the Leader of the Opposition in the largest of the suite of offices allocated to him in the red-brick Norman Shaw South, one of the Palace of Westminster's less glamorous buildings. Shadow Cabinet meetings are now also held in the same building, in a room which is mostly notable for being unbearably stuffy when the windows are closed, and impossibly noisy when they're open. Every so often, when there is a change of government, the leadership team of the victorious party will excitedly move into No. 10, while their beaten opponents will decamp the other way. Oppositions get to choose the decor of their offices, meaning that a defeated former government is likely to find the walls of its new space adorned with its rival's posters.

Norman Shaw South has been the Leader of the Opposition's base only since Michael Howard's leadership of the Conservative Party. Previous opposition leaders used a much smaller set of offices behind the Speaker's chair, near what is now called the Old Shadow Cabinet Room. George Osborne told us that in 1997, as a Tory staffer in the aftermath of their landslide defeat, 'I walked into the shadow Cabinet block which no Tory had been into for eighteen years, I was the first person there.' Leaders generally prepared for PMQs there, but at least once Tony Blair took his PMQs team out onto the terrace: Alastair Campbell told his diary that it was 'searingly hot. TB has a capacity to endure any temperature, loves the sun, held his face up to it almost as if he was in conversation with it, while the rest of us were longing to go inside to cool down.'[103]

Whatever strategy the Leader of the Opposition chooses – attacking or defensive, topical or left-field, forensic or rhetorical, jokey or menacing, crowdsourced or research-based – he and his team need to do the work to make sure he has a set of questions that flows logically, is factually accurate, has a political edge, reaches a strong conclusion and doesn't set up easy attacks by the Prime Minister. It isn't as easy as it sounds. Getting it right, and making the questions as effective as possible, can take hours. This chapter looks at what goes on in the room where Leaders of the Opposition, and their teams, prepare: the work that's being done, the pressures and frustrations they are worrying about, the material they rely on, the way they anticipate answers and attacks and the way they rehearse.

PMQs prep took up a significant chunk of Ed Miliband's, and

our, week, as it did for many previous opposition leaders and their teams. PMQs is a big platform, and an important thing to get right. As Osborne told us, 'If you fail, the Leader of the Opposition doesn't really have many other opportunities during the week to correct that. A Prime Minister, there'll always be a summit with the American President, there'll always be something else going on. So Prime Ministers can quickly recover, whereas I think Leaders of the Opposition live with the defeat for more days.'

For the participants on both sides, the sheer relentlessness of PMQs is the toughest thing about it. We certainly felt this over years of PMQs prep with Ed Miliband, who told us, 'I actually think the tricky thing about PMQs is not *doing it* – this is not to demean the people who do it once in a blue moon – but I think the tricky thing is the grind. For me, it wasn't doing it once, it was doing it 127 times. [In fact, it was worse than that: Ed did PMQs 135 times as Leader of the Opposition.] I think people underestimate the grind. I remember Cameron saying to me once, "You'll wake up on a Wednesday and you'll think, well, thank goodness it's not PMQs today," when you're on a recess. Because it's like painting the Forth Bridge. It might have gone well, but by Thursday, Friday, you're thinking, "Well, what are we going to do next week?"'

David Cameron told us that he preferred answering the questions at PMQs as Prime Minister to asking them as Leader of the Opposition: 'I found that in some ways easier, because the Leader of the Opposition is a miserable job. You've got to raise everything, you've got to have an answer to everything, but you're not responsible for anything, and I found it very frustrating. You have to have a position on everything but you don't have the briefing, you don't have the expertise backing you up, and the deep resources of the civil service, and in the end you can't actually *do* anything; all you have are your words and your positions. And of course as Leader of the Opposition you don't get the last word, so you really have to do well all the way through in order to be judged the victor.'

Under Ed, the drafting process for Wednesday's PMQs started almost a week in advance, with a memo commissioned at a Labour HQ policy team meeting on a Thursday afternoon and put in Ed's box on Friday evenings for him to read over the weekend. This was much too early, most weeks, to get a sense of what the likely topics would be; the memo was more useful as a management tool to encourage policy officers to think about the most politically charged and useful issues in their areas of expertise, and to think about whether they might be viable PMQs topics and, if not, why not – a much smaller-scale, lower-resourced equivalent of the government's pre-PMQs trawl of departments to work out where the risks are. Each section of the memo contained a brief summary of the political case for devoting PMQs questions to a given topic, along with key facts, expected prime ministerial rebuttal and a small number of draft questions.

The memo may not have had much impact on the following week's PMQs, but it was a major reason why Labour HQ's policy team stopped going out to lunch on Fridays.

Ed's first PMQs meeting would be on a Monday – often first thing in the morning – when he would give his assessment of what the best topics were likely to be. This was inevitably influenced as much by the Sunday papers and political shows, which set the agenda at the start of the week, as by the memo, which had been drafted without the benefit of seeing them, but often there would be at least some overlap between them. Ed would then commission rough draft sets of questions on his chosen topics, which we would write by the end of the day for him to review overnight.

After a bit of practice, drafting a set became reasonably formulaic, and the first go would end up something like this, attempting to build an argument over the six questions:

1. Short, tight, often sarcastic opening question designed to draw stock response from the PM's briefing book.
2. Rejoinder including rebuttal of predicted stock government response, followed by factual question narrowing down the subject of the opening question.
3. Rejoinder containing correct answer to unanswered factual question, followed by another factual question either pursuing the previous question or moving to a closely related issue.
4. Rejoinder containing correct answer to second unanswered factual question, followed by quote critical of the government's position from either an expert or someone who should be a political ally of the Prime Minister.
5. More detailed critique of government policy on the issue at hand/ another quote.
6. WRAP – Closing question containing the summary of the opposition's characterisation of the government, ideally with a punchy phrase that could be clipped by broadcasters.

These early sets never made it to noon on a Wednesday. William Hague told us that the same was true of the preliminary draft sets he commissioned from his team: 'It was very useful to have somebody draft some questions but they hardly ever survived. But of course you need someone to trigger you off, so it doesn't mean it's not valuable, you need someone to get you going, so you can at least say no, not those, which makes you think what it *should* be.'

Ed would send comments the following morning and we would redraft the set or sets in time for the main Tuesday evening meeting. For the first couple of years of Ed's leadership, this would start around 5 or 6 p.m. and regularly dragged on until 11 p.m., with a cast of far too many people, and relevant shadow ministers and their advisers being called in and out, before the team reconvened at 7 a.m. or 8 a.m. on the Wednesday. Subsequently, as Ed's staff got a tighter grip on the diary, the Tuesday evening meeting got much shorter.

On one occasion in 2011, in advance of a PMQs in which he challenged David Cameron over the impact of welfare reforms on cancer patients, Ed took home a copy of Hansard containing a thirty-page committee stage debate in which the relevant reform had been discussed, to make sure he properly understood how the argument worked. That kind of attention to detail made Ed a good special adviser to Gordon Brown at the Treasury, but it's not strictly speaking the Leader of the Opposition's job. We considered briefing a story about Ed's overnight reading material to the press afterwards – the PMQs exchange had gone well, not least because Cameron was evidently less well briefed on the issue than Ed was – but decided it would make him look nerdy.

The Tuesday night draft set of questions would be emailed for comment to various people who were not part of the prep team: advisers as well as shadow ministers with responsibility for the policy area we were asking about. On Wednesday mornings we would joke about whether anything had come back from the 'peanut gallery'. Sending it round was largely done to make sure people felt involved; they would often email back asking why we weren't pursuing a tactic we'd already worked through and ruled out. As Ed says, 'If you've not been in the conversation as it has proceeded you might ask, "Well, why aren't you doing that?" but you'd have no idea that we'd already bottomed out the fact that that wasn't going to work.'

The PMQs prep team was quite distinct from the advisers who worked closely with Ed on other policy, strategy and media issues and who were in general more central to his leadership. Ed explains, 'You've got to let other people get on with their work, otherwise everyone gets sucked into the giant vortex.' This was a lesson we didn't learn immediately. Ed told us, 'Too many people who do PMQs have far too many people in the room. That's something we learned over time. We kicked lots of people out. Otherwise you can't think straight.' By the last couple of years of the 2010–15 parliament the regular prep team, along with the two of us, was Ed's private secretary, Simon Alcock; his parliamentary private secretary, Karen Buck; Simon Puddick from the Labour whips' office; and Labour's longest-serving PMQs veteran, the Labour peer Bruce Grocott.

'Bruce is basically the best,' says Theo Bertram, who worked with him when he prepared Tony Blair and Gordon Brown for PMQs in No. 10. 'What Bruce doesn't know about PMQs you don't need to know. You'd hear Gordon say a line and Bruce would say, "The rhythm's not quite right," and that is something that Gordon would struggle with. Gordon would know that it needs facts and it needs words, and think if you just put them into a sentence it doesn't matter, whereas actually there is a degree of poetry, rhythm.' Bruce's input, especially into the phrasing of questions, was always invaluable: he would always tell us that he could tell we were going to have a good PMQs if we could fit the entire set of six questions on one page.

On Wednesday we would take stock, based on that morning's media agenda. Ed would make a decision and then we would either start again or, more commonly, refine the existing questions further, including several run-throughs with one of us playing David Cameron, until around 11 a.m., by which time everything would be broadly settled and one of us would go and write a briefing note for journalists setting out the key facts Ed was using and their sources, along with suggested tweets which would be emailed to MPs and others during PMQs.

This whole process was substantially more time-consuming and labour-intensive than that employed in opposition by John Smith, who we were told would often write his PMQs questions by himself. Tony Blair kept his PMQs prep team in opposition similarly tight, and did a lot of the work alone: 'I only had a very small number of people, three, four maximum. As Leader of the Opposition it would basically be Alastair [Campbell] and Jonathan [Powell] probably. And most of it I would do myself, because the thinking time, you've got to think it out, you know, what is the point you're trying to make, where are they liable to come back at you? You've got to make sure you're not asking a question with a dirty great big vulnerability of your own.'

Neil Kinnock used to convene his team in his House of Commons office, with some sandwiches and pork pies, at around eleven o'clock on Tuesdays and Thursdays for an hour or so: 'It started off with the office team, particularly Charles [Clarke], Dick Clements, Pat Hewitt,

John Reid, but they tended to come in when their area of expertise was going to be the focus. Henry Neuberger, who was my economic adviser then, would come in with any statistics I wanted, because apart from the fact that he had great access he was also encyclopaedic, as indeed was John Eatwell afterwards, bloody marvellous. So that was the team, and then, after I don't know how long, maybe a year, maybe a bit more, I decided to get in Bruce [Grocott] and Derek [Fatchett] because they were grounded, loyal, great observers of the scene, understood Parliament, sometimes simply as sounding boards, sometimes to say to them, "Listen I'm going to go on health and, you know, bed occupancy, how should I approach it?" That kind of thing. But that's how we did it. I always wrote the questions myself, they were then typed up by Sue [Nye] or by Jan [Royall] and then we'd go through the text to try and ensure that we weren't wasting words because I was obviously also contending with the "Welsh windbag" thing, although if you look at Hansard you'll see that Thatcher's answers were almost without exception longer than my questions.'

We would have been grateful for sandwiches and pork pies. Often we would be summoned for a meeting in the Leader's office which would be billed as one hour maximum but suddenly we would find ourselves in a hostage situation where the extra minutes stretched into hours. Day would turn to night. Beards would visibly grow and the sound of rumbling stomachs would be deafening. It is very hard to see a crisp, clear intelligent argument or find that magic killer fact or statistic when your blood sugar is crashing and you would happily start eating the old copy of the Tory manifesto lying on the table.

Too much of the time preparing for PMQs is spent thinking about food. In the first few weeks of Ed's leadership of the Labour Party, the food was a perk of the job, as we were often treated to a quality takeaway selection. But this was a false dawn: the office soon decided to impose some severe internal austerity and the food stopped coming. The next time the Leader of the Opposition's office enjoyed that kind of feast was when Oliver Letwin ordered a pizza during the late-night negotiations on the Leveson Inquiry. After the ban on fast food, until Ed's office got a grip on the diary and enabled us all to get out early enough to eat at home, we would all troop wearily down to Portcullis House and have a late-night dinner from the canteen which was basically a repeat of whatever we had had for lunch. It did not make for a happy workforce.

The worst thing to do was to take any sugar-based snacks into the prep room, where you would be stared at in a desperate manner until you were forced to ask the Leader of the Opposition through gritted teeth whether he would like some of your Maltesers, which in reality meant handing over the entire packet. Anything for the cause. Whatever meagre snacks were provided by the office were dependent on the diet regime of the leader. Sometimes there was fruit. Sometimes nuts and seeds. On a few occasions there were slices of apples with an unappetising smear of something called 'nut butter', which is like peanut butter but with less taste.

Breakfast was no less challenging from a hunger management point of view. We would start very early. Again, in the early days there was a coffee-and-bacon-sandwich run (we never spotted any political risks in the way Ed ate bacon sandwiches) and the moment they arrived would feel like winning the lottery. Under the new regime, that stopped and so did any opportunity to get breakfast. Some of us who started at 7 a.m. would start getting rumbling stomachs at around eight when Bruce Grocott would arrive full of energy, good humour and tales from the Lords tearoom involving the morning's gossip and details about the delicious fry-up he had just enjoyed. We would all almost be weeping with envy at this point.

Ed got into the habit of stopping his car at Pret A Manger near Leicester Square at about 6.30 a.m. One of the baristas would often give Ed a free coffee and tell him they were rooting for him. Ed's healthy breakfast – often something light like a fruit salad – would often leave him hungry again by about ten and Bruce was always chiding us to make sure he got a 'proper breakfast'. Harriet Harman, when she stood in for Ed, would give us all a breakfast break when we were allowed to escape for twenty minutes to clear our head and get some food. It made a difference. We could catch our breath, step outside the bubble of the room, and get a bacon sandwich.

Other politicians had a PMQs-related diet routine too. Tony Blair wrote in his memoirs that on Wednesdays 'I made sure I had a proper breakfast, and just before the ordeal began, I would eat a banana to give myself energy. It seems daft, but I was finding that my energy levels, and thus my mental agility, were dropping after ten minutes. It really made a difference. At 12.28 I was still alive to the risks and up to repelling the assault.'[104] Margaret Thatcher would always have a bowl of soup and a glass of water in her study in Downing Street. William Hague told us that he took the advice of his chief of staff, Seb Coe, and had a cup of sugary tea: 'Spreading sugar on your larynx helps your ability to give volume to your voice. An alternative version is to drink port, but that doesn't help so much with Prime Minister's Questions.' Harold Wilson, according to his press secretary, Joe Haines, had a less healthy approach: 'He always used to throw down a brandy at 3.10. And then it got to two brandies. He went in one day and the questions dragged on until 3.40. He came out and people flooded into the room and a private secretary said he'd done well. I told him his voice was slurred and that he couldn't drink two brandies and perform.'[105]

Many Leaders of the Opposition have cleared large chunks of their diary for PMQs prep. Alastair Campbell says that in opposition Tony Blair 'would really, really want to think about it the day before. There would certainly be a couple of hours blocked out in the diary to make sure that was all we talked about. And sometimes it was just really tedious because it was three questions, wasn't it? That was all we were having to do, so what we would do is go backwards and forwards. I used to say to him, "Why are we taking hours to do this? You have three questions, John Major's got a country to run and he's got to look after you and he's got to deal with the Lib Dems and he's got to deal with his backbenchers, I mean come on."' For William Hague, 'The machine would start, the cogs would start to turn including mentally on Monday night really, and then on Tuesday we'd have a meeting about it and commission work. And I would say, "Right, work up a set of questions on this subject or another one on that subject and on Wednesday morning we'll see where we are and choose."'

George Osborne, who worked on PMQs with every Conservative Leader of the Opposition from 1997 through to 2010, told us that Hague 'just wanted to demonstrate that there was some fight left in the Tory Party, that you could rally the parliamentary troops and whack this apparently impregnable Prime Minister around the head, and would therefore put a lot of time into preparing for it, although all of the Leaders of the Opposition I worked with did put a lot of time into it.' PMQs, as Osborne says, was all Hague had. 'We had nothing. I mean, we were annihilated to 160 MPs, even Labour at its worst was 230 MPs. We had 160 MPs, just been shattered by Blair. Blair had a 42-point poll lead. Not a two-point poll lead, or a fourteen-point poll lead, but a 42-point poll lead.' Hague himself told us: 'It was an important thing because we had nothing else going for us at all in the Conservative Party at that time, we were completely flat on our backs politically, and so it was important to show that we could win something, we could win an argument, we could win an exchange of views, there was hope. It was an opportunity to raise morale, that is more important actually than for a party that is one step away from power, to show that when you've just lost half your seats and there's a vast majority on the other side, that you can still sock it to them. So we did approach it with that psychology, that it was important. And also I suppose we detected that while Tony Blair was so good at so many things, he was a brilliant operator of course at politics in almost every way, you just got that sense at the beginning that this he was not as comfortable with as he was with everything else. And since I was brought up from being thirteen at school to debate, it was the other way round, I was more comfortable with this than everything else, so we also decided to put a lot of effort into it because of that.'

Harriet Harman told us something very similar about her approach to leading Labour in the immediate aftermath of the party's defeat in 2010 and Gordon Brown's resignation: 'The feeling of being ejected to the wrong side of the House of Commons and how miserable everybody was because these were former Cabinet members consigned to opposition, looking at the crowing Tories, sitting in our places – what should have been our places – and there was such a sense of being rejected by the country and being suddenly plunged into being unable to do anything except watch the Tories just do terrible things with government. The party was raw from the defeat both inside and outside the House of Commons, so it was an important moment to show everybody that we still felt proud of who we were. We had our heads held high, we were beaten but we were not crushed and we were still proud. So that was an incredibly important moment to do well then, not for me but for the sake of the party, that was my job then. It's all so grim being in defeat, you've got to do well in Prime Minister's Questions for your own side so that there can be some pride in the team. You know, you've lost but you're not losers.'

William Hague's confident and effective PMQs performances restored some Conservative pride and sometimes embarrassed Tony Blair, but they did not change either party's fortunes, and the Conservatives made no impression on Labour's majority at the 2001 general election. Hague was replaced by Iain Duncan Smith, who faced a number of challenges at PMQs. The most important was that he just wasn't very good at it. Alastair Campbell says, 'It was hard to take IDS seriously. We did try. Tony just couldn't see the point of him really.' But Duncan Smith was also hampered by the wider political context. The announcement of his election as Conservative Party leader had had to be delayed for two days because of the 9/11 attacks, and his decision to back the Labour government's broad strategy in Afghanistan and later Iraq meant not only that on the biggest political issue of the day he was not opposing the government, but also that on the issues where he did attempt to oppose the government there was less public attention. Broad agreement on foreign policy between the main parties is not unusual; but most of the time foreign policy does not dominate domestic politics in the way it did after 9/11. At PMQs, he offered so little challenge to Tony Blair that Osborne says, 'There was some evidence, I thought, of Blair backing off, and not destroying him every week.'

After Duncan Smith had had a few months in the job, Osborne told us, 'It was decided that they needed a bit more help at Prime Minister's Questions, so three new Tory backbenchers were drafted in to help every morning, four actually: me, David Cameron, Boris Johnson and Paul Goodman, who now edits ConservativeHome. And the four of us would turn up, he moved the start to seven in the morning, so really early, and the four of us would help, which in hindsight was quite an interesting combo. Boris was funny because he was editing *The Spectator* at the time and Wednesday was the going-to-press day so he would always try to slip out of the room at about 8.30 in the morning going "Ah, you've got him nailed to the floor, Leader, it's like jelly, you're going to absolutely..." and then skip out. But David and I would do a lot of prep with him for it.'

Cameron combined the early starts with caring for his disabled son Ivan – one member of the briefing team 'recalls him quietly saying one morning that he had come direct from hospital where he had spent the night'.[106] Another account quotes a source in Duncan Smith's office as thinking that the ambitious backbenchers were a little too big for their boots: 'They were pros and better at it than Iain, but thought they knew it all, and would talk over him in the meetings or put their feet up on coffee tables ... At one point Osborne turned to Johnson and said: "The simple reality is that the Conservative Party is not going to recover until Tony Blair ceases to be Prime Minister."'[107] He was right.

In 2005, Cameron moved on from preparing others for PMQs to asking them himself as leader of the Conservative Party. Osborne was promoted too, to shadow Chancellor, but kept his role on the PMQs prep team. As he told us, it was inexplicable to him that anyone who was given the opportunity to be in the room for PMQs might turn it down: 'It always struck me as an extraordinary mistake that a series of MPs who were drafted in to help would come in and drift away when it was clearly the only place to be, and even as Chancellor I, every Wednesday, would spend the whole morning with Prime Minister's Questions prep, as shadow Chancellor I did and then as Chancellor. But whether it's the Leader of the Opposition or the government, you're there with the leader, you get to hear what they think about everyone else, and you pick up all the gossip, but you're also there as all the decisions are made on how to deal with a problem.'

In opposition Cameron prepared for an hour on Monday, a couple of hours on Tuesday and then for the whole of Wednesday morning. On Wednesdays, he told us, 'I used to cycle in in the morning from home, and that was when I used to think it through, there's something about the combination of fresh air and thinking through how to make either two lots of three or one lot of six. And that was close to a ritual because that got me in the mood. It's a responsibility but a bit of a chore as well, sort of "Oh God, Wednesday", you had to get yourself a bit pumped as Leader of the Opposition. As Prime Minister you don't need to get yourself pumped, you're fully pumped because you're about to answer questions for half an hour.'

By mid-morning on a Wednesday, journalists are speculating on Twitter about what the Leader of the Opposition is going to ask about. We would often read these tweets in the prep room with the benefit of having stress-tested options the journalists thought were viable and discovered hidden vulnerabilities, or sometimes in bafflement that they thought a particular topic was a sensible strategy. It isn't uncommon for journalists to insist on Twitter, or in their early-morning email newsletters, that a story they have recently written is a likely PMQs topic, whether out of wishful thinking or as a form of self-promotion.

Occasionally journalists do influence what is said in PMQs. In 2012, George Osborne's Budget put a series of new taxes on charities, churches, caravans and, most notoriously, pasties, before he was forced within weeks into an embarrassing succession of U-turns. Several months earlier, Tim Shipman, then of the *Daily Mail* and now of the *Sunday Times*, had drawn up what he calls a 'Richter scale of chaos', with the word 'omnishambles', from the BBC political comedy series *The Thick of It*, at the top. This became an in-joke among political journalists, and started being used privately even in Downing Street. As the Budget unravelled, the *Times* columnist Rachel Sylvester quoted a government source saying, 'I think the technical term is omnishambles,'[108] and Shipman called us on a Wednesday morning to suggest that Ed should use it. He did. 'Over the past month we have seen the charity tax shambles, the churches tax shambles, the caravan tax shambles and the pasty tax shambles, so we are all keen to hear the Prime Minister's view on why he thinks, four weeks on from the Budget, even people within Downing Street are calling it an omnishambles Budget,' said Ed.[109] The name stuck.

There are other outside influences, too. For a while, at least one bookmaker offered odds on the topic Ed Miliband would choose for his questions to David Cameron. In the prep room we half-seriously suggested putting a substantial amount of the Labour Party's money on a long-odds obscure topic, then asking about it, in order to fund Labour's election campaign. It might have been the justification Ed needed for his long-held, never-fulfilled ambition to ask about the abolition of the Agricultural Wages Board. We remain uncertain about whether the bookies would have paid out if they had found out we'd done this, and indeed uncertain about the ethics of doing it if we could have got away with it. We never tried.

The last thing you want on a Wednesday morning is what looks like an open goal. This happens when a particular political story is so dominant, and so bad for the government, that it is obvious not only that the Leader of the Opposition is going to ask about it, but that he should win easily. Any emerging consensus among political journalists that PMQs will be an open goal is a disaster, because at PMQs there's actually no such thing as an open goal – the Prime Minister is always still standing in front of it – and because it means that anything other than a decisive win looks like a defeat for the Leader of the Opposition. Harold Macmillan's view of the accuracy of any media consensus – 'usually when the press would say that something big was going to happen, it always petered out'[110] – still holds true, but that doesn't mean that the media consensus has no effect. As Danny Finkelstein says, 'One of the most difficult question times to ever do was when the government was in real trouble. Then it was really hard, because what else could you add? You ended up looking cheap, or you weren't adding anything, or people said you'd missed an open goal: what were you supposed to do, shoot him? What did people expect to happen? That he was going to trip over and hit his head?' David Cameron told us: 'My general rule was that if you went in thinking you were going to do well you did badly, and if you went in thinking you would do badly you'd do well. And that's partly expectations and partly how you respond. And I found that as Leader of the Opposition, if you thought, "Oh my God, today we are going to just nail this," that was always a disaster.'

If there's an open goal that you have no choice but to ask about, you've already lost the element of surprise. The Prime Minister's team is working on detailed lines in the certain knowledge that you will ask her about it. Whatever else happens, there is no prospect that she will be caught out or lost for words. You can be briefed as much as you like, but she will have even more information than you and will be able to obfuscate and create an element of doubt in the audience's mind. And if everyone already thinks it's an open goal, you almost certainly don't have any new facts of your own to deploy. The story, whatever it is, is already bad for the government. You can keep it that way if you do well, or you can let the government off the hook if you don't. What the 'open goal' narrative does is to raise expectations so high that only a completely dominant performance will satisfy them. And if you realise all this and decide to ask about something else, then you don't just look weak; you start to make people wonder if the story everyone thought you'd ask about is as bad for the government as they all assumed it was, and provide the opportunity to move the agenda on.

Perhaps the most annoying so-called 'open goal' we ever worked on with Ed Miliband was the PMQs following the resignation of Maria Miller as Culture Secretary in 2014 over her expenses. Miller resigned on a Wednesday morning, just a few hours before PMQs, after her position got more and more untenable. It was a major political story, and a huge embarrassment for the government, which was impossible to ignore at PMQs. The problem was that by the time PMQs came around, the story had already happened. While it certainly wasn't comfortable for David Cameron, who would have preferred his minister not to have had to resign, and would have preferred not to have had to talk about it, he had an ungainsayable response to every question: variants on 'Well, she's resigned now, what more do you want?'

It was made worse by the fact that Ed, having been bitten before by calling unsuccessfully for scandal-hit ministers to resign, had deliberately not called for Miller's resignation before the event. This meant that Cameron could rightly point out, 'He seems to be the first Leader of the Opposition, probably in history, to come to this House and make his first suggestion that someone should resign after they have already resigned.'[111] The biggest frustration for the opposition prep team on occasions like this is the journalists who insist that the Leader of the Opposition should have done better, without presenting an alternative line of questioning that looks as if it would have been more successful.

Sometimes an open goal turns up at very short notice indeed. Theresa May's Chancellor Philip Hammond created one for Jeremy Corbyn less than half an hour before PMQs on 15 March 2017, by publishing a letter announcing that he was no longer proceeding with a controversial increase in national insurance contributions which he had announced at the Budget just a week previously. While Corbyn's task was harder than it looked, it was easier than he made it. Four out of his six questions were not in fact questions, but statements, giving May an easy out: 'I do not think the right honourable gentleman has got the hang of this. He is supposed to ask me a question when he stands up.'[112] And Corbyn's question about how May would pay for the 'black hole' in her Budget which the U-turn had created was a good example of inadequate bombproofing, since it left May with an obvious and predictable answer: 'If the right honourable gentleman is so concerned about balancing the books, why is it Labour party policy to borrow half a trillion pounds and bankrupt Britain?'[113] Irritating though it is when people like us come up with suggested lines of questioning after the event, this was an occasion when some simple, deadpan contrasting of the Prime Minister's position before the U-turn with her position after it would have paid dividends.

Your questions might look good on paper, but PMQs is a joust, not a speech. So your set needs to be tested in simulated combat. In prep sessions with Ed Miliband, we would hold brief run-throughs of the question sets, with one of us playing David Cameron. For the Conservatives in opposition after 1997, George Osborne played Tony Blair: 'I ended up mimicking him, and playing the Prime Minister to William Hague, and David Cameron when he was shadowing him, and indeed Michael Howard and Iain Duncan Smith. What a great way to spend your life.' Danny Finkelstein told us that it was 'proper mimicry, he can properly mimic the voice of all sorts of people including very funnily Blair and Brown. And he would literally give you Blair's answer in Blair's voice, which was extremely funny, and Blair's answers were very clever, and they were very funny *because* they were clever answers, and George could think his way out of the question in Blair's head, and then you thought, "Well, I'm not going to follow that because Blair will say that."' Finkelstein remembers Osborne's Blair impersonation as 'a very important part of the process because we were working out where Blair would go'.

Mimicry in run-throughs is risky if you don't have a good mimic: in Ed Miliband's team we never did have one, so we tried to focus on getting the answers right rather than the voice. If you end up producing a self-conscious impersonation, rather than just trying to get the phrasing and choices as accurate as possible, then the rehearsal risks becoming more about showcasing the talents of the stand-in than meeting the demands of the forthcoming real event.

Osborne told us: 'I was the only person who had continuously served, I never went out and did anything else between 1994 and 2017, so I ended up having this ridiculous encyclopaedic knowledge of every question that had been asked and what the answers were likely to be and remembering, well, hold on, didn't they say something different eleven years ago?' He prepared for playing Blair by 'paying attention to the way he answers questions, and thinking of the snappiest and toughest responses. I would read everything, but I did this as Chancellor, I would make sure I read everything Ed Miliband and Ed Balls said, so I knew.'

As a stand-in, you need to have a good knowledge of government policy, of the arguments and language the government is currently using to defend its policies, and of the most recent attacks the government has launched on the opposition. You need to be comfortable using the language of your opponents, and make sure you have read the papers looking out for stories attacking your side which the Prime Minister can use against you. Some of these stories will have been placed by your opponents, and others will be 'friendly fire' – unhelpful quotes by people on your own side which the Prime Minister can embarrass you with by reading back.

In a typical run-through, if Ed Miliband was asking about the

NHS, for example, 'David Cameron' would open with something like this: 'The NHS is under pressure, but it is receiving record levels of funding under this government, and thanks to our investment and reform it is now performing over a million more operations every year and has thousands more doctors and nurses and thousands fewer bureaucrats. That wouldn't be the case if we had taken the advice of the shadow Health Secretary and cut NHS funding.' If Ed was asking about the economy, 'Cameron' would complain about the deficit and Labour's mismanagement of the economy and defend the government's long-term economic plan. None of this was hard. Playing the Prime Minister in rehearsals is much easier than being the Prime Minister in real life.

Knowing what the government's top lines are isn't that difficult. It is the government's job to set out its main arguments on all policy areas over and over again. So pulling together a rough facsimile of the Prime Minister's briefing book is a pretty straightforward task. Between 2010 and about 2014 the Conservative Party's own website had a fairly comprehensive policy section, broken down issue by issue at just the right length and presented in a usefully political way: a critique of the previous Labour government, key Conservative policies and a narrative about why they were being pursued, and some facts and figures which supported the arguments. We printed it out and used it in PMQs prep as the basis for anticipating Cameron's main lines. It didn't contain the up-to-date figures at the real Prime Minister's disposal, but it was good enough.

This was supplemented by the Labour HQ policy team's comprehensive catalogue of David Cameron quotes – a document several thousand pages long and growing by the day, from which we could extract shorter compilations of the best quotes on the topics of the week. This was useful not only for anticipating his answers, but also for drafting questions and rejoinders, when we could expose an inconsistency between what Cameron was saying about an issue now and what he used to say in the past. One of the worst things for any opposition research team when the Prime Minister of an existing government changes, such as the transition from Cameron to Theresa May in 2016, is the sudden irrelevance of vast quantities of information about everything the outgoing Prime Minister has said, and of tens of thousands of hours of work over a decade or so. Instantly a massive quotes catalogue is dead, replaced with a much shorter one which, in May's case, is mostly about the Home Office.

In Ed Miliband's very first PMQs, asking about the government's plans to remove child benefit from higher-rate taxpayers, the Cameron quotes catalogue turned up a pre-election promise: 'I'm not going to flannel you. I'm going to give it to you straight. I like child benefit ... I wouldn't change child benefit, I wouldn't means-test it, I don't think that's a good idea.' Ed quoted it, and then asked, 'I agree with the Prime Minister: why doesn't he?'[114] – a classic PMQs device, used over and over again by different leaders, and only possible with a good research operation.

We would also compile a dossier of the most damaging stories in the last week's papers – a document privately referred to as the 'bucket of shit' – to help us to anticipate Cameron's most topical attacks. In addition to being a useful crib sheet for the person playing Cameron, this was also handed to Ed at the end of Tuesday prep for him to read overnight, which meant that he knew what might be coming but was also reminded of the most unhelpful things his colleagues had been saying to the papers. Handing Ed the bucket of shit always felt somewhat socially awkward, especially when – as was sometimes the case – it was the first time he had seen a viciously personal headline attacking him.

Not all of the quotes in the bucket of shit were deliberately damaging: some of them were things people on our side had said in an attempt to be helpful, but which ended up causing more problems for us than for the Conservatives. One of these was by Ed himself, in an interview early in his leadership, in which he said that 'in terms of policy, but not in terms of values, we start with a blank page'.[115] This was not a mad position for someone who knew he was in the early stages of building towards an election in four and a half years and didn't need to announce all of his policies straight away, but it was immediately obvious to the PMQs prep team that it was not ideal. It was duly seized upon by David Cameron, who used it against Ed over and over again at PMQs, starting just after the interview was published ('They are having a policy review, and the Leader of the Opposition says: "In terms of policy … we start with a blank page." That would be a great help at the G20')[116] and going on for years. This is Cameron at a PMQs in 2013: 'We have learned this week that Labour has no economic policy, no foreign policy and no leadership, either. He promised us a blank sheet of paper; three years in, I think we can agree he has delivered.'[117]

Nuanced arguments made elsewhere can be a gift for the leaders in the House of Commons Chamber. In real life, it can be a good persuasive strategy to set out common ground before drawing attention to important differences in approach. In real life, it can be sensible to recognise that you understand where your opponent is coming from, to show that you are fair-minded and capable of appreciating how arguments work even if you disagree with them. But this approach can backfire.

As Ed's first shadow Health Secretary, John Healey tried to make some nuanced points about Andrew Lansley's NHS reforms. His argument was that Lansley was an ideological Conservative with a deliberate and dangerous plan for the NHS – not pursuing a random or chaotic reorganisation, but a man who knew exactly what he was doing in trying to introduce free-market competition on the basis of a preference for the private sector. Whatever the merits of the argument, the way he made it was perfectly gift-wrapped for David Cameron to deploy it at PMQs.

'No one in the House of Commons knows more about the NHS than Andrew Lansley,' Healey said in a speech to the health think tank the King's Fund in January 2011. 'Andrew Lansley spent six years in opposition as shadow Health Secretary. No one has visited more of the NHS. No one has talked to more people who work in the NHS than Andrew Lansley … these plans are consistent, coherent and comprehensive. I would expect nothing less from Andrew Lansley.'[118] As Cameron said gleefully, 'I could not have put it better myself.'[119] Cameron quoted Healey back at Ed Miliband again and again, entirely predictably, leading to gallows humour in our prep sessions. There's a lesson here for all politicians: if you're being quoted out of context, you're being quoted.

In some of Ed's early prep sessions, we tried rehearsing with him standing at one end of the table with his notes on a yellow plastic box to simulate the correct height of the dispatch box, and the rest of us yelling and braying at him like Tory backbenchers as he tried to read out his questions. The yelling was, frankly, embarrassing for all concerned and soon petered out, but the box stayed in use on occasion for rehearsals. Years later, in Jeremy Corbyn's early PMQs prep sessions in the same Leader's office, the yellow plastic box was still there, cast to the side of the room, its former purpose unknown to the new Leader's team. Corbyn, too, would hold run-throughs of his questions, with most of his office present both to offer comments and to play extraordinarily half-hearted Tory MPs – but these would be held much later in the process, at around 11.15 on Wednesday, when it was far too late to make any significant changes in response to staff comments or to difficult answers or attacks from the stand-in 'Prime Minister'. These were run-throughs as confidence-builders rather than as opportunities for honing the questions.

One of the most surprising things about Corbyn's early PMQs prep sessions was his own surprise at the ability of the stand-in to predict David Cameron's answers. He remarked on this several times in his first few months, slightly to our embarrassment. Corbyn acted as if this was some form of telepathy, rather than the product of being interested in politics and paying attention to what Cameron and the Tories were saying about things. Of course, until being elected Labour leader Corbyn had spent more intellectual effort on internal Labour Party debates than on engaging seriously with what the Tories were thinking and saying. Addressing people who didn't simply take it as read that the Conservative Party was bad and wrong seemed to be a new experience for him. Making political arguments to an audience that doesn't already agree with you and share your basic assumptions is a different challenge from addressing rallies or even taking part in leadership contests, and this made PMQs an important part of Corbyn's learning curve.

There are two pitfalls for the person who plays the Prime Minister in a PMQs run-through. One is missing an important argument or attack which the PM goes on to use in the Chamber, leaving the Leader of the Opposition wrong-footed: if that happens, you feel personally responsible for your boss's humiliation. Danny Finkelstein remembers an occasion in 2001 when William Hague's team convinced themselves that Tony Blair could not possibly answer a question they had written. Blair had said that the government would decide whether to enter the single currency or not 'early in the next parliament'. Hague's team decided to ask him exactly what this meant. 'George [Osborne] tried out various answers and then he said, "He's not going to answer this question." And I kept saying, "What happens if he answers the question? What do we do then?" And George and William said, "He can't answer this question, if he answers this question he'll trap himself into a decision about what 'early in the next parliament' is, then he'll be stuck having to do it." So the idea was to go: "Is it one year? Is it two years?" You keep going through the whole set of questions, proving that "early in the next parliament" was valueless. It was a very good question because if he didn't answer it, it would be clear that it was valueless, so he had to answer it, but on the other hand he mustn't answer it, because he'd get into terrible trouble with everyone and it would be a real headache.'

It was a good theory. Here's what actually happened on question one:

WILLIAM HAGUE: The Foreign Secretary repeated this week that the government, if re-elected, would make an assessment on joining the euro early in the next parliament. Does 'early' mean in the first two years of that parliament?

TONY BLAIR: 'Early in the next parliament' means exactly what it says. It would of course be within two years.[120]

That was the end of that. But as Finkelstein pointed out, it wasn't entirely triumphant for Blair: 'Then he has to do it, because he answered in PMQs, so he then had to deliver it. So that was an example of when PMQs shifted policy, because he's there and he has to answer it.' After that, says Finkelstein, Hague's prep team developed a new rule about Blair's ability to deal with what looked like unanswerable questions: 'He can always do *anything*, he can always answer anything, he can do what he wants. So when you said, "Well, he can't do *x*" – yes, he can. You'd always think, "Oh, Blair can't rule that out," and then he'd just rule it out. You know, "Blair can't do that because it's too right wing" – no, he could.'

The other pitfall for the stand-in is the opposite problem: hitting your boss with an attack which the Prime Minister doesn't use, leaving you exposed as the only person in the room whose brain is hostile enough to have come up with that particular line. This isn't so bad when you spot a political opening in a particular line of argument, and help change the questions before they get as far as the Chamber. But when you come up with attack lines the Prime Minister doesn't hit on it's easy to feel as if you're the bad guy. You have to be comfortable thinking of the most cutting things you can about your own party leader, and saying them to his face. Even the shadow Cabinet doesn't do that. Usually.

During Jeremy Corbyn's first PMQs prep session one of us, playing the stand-in 'David Cameron', threw a number of obvious but quite robust attacks at him, including the line 'The Leader of the Opposition and I may not agree on much, but we do have one thing in common: I've spent my whole career opposing the Labour Party, and so has he' – which we still think would have worked well for Cameron if only he'd thought of it. But in the Chamber shortly afterwards, the real David Cameron remained scrupulously polite and more or less avoided attacks at all during the leaders' exchanges. Watching from upstairs, as Cameron failed to use a series of vicious attacks which had just been thrown at Corbyn by a Labour HQ staffer in front of loyal veterans of his own leadership campaign, was a bit uncomfortable.

Part of the purpose of run-throughs is to bombproof the script. The whole thing needs to be checked over for trigger words. If your party is widely and credibly perceived to be in chaos, or your leadership weak – these things generally go in phases for all parties, although some phases are longer than others – then attacks using the words 'chaos' or 'weak', even where justified, will provoke howls from the other side and an embarrassed silence from your own. Spotting the danger words or phrases requires self-awareness, an understanding of what the media, the public and your opponents think are your main weaknesses, a thick skin and an eye for any opportunity for mockery – all key talents for any effective politician. And you have to have the discipline, having spotted the risk, to change your attack even if it means forgoing what is objectively the most powerful criticism of your opponent right now. If you can't make a valid point without being laughed at, then make a different point.

In rehearsing for one of Ed Miliband's early PMQs we removed the (accurate at the time) line on the state of the economy 'There are five people applying for every job' from the script after a run-through in which one of us, as the stand-in 'David Cameron', responded to the newly elected Labour leader, 'There were five people applying for your job – looks like they picked the wrong one.' The Prime Minister probably wouldn't have spotted it in the heat of battle, but the risk was too great. It was to Ed's credit, and our benefit in keeping our jobs, that he responded to abuse like this in the privacy of the PMQs prep room with good humour and a recognition that it was better to think about what might be coming than shoot the messenger.

Ming Campbell's credibility as leader of the Liberal Democrats dissolved on just his second post-leadership-election PMQs in 2006 when he asked what must have looked like a perfectly appropriate and topical question. When the 64-year-old Campbell raised the need for the government to give 'accurate and complete information about pensions', Tory backbencher Eric Forth called out, 'Declare your interest!' MPs collapsed in laughter, and the rest of Campbell's question, and his second question, and ultimately his leadership of his party, were rendered irrelevant.[121] 'Avoid asking about pensions while being relatively old' might look like an unreasonable rule, but if you leave an opening for a good heckle, someone might just take it.

Nick Clegg, who took over from Campbell as Liberal Democrat leader, made a similar mistake at a PMQs in December 2008. Some months earlier he had given an ill-advised interview to *GQ* magazine in which Piers Morgan asked him how many women he had slept with, to which he replied, 'No more than thirty ... it's a lot less than that.'[122] He was never allowed to forget it, or to shed his accidental and almost certainly unjustified reputation as a boastful lothario. Attempting to ask Gordon Brown a completely reasonable question about tax credits, with reference to the personal experience of a real constituent, Clegg opened his question with 'Recently, a single mother with small children came to see me in Sheffield...' The Speaker had to intervene to calm the hilarity.[123] The joke was still going six years later, when we set him up with a straightforward sucker punch from Harriet Harman at one of their PMQs encounters:

HARRIET HARMAN: Since he became Deputy Prime Minister, he has had the opportunity to appoint seven Cabinet members. Will he remind the House how many have been women?

NICK CLEGG: The right honourable and learned lady knows exactly who the members of the Cabinet are from the Liberal Democrat team. I would remind her, however, that millions of women in this country have got from this government what they never got from her government: better pensions; more jobs; tax cuts; shared parental leave; better child care; and more flexible working. Instead of scoring Westminster points, why does she not do the right thing for millions of women around the country?

HARRIET HARMAN: The right honourable gentleman is reluctant to answer the question, which is unlike him, because normally when he is asked about numbers and women, he is quite forthcoming.[124]

Childish? Of course. Annoying? Undoubtedly. Funny? We think so. Are we proud of ourselves? Yes. Yes, we are.

Bombproofing can be taken too far. In October 2013 Ed Miliband agonised over whether to use a line we provided for him to attack

David Cameron's loss of commitment to the green agenda – 'He's gone from hug a husky to gas a badger' – because of the distinctive white patch in his black hair which, now he came to mention it, was vaguely badgeresque. 'Am I a badger?' he repeatedly asked us. We did not think he was a badger. He called several baffled shadow Cabinet members to ask them, 'Am I a badger?' They didn't think he was a badger, but frankly hadn't ever really considered it before. Ed was persuaded that he was not a badger. He used the line. Cameron failed to come back with 'Gas a badger? *You're* a badger!' In all of the post-PMQs commentary, nobody accused him of being a badger.

These last-minute panics would go right to the wire. At about 11.45, after a morning of discussions, redrafts and run-throughs, it was time for Ed to begin the walk from his office in Norman Shaw South to the Chamber. It was always a highly stressed and harassed moment. Simon Alcock would have diligently printed out his pack of questions, rejoinders and any extra information, but just as we were about to leave Ed would often ask for fresh facts or statistics. There would then be a flurry of pleading with him that it was too late and that he really did have every fact and figure that he needed. After tense negotiation, Ed would grumpily concede and suddenly we would be late. Ed is tall with a quick, long-legged stride: often Karen Buck and the rest of the entourage would struggle to keep up, trotting along behind as he asked us questions about whether he had the right information. We would dash down the stairs, then across Portcullis House where we would begin to bump into MPs as we moved towards the escalators down into the underpass which takes you to the older part of the Palace of Westminster. There would always be shouts of good luck and best wishes from Labour colleagues; you could tell from people's expressions that they were sincere. They all wanted to see the boss do well. We would veer off towards a suite of rooms reserved for the Leader of the Opposition close to the Chamber. Ed would gather his final thoughts quietly in his study and go through his questions. Ed Balls would arrive, ready to take his seat on the front bench next to the leader, and after reassuring him that he definitely didn't need any new material at 11.58 a.m., they would charge along the corridor. As they entered the Chamber it would already be packed with MPs, most of them uninterested in the departmental question session that precedes PMQs, barely listening to it, but in their places ready for the main event.

4

THE ANSWERS

The fact that Prime Minister's Questions is called Prime Minister's Questions often misleads people into assuming that the Prime Minister will spend the session answering questions. The fact that she doesn't always do so makes some people think that the whole exercise is fake and that all politicians are slippery, or at least makes them cross with the Prime Minister of the day. So it's worth thinking about what the Prime Minister is trying to achieve at PMQs, and why she doesn't simply give the fullest factual answer she reasonably can to every question and leave it at that.

For a start, answering the questions is not the Prime Minister's main priority. She is trying to get a message across too. She wants to set out the government's position and narrative, contrast it favourably with that of the opposition, contrast herself favourably with the Leader of the Opposition – a person who is presenting himself as an alternative candidate for her job – and generally to exude confidence and competence, to look as if she knows what she's doing. Of course, in order to achieve some of this she will have to give the general impression of answering questions, but it is the general impression that matters. And of course, the Leader of the Opposition is trying to achieve roughly the equivalent things from the other side, and to do so by giving the general impression of asking questions.

As Danny Finkelstein says, 'Often Prime Minister's Questions involves making points which you artfully contrive to put a question mark on the end of and that's part of the skill, and then the response will be the same, making a political point which you artfully contrive to make sound like the answer to the question.' Almost invariably, the questions from the opposition – when they are questions at all – are questions the Prime Minister doesn't want to give a straight answer to. That's the whole point of them – if the Prime Minister hears them and *does* want to give a straight answer, then they're almost certainly bad questions. Just as we shouldn't be surprised that the Leader of the Opposition's questions aren't variants on 'Please tell us about your education policy for a bit', so we shouldn't be surprised or scandalised that questions whose basic thrust is 'Are you rubbish? Is your government rubbish? Why are you and your government rubbish?' are not responded to by the Prime Minister with answers whose basic content is 'Yes, I'm rubbish, my government is rubbish, the main reason for this is that we're rubbish.' Of *course* the Prime Minister, like anyone who is asked a hostile question in a public forum, is going to shift it onto her terms and answer it in a way that presents her case in the best way possible – which may mean dodging the specific question that's been asked.

Highlighting the fact that the Prime Minister hasn't answered the question is part of the Opposition's job, but being surprised that she hasn't answered it is silly, given the options available to her. Leaders of the Opposition might not be accountable to Parliament in the same way as Prime Ministers, or have to answer questions there, but in media interviews or public meetings they use techniques to avoid difficult questions too. (Sometimes they simply refuse to take part in media interviews, which is of course a highly effective technique for avoiding difficult questions, with the added advantage that political opponents can't even point and laugh at evasive answers, because there aren't any.) Complaints that politicians don't give straight answers to straight questions are not wrong, but it's worth bearing in mind that most people in most jobs don't even get *asked* straight questions, or at least not in front of an audience.

David Cameron told us that answering the question properly, where possible, is important: 'Where you could give a straight answer or a factual answer I would try to be direct. I think people get really infuriated by the lack of directness of politicians even when there is a direct answer.' But there are some questions that can't be answered: sometimes for reasons of national security, sometimes because the Prime Minister simply doesn't know ('It's perfectly acceptable to say, "I don't have that information, I'll write to the honourable gentleman," you just can't say that six times in one Prime Minister's Questions'). And there are some questions that simply shouldn't be answered: 'There's the conditional question which you don't have to answer, you know, "If you lose the vote in Parliament tonight will you resign?" to which the answer is "We're not going to lose the vote." Always think to yourself, "Don't accept a conditional question."'

It's a constant in politics that both sides think that they are doing the right thing and their opponents are acting unfairly. Cameron thought that he was answering the questions as fully as possible; Labour thought he was dodging them. Harriet Harman told us: 'One of the problems under David Cameron was that he just started to spout all sorts of figures that were wrong on everything, and previously there had been much more of an attempt from Prime Ministers to be actually accurate in what they were saying, and he was very cavalier, and that slightly degraded the occasion.' The truth is somewhere in between: the factual claims in Cameron's answers were, by and large, accurate, but they did not always relate directly to the exact questions being asked. And a lot of the time, Cameron's pivot (a pivot all Prime Ministers make) away from factual answers towards political attack and other material tended to come very quickly.

The charge that Prime Ministers don't answer the questions at PMQs goes back a long way, but Neil Kinnock believes that it was Margaret Thatcher who invented the modern technique of compiling and then sticking to a prepared PMQs script. 'Since time immemorial politicians have not answered questions. That's one phenomenon where you avoid giving the answer that the other side wants and giving the answer that you don't want. I mean, you can go back to the Greeks, fine, OK. But her technique was something different: this isn't avoiding answering the question, it's answering the question you wanted to be asked, and simply getting up and bulldozing whatever response had previously been drafted, or response that suited what she wanted to say.'

John Whittingdale, who worked with Margaret Thatcher on PMQs, told us, 'I wouldn't entirely disagree. It wasn't even reading

from a book. Let us say the question was about the health service –
and it was, a lot, because like every Tory government, health is always
a difficult issue, lots of problems – it didn't matter in a sense what
the question was, the answer was "Real-terms increase in expenditure
every single year, now spending record amounts." And you would use
that. If health came up you'd press the button and that's the answer.
And it probably was the best answer to give.' The reason it was the
best answer is that it was true: in the 1980s there really were problems
in the NHS which Neil Kinnock wanted to highlight, but there really
was record NHS expenditure. Similarly, Labour leaders since the
middle of the 2010–15 parliament have wanted to point to stagnating
wages for working people, and Conservative Prime Ministers have
wanted to point to record levels of employment. They're both right.

The Prime Minister must not lie – if she misleads the House,
saying something that can be shown to be untrue, she can be forced
to correct the record, which is embarrassing – but she can tell a
precise and narrow truth which sounds to the casual listener like a
general and broad truth. For example, accused by Jeremy Corbyn in
September 2017 of cutting the pay of public sector workers, Theresa
May explained that, in fact, 'A new police officer in 2010, thanks to
progression pay, annual basic salary increases and the increase in the
personal allowance, which is a tax cut for people, has actually seen an
increase in their pay of over £9,000 since 2010 – a real-terms increase
of 32 per cent.'[125] This sounds impressive: you might have thought that
police pay was being cut, but here's the Prime Minister saying police
pay has risen. Or is she?

In fact, as Tim Harford explained later on the BBC's *More or
Less*, this example was carefully chosen: 'Police officers joining the

force in 2010 were at a particular sweet spot in measuring pay. They were the last to join before public sector pay was frozen for two years in April 2011. They joined before the police pay reforms of 2013, which changed the pay increment scales. And they joined before the then Chancellor, George Osborne, started to raise the personal allowance for income tax. So these are the police officers that would have experienced some of the greatest benefit.'[126] Very few police officers came into this category but, crucially, Theresa May did not lie.

Prime Ministers can use figures like these with confidence that the Leader of the Opposition will not be in a position to unpick them on the spot – as Jeremy Corbyn didn't on this occasion. The job of doing so is left to party policy staff on both sides as they attempt to interest journalists in 'The Prime Minister/Leader of the Opposition was wrong at PMQs' stories, as well as to programmes like *More or Less* and various fact-checking websites, which go over the factual claims made by the leaders and almost invariably conclude that they are all, strictly speaking, true. So when one side claims that NHS waiting lists and waiting times have gone up and the other side claims that, on the contrary, the NHS has more money and is performing more operations than ever before, nobody is lying – but everybody is picking the facts that suit their argument best.

William Hague, who as well as spending four years asking Tony Blair questions at PMQs also had experience of answering departmental questions as a government minister under both John Major and David Cameron, and of standing in for Cameron to answer at PMQs on a few occasions, told us: 'Having done the preparation on both sides, in a way it's harder work for the Leader of the Opposition because you're really choosing the subject, whereas the Prime

Minister is just reacting, and that's a case of knowing your brief and of course being ready with some counterstrikes on opposition leaders, but mainly it's a question of knowing your stuff well and performing competently anyway. And on two occasions I stood in for David Cameron when both he and Nick Clegg were away during the coalition, so I did the answers to Prime Minister's Questions: well, I found that quite a doddle compared to doing the questions, interestingly. I didn't find any difficulty at all in answering. That sounds like a very arrogant thing to say, but I didn't compared to all those years asking the questions. You still have to go through your housing brief, your health brief, your tax brief, but on the other hand if you're the Prime Minister you should know a lot of that stuff anyway, and then you have to go through all the constituencies of the members who you know are going to be asking questions and so on, so there's still plenty of work for a Prime Minister in preparing the answers.'

Hague might sound a bit blasé in saying 'You should know a lot of that stuff anyway', but he's right. Knowing the basic facts is less hard than it sounds. Any remotely competent Prime Minister will already know the government's narrative, including the key facts that are needed to support it, on any given policy area. The same is true, of course, of any remotely competent Leader of the Opposition – one of the most important jobs of any opposition politician is to know the government's case. You can't identify weaknesses in something you've never bothered to look at. Ask any professional politician about health, or housing, or education, or the economy – not just at PMQs, but on *Question Time* or *Any Questions?*, or in a media interview, or if you bump into them in the street – and they ought to have a decent answer, combining some facts with a political argument. It's not difficult; it's every politician's job.

Part of this is knowing 'the line', but more important is knowing how the logic of your side's argument works. And there's nothing wrong with knowing 'the line' anyway: politicians who make their careers out of ostentatiously refusing to follow 'the line' often discover, when they get into leadership positions, that it's worth working out what 'the line' is and not only encouraging their colleagues to follow it but disciplining them for failing to do so.

The Prime Minister carries a large folder full of briefing material, the compilation of which will be discussed in the next chapter. She will usually open her briefing folder to the relevant page once she hears the topic of the question, and will be able to glance down at it to make sure that specific statistics are right, but she should already know what to say. Sometimes she will answer without reference to the book at all: on 15 March 2017, when Jeremy Corbyn asked Theresa May about that morning's U-turn on the rise in national insurance contributions which had been announced in the previous week's Budget, it was noticeable that May's folder was closed and she was able to answer confidently and off the cuff – partly because she was not being pressed on detail.

So the basic skeleton of the Prime Minister's first answer is normally not an immediate dodge, but a general script – written down but also, usually, known off by heart – on the approximate topic of the question. Her briefing folder will contain scripts, with key lines, facts, statistics and attacks, for all policy areas, and for particularly contentious current issues which are predictable PMQs topics. Even if the Leader of the Opposition doesn't pick the most obvious topic for his set of questions, the chances are that at least one backbencher will do so.

At almost any PMQs, the first couple of answers to the first couple of questions from the Leader of the Opposition will very obviously, once you tune yourself into it, be based on one of these scripts. This will usually require a sidestep from the specific question that the Prime Minister has been asked – but only a small one, and the answer will still be relevant, even if not completely on point. George Osborne explained to us how the discipline of answering up to six questions on the same topic without repeating yourself works: 'You don't want to have the same answer six times in a row, so you need to have six different answers to the NHS crisis, you've got to think of, well, they'll probably ask about the latest waiting time target miss, so you need to know the answer to that, but then maybe you need the quote from Frank Field saying that the Labour opposition is being irresponsible, you know, the chair of the Labour health authority who has just written a letter thanking Downing Street for some money.' Giles Kenningham, a No. 10 adviser under David Cameron, explained how Cameron's PMQs team mapped out each set of answers:

Answers one and two and would tackle the question head-on in some factual way to knock back the substance of the attack. Answers three and four were the pivot, bouncing out of a defensive position and on to the offensive by turning the issue to Labour policy in some way, for example saying that you could only have a strong NHS with a strong economy. That way we brought the argument back to our strategic political strength. Answers five and six were where we deployed the payoff lines that we wanted our MPs, the media and voters to hear.[127]

The attack material the Prime Minister is using, if deployed properly, has the additional function of allowing her some variety in her answers while staying more or less relevant to her opponent's line of questioning. The sidesteps the Prime Minister is making, pivoting away from the specific question she is being asked, fall into a few different categories. Many of the pivots involve denying your opponent's right to ask this question, or questions on this subject, in the first place. There's the pivot to irrelevant good news: 'I notice he's not asking about the excellent economic figures that are out today.' There's the pivot to your opponent's party's record: the 'I'll take no lectures' sidestep, as in 'I'll take no lectures on this from the people who wrecked the economy/sold the gold/failed to invest in our public services/trebled immigration/saw unemployment rise.' There's the pivot to your opponent's party's current policy: 'He's spent the money he says he wants to use to pay for this ten times over, so he's in no position to ask me about it.' There's even the pivot to more-in-sorrow-than-in-anger disappointment that your opponent is seeking to politicise an issue like this. For example, here's David Cameron, pressed by Ed Miliband on cuts to the Environment Agency and a lack of investment in flood defences, following severe floods in February 2014: 'I am only sorry that the right honourable gentleman seeks to divide the House, when we should be coming together for the nation.'[128] The idea is to get the audience nodding along – after all, we really *should* be coming together for the nation at a time of crisis – before anyone has noticed that cutting flood defence funding is not something on which the whole nation necessarily agrees, and is a perfectly legitimate topic for political discussion when there are severe floods.

For a decade as Prime Minister Tony Blair was a master of these pivots, and in particular of the art of the good-natured acknowledgement of imperfection: I'm a reasonable person, of course I don't know everything, but things are generally going in the right direction and certainly better than they would be under my opponents. Many politicians, in trying to project strength and infallibility, end up exposing their own weakness; recognising the absurdity of the whole enterprise and knowing what you can afford to concede leaves you in a much stronger place. None of Blair's successors, whatever their other strengths or weaknesses, have so far quite demonstrated his ability to shrug off criticism amiably before going in for the kill.

Blair's easy, confident tone, mildly amused, lightly exasperated that he had to deal with such silly questions, was the springboard to attacks on his opponents: it's all very well to find fault, and it's true that not everything is perfect, but for these Tories who ran the country into the ground for eighteen years to have the nerve to complain is a bit much, frankly. The rhetorical move from the perfectly reasonable 'It's unfair to blame me for everything that's gone wrong' to the absurd, once you think about it, 'Everything that's gone wrong is actually their fault' is difficult for an opponent to expose without making similar concessions of weakness – and it is harder to do in the Leader of the Opposition's offensive starting posture than the Prime Minister's initially defensive one.

Occasionally, the Prime Minister can win by answering the exact question that's been asked, in as much detail as has been asked for.

This is very unusual: its main effect is to make the Prime Minister look good, and since this is the last thing the Leader of the Opposition wants or expects it's the sign of poor preparation on the opposition side more than it is of a well-briefed Prime Minister. As George Osborne told us, 'The Leader of the Opposition has got to get the first serve in. You're absolutely on the back foot if your first question is "How many asylum seekers…?" and the Prime Minister says, "Well, I'll tell you: 210,000, but we're dealing with the list."'

Other than giving a perfect, detailed answer, perhaps the most effective way of knocking the stuffing out of your opponent is to concede their point, undermining whatever they were planning to say next and making their attack on you irrelevant. This has the added advantage that the *coup de théâtre* of ruining their flow tends to overshadow the inconvenient fact that you have just dropped your policy. Here's David Cameron in 2011 wrecking Ed Miliband's big attack on his plans for selling off Britain's forests, by suddenly dropping his plans to sell off Britain's forests.

ED MILIBAND: Can the Prime Minister tell us whether he is happy with his flagship policy on forestry?

DAVID CAMERON: The short answer to that is no. As I have said before in this House, it is a consultation that has been put forward, and we have had a range of interesting responses to it, but what is important is that we should be making sure that, whatever happens, we increase access to our forests, we increase biodiversity and we do not make the mistake that was made under the last government, where they sold forests with no access rights at all.

ED MILIBAND: Even the right honourable gentleman must appreciate the irony: he, the guy who made the tree the symbol of the Conservative party, flogging them off up and down this country. He says that they are consulting on the policy; they are actually consulting on how to flog off the forests, not on whether to flog off the forests. Is the Prime Minister now saying that he might drop the policy completely?

DAVID CAMERON: I would have thought that the whole point of a consultation is that you put forward some proposals, you listen to the answer and then you make a decision. I know it is a totally alien concept, but what is so complicated about that?

ED MILIBAND: Everybody knows that the right honourable gentleman is going to have to drop this ludicrous policy. Let me give him the chance to do so. Nobody voted for the policy; 500,000 people have signed a petition against it. When he gets up at the dispatch box, why does he say not that he is postponing the sale, but that he is cancelling it?

DAVID CAMERON: I think, once again, that the right honourable gentleman wrote the questions before he listened to the answers, and I think the bandwagon has just hit a bit of a tree.[129]

The fact that this unexpectedly dropped Ed Miliband in it was a better story than the fact that it also dropped Environment Secretary Caroline Spelman in it. Cameron won this exchange by doing what Ed wanted him to do, because doing what Ed wanted him to do was the last thing Ed wanted him to do.

Theresa May was similarly able to wrong-foot Jeremy Corbyn in January 2017, when it was highly predictable that he would ask her to publish a White Paper on the government's plans for leaving the European Union – something many of her own backbenchers were calling for. Rather than wait for him to ask, and be forced to dissemble or make an embarrassing concession to her principal opponent, she arranged for a Tory backbencher to ask the same question just before Corbyn stood up, and told him that a White Paper would indeed be published. Corbyn, not the greatest improviser, was reduced to asking why it had taken so long and when *exactly* the White Paper would come out – not questions anyone really cared about.[130]

In both cases, Cameron and May could exit the main PMQs exchanges with the cheers of their backbenchers ringing in their ears and the opposition silenced, by executing a perfect tactical retreat which in other circumstances could have been humiliating.

There are certain specific question techniques against which Prime Ministers can develop specific defences. Theresa May took some time to hit on a tactic to deal with Jeremy Corbyn's crowdsourced questions from members of the public, which was to ask him to send them to her so that she could deal with them personally, and then – when he failed to do so for weeks on end – to point out that he hadn't, implying that he was more interested in political point-scoring than in working together to solve people's problems. For example, on 11 October 2017 Corbyn read from a letter sent to him by a member of the public called Georgina, to which May replied, 'I would be happy to look at the case of Georgina if he would like to send me those details.'[131] More than a month later she was able to reply to a different letter-based question from Corbyn by saying, 'In an earlier Prime Minister's Questions, he raised a specific case of an individual who had written to him about her experience on universal credit – I think it was Georgina. As far as I am aware, he has so far not sent that letter to me, despite the fact that I asked for it.'[132] A member of her team told us they were delighted by Corbyn's team's negligence and the political opportunity it left for her.

PMQs is, at least in theory, a one-way process. The Prime Minister answers questions; she does not ask them. But asking questions back can still be a good answering tactic. After all, the Leader of the Opposition may not run the government, but he still has policies and decisions and problems that people might be interested in knowing his position on. He is perfectly entitled not to answer questions put back to him at PMQs: indeed, there are standard formulas for responding to them, which are 'The Prime Minister seems to have forgotten that it's my job to ask the questions and her job to answer them,' or 'If the Prime Minister wants to ask me questions, I'm happy to swap sides,' or 'If the Prime Minister is so keen to question me, why doesn't she go ahead and call an election?' Somehow, these can all still raise a cheer from opposition backbenchers, and it's not unheard of for journalists who really ought to know better to describe a response from this category as 'a clever line'. Nevertheless, it's not at all unusual for the Prime Minister to try to challenge questioners by asking them what their policy is on the issue under discussion, or asking if they agree with some embarrassing quote from someone on their own side.

David Cameron did this very effectively in what turned out to be Ed Miliband's last ever PMQs as Labour leader, in March 2015. Ed asked Cameron to rule out raising VAT if he won the election (Labour had calculated that the spending plans the Conservatives had announced meant that he couldn't) and Cameron did just that. 'We'd thought that one through,' he told us. 'George and I discussed it, and I said, "If he asks that, I'm going to pre-announce that part of the manifesto, because this is such an important day."' Ed stood up and asked 'a straight question: will he now rule out a rise in VAT?' Cameron responded with the one answer we'd thought he couldn't give: 'Straight questions deserve straight answers, and the answer is yes.'[133] Then Cameron turned the tables, asking Ed three times if he could rule out raising national insurance contributions. He could not. Ed maintains that it wasn't important: 'It didn't matter. We got Ed Balls to go out later on, to deal with the national insurance issue. If we're honest it was awkward at the time, but who remembers?' Well, we remember, and there are reasons why that PMQs ended up being Ed's last.

We were right, incidentally, that Conservative spending plans set out before the 2015 election turned out to be as undeliverable as the Labour policy team had calculated, but it wasn't much consolation when the Tories won the election and then promptly dumped them.

One of the biggest advantages the Prime Minister has in her exchanges with the Leader of the Opposition is the last word. After the sixth question, she has the chance to give an answer which will have no comeback from him. This is where she can unload, with a big attack on her opponent, or a contrast between the two sides. Margaret Thatcher would do this after Neil Kinnock's third question, as John Whittingdale remembers: 'If you're doing three questions and you know that after the third one he's not going to have a comeback, that's probably when you punch him hard. She used to refer back to the chaos of the late '70s right up until she left office, and it was still within most people's memory then, so it was fair enough to do.' Now, of course, the big attack comes after question six.

The sixth answer may start with something more or less relevant to the sixth question – which will often itself be a broad attack on the government – but it will quickly pivot to something wider, and generally scripted. Investment versus cuts, a long-term economic plan versus spiralling debt, talk versus action, strength versus weakness, competence versus chaos: whatever the chosen dividing line is. The Prime Minister is waiting for the right moment to unload, as William Hague told us: 'You've got your best line ready for the end, and that's why David Cameron often used to turn to me during PMQs saying, "Was that five or six? Is this the sixth?" and it is difficult to keep track of the number actually. His most common question was not "What is the answer to this?"; it's "Was that the fifth?" because you'd be getting ready your best answer for the fifth or sixth question.'

Cameron knew that even if he was in trouble from the substance of Ed Miliband's questioning, the last word on the sixth answer would help him escape. George Osborne's analysis to us of Ed's PMQs performances, and the best way of attacking him, largely reflects what we knew in Ed's prep team: 'I thought he was pretty good, he had good jokes and he was clever and definitely if you'd had a bad time, there'd been some row in the Cabinet or something, you could expect that you'd be on the ropes. But partly because there was always a question mark over Ed Miliband's leadership, particularly after the initial months, you could always as the Prime Minister say, "Weak leader, not supported by his party."' There were certain attacks Cameron could keep going back to, such as Ed's decision to stand against his brother David for the Labour leadership. Here's an example from December 2011: when Ed asked about divisions between the Conservatives and their Liberal Democrat coalition partners, Cameron responded, 'It's not that bad – it's not like we're brothers or anything.'[134] Cameron says, 'I think we thought that was fair game. He had taken on his brother, it was totally fair enough, and we knew it was one of those things that just worked. It worked in the public.'

The Prime Minister is given some leeway to attack the opposition, but this is not infinite. The Speaker can cut off answers that appear to him to have nothing to do with the Prime Minister's responsibilities. In April 2014 an attempt by Cameron to give a sixth answer which had absolutely nothing to do with the topic of Ed's six questions – the privatisation of Royal Mail – was slapped down by John Bercow, wrecking the planned attack on Labour:

DAVID CAMERON: Six questions and not a mention of GDP; not a mention of what happened to employment figures while we were away; and not a mention of the fact that the deficit is getting better. We know that the right honourable gentleman has a new adviser from America. It is Mr [David] Axelrod, and this is what the right honourable gentleman has been advised to say. Let me share it with the House as it is excellent advice. It is that 'there's a better future ahead of us' but we must not 'go backward to the policies that put us in this mess in the first place'. I do not know what Labour are paying him—

MR SPEAKER: Order.

DAVID CAMERON: I have not finished— [*Interruption*]

MR SPEAKER: In response to that question, the Prime Minister has finished, and he can take it from me that he has finished.[135]

Bercow similarly intervened on a Labour Prime Minister in November 2009, when the answer to a planted question on the NHS from a Labour backbencher, designed to allow Gordon Brown to highlight an embarrassing comment from shadow Health Secretary Andrew Lansley, was cut off before the punchline:

> GORDON BROWN: We will not only make promises to improve cancer care in the National Health Service, we will deliver on these promises. We will not only have a two-week maximum before people can see a consultant, we will move to a one-week maximum before people can actually have the diagnostic tests they need. However, I think that people should be warned about the National Health Service, because the shadow Health Secretary said yesterday—
>
> MR SPEAKER: Order. I do not think that we need to go into that today, Prime Minister. I call Mr David Cameron.[136]

This is not just embarrassing for the Prime Minister; it stops a key attack line from getting aired. The way to avoid it is for the Prime Minister to keep her references to her opponents tight and relevant to the line of questioning. But dubious attacks do slip through the net. In December 2017 Jeremy Corbyn, uncharacteristically, asked Theresa May six questions about Brexit. May's sixth answer had absolutely nothing at all to do with anything he had said:

> Week in, week out, the right honourable gentleman comes to this House making promises he knows he cannot deliver, and Labour members keep doing it. At the election, he told

students that they would write off their student debt, and then he said, 'I did not commit to write off the debt'. But what is the Labour Party doing? It is putting around leaflets that say 'Labour will cancel existing student debt'. It is time he apologised for the grossly misleading Labour leaflets.[137]

Not only had Corbyn not mentioned student debt in his set of six questions; he had not even made a promise of any sort, let alone one which could be characterised as undeliverable. May got away with this, and video of her giving this answer was clipped by the Conservative Party and shared on social media for the benefit of an audience which may not have seen PMQs or realised just how irrelevant her attack was – for more on the increasing use of this tactic by both sides see Chapter 9. She was lucky.

Nevertheless, the sixth answer is the Prime Minister's biggest opportunity to broaden the argument from the specific topic of the Leader of the Opposition's questions to something just general enough to get past the Speaker, a wider attack on her opponents and defence of her programme. Tony Blair explained in his memoirs that he took the characterisation of his opponents very seriously:

With each successive Tory leader, I would develop a line of attack, but I only did so after a lot of thought. Usually I did it based on close observation at PMQs. I never made it overly harsh. I always tried to make it telling. The aim was to get the non-politician nodding. I would wonder not what appealed to a Labour Party conference in full throttle, but what would appeal to my old mates at the Bar, who wanted a reasonable case to be made; and who, if it were made, would rally. So I defined Major as weak; Hague as better at jokes than judgement; Howard as an opportunist; Cameron as a flip-flop, not knowing where he wanted to go. (The Tories did my work for me in undermining Iain Duncan Smith.) Expressed like that, these attacks seem flat, rather mundane almost, and not exactly inspiring, but that's their appeal. Any one of those charges, if it comes to be believed, is actually fatal. Yes, it's not like calling your opponent a liar, or a fraud, or a villain or a hypocrite, but the middle-ground floating voter kind of shrugs their shoulders at those claims. They don't chime. They're too over the top, too heavy, and they represent an insult, not an argument. Whereas the lesser charge, because it's more accurate and precisely because it's more low-key, can stick. And if it does, that's that. Because in each case, it means they're not a good leader. So game over.[138]

Blair also had the skill, which he didn't only deploy at PMQs, of thinking through the logic of an argument and being able to state it in simple terms. George Osborne says: 'Blair was very, very good. His devastating thing was he can frame an argument, and deconstruct the argument. I think the clever way to do it is to tell a story of why you're doing something and make the other person look small or brittle or point holes and say, "I thought you were supposed to be in favour of this."'

The importance of the ring of truth in political attack is often underestimated. For example, the idea of Theresa May as robotic, unable to think outside the tramlines of a prepared script or adjust to changing circumstances, is both more plausible to the non-partisan observer and more powerful than the idea that she has – as some Labour supporters might believe and want to tell the public – evil motives. Think of what might make even a leader's own supporters wince with embarrassed recognition, rather than sincerely reject as unfair, and keep punching that bruise. You might still never win those supporters round, but if they can see the truth in your attack, more neutral viewers will see it too, and they're your real targets. And of course, if the other side's MPs think you're on to something in your attack on their leader, then all the more chance of outbreaks of disquiet and leadership speculation.

Attacks have to be consistent. Sometimes two attack lines are possible but come into conflict with each other. And sometimes parties just don't know what their best characterisation of their opponent is. Alastair Campbell thought that John Major and the Conservatives had this problem in the mid-1990s when Tony Blair was Leader of the Opposition: 'You could tell they were really struggling to work out how to deal with Tony, a bit like we were with Cameron. Is he Bambi, is he Stalin, is he a control freak, is he a flibbertigibbet – they were a little bit all over the place.'

Theresa May managed to shoehorn two incompatible attacks into one PMQs session in September 2017 when she attacked Labour's failure to act for thirteen years in government on the issue Jeremy Corbyn was asking her about and then, three questions later, attacked Corbyn for not backing the exact same Labour government which, she had just claimed, had been so ineffective. It might have been true to say of Corbyn that 'for years [he] sat on the Labour benches and did not support Labour policy',[139] but it wasn't wise, given what she had said a few moments before about how useless Labour policy had been at the time. You have to choose one line, and stick with it. Either the Labour Party had not changed under Corbyn's leadership, or it had. Of course, this kind of inconsistency isn't the end of the world, and most viewers won't even spot it, but it gives a useful indication of a research and attack operation that isn't firing on all cylinders, and a party that doesn't know what its best argument is.

In fact, too many of May's PMQs attacks on Labour raised suspicions that she didn't know how to deal with its change of direction under Corbyn. She had some good moments that drew an effective contrast between herself and her opposite number: one closing line in February 2017, 'He can lead a protest, I am leading a country,'[140] stands out. But too often, she relied on David Cameron's old briefing book.

For example, in October 2016 she attacked Labour's approach to the NHS by using a quote that dated all the way back to the 2010 Labour leadership contest: 'a former shadow Health Secretary said that it would be "irresponsible" to put more money into the National Health Service'.[141] This was an attack with which we, as members of Ed Miliband's old PMQs prep team, were drearily acquainted. Andy Burnham had claimed that the Conservative policy of increasing NHS funding without protecting social care spending was 'irresponsible' because it would lead to even bigger cuts in social care; this was then hung around his neck by David Cameron at PMQs and elsewhere as a much more straightforward, bald claim that increasing NHS spending was irresponsible. Whatever the merits of Burnham's prediction about social care (it turned out to be completely accurate) or the wisdom of his expressing it in the terms he chose (it turned out to be hugely unhelpful), six years on, with Jeremy Corbyn leading the Labour Party and Burnham no longer even in the shadow Cabinet, the survival of this attack was, frankly, baffling. If you're attacking Jeremy Corbyn's Labour Party for wanting to cut public services, you're doing it wrong.

This points to a truth at the core of PMQs: even if the Prime Minister isn't always answering the specific questions that are being asked, she is answering, both explicitly and implicitly, bigger political questions about who should be running the country. The subtext of all questions in the leaders' exchanges at PMQs is 'Who should be running the country: you or me?' The subtext of all of the Prime Minister's answers is 'I should be running the country, not you,' and then the content of those answers – their substance, rhetoric and political attack – as well as the delivery of those answers, is what either backs up or undermines that subtext. So the heart of the Prime Minister's task is not knowing the facts, but framing the argument. Danny Finkelstein says: 'I think what Tony Blair and William Hague proved actually is that the core of Prime Minister's Questions is the argument. Tony Blair was very good at Prime Minister's Questions because he was extremely good at defining the right, the correct, *actual* answer to questions. And I think David Cameron also relied on this. That is the heart of Prime Minister's Questions.'

5

NO. 10 DOWNING STREET

The most obvious disadvantage the Prime Minister has at PMQs is the fact that she doesn't know what's coming. As Harriet Harman says, 'It is like an exam in public where the curriculum is the entire world, its past and future.' But it is also easy to overstate how hard this is. While it's certainly true that the Prime Minister can't predict the questions from the Leader of the Opposition with complete accuracy, she can do so with some confidence – or at least narrow them down to a shortlist of likely topics. Although it's impossible to prepare for the ambushes described in Chapter 2, which are designed to take the Prime Minister entirely by surprise with information which has never previously been in the public domain and which No. 10 never even knew existed, in general the constraints on the Leader of the Opposition, and the options available to him, are just as obvious in 10 Downing Street as they are in Norman Shaw South.

One of Theresa May's advisers told us that her team has a very high success rate in predicting what Jeremy Corbyn's main subject at PMQs will be, and added, 'Usually there's a discussion that takes place for thirty seconds in which we say, "Well, he could ask about Brexit," and then someone reminds us that he won't ask about Brexit.' Alastair Campbell can only recall one occasion during his years working in No. 10 when Tony Blair's team did not successfully predict the Leader of the Opposition's chosen topic. Margaret Thatcher and her team similarly found Neil Kinnock's PMQs topics easy to guess, as John Whittingdale told us: 'Neil, I would have to say, was quite predictable; he was not one who would from way outside left-field suddenly pluck a topic. Normally we would guess, I'd say 80 per cent of the time we would guess and the next 15 per cent we probably hadn't guessed for that week but it wouldn't be something we hadn't covered in the past, and only 5 per cent would it be literally something she didn't even know about.' To be fair to Kinnock, he was perfectly aware of his predictability, which was deliberate: 'My tendency was to ask a question that could fairly easily be anticipated because it was the major headline issue of the day, on which it was important for the Prime Minister to be asked, and to try and get a response.'

Guessing the topic correctly does not mean that preparation is easy. The amount of time the Prime Minister has to spend preparing for PMQs has grown along with the event's significance. Harold Macmillan said of PMQs that 'in many ways, this is the most anxious work; I would never have lunched out on question day'.[142] For his most recent successors, PMQs does more than get in the way of lunch. Tony Blair says, 'Sunday night it would be a smallish cloud on the horizon, Tuesday, Wednesday it was full-on.' Prime ministerial diaries have to be cleared. As Gabby Bertin, one of David Cameron's advisers, told us, 'It halts life for two days really.' There are no media appearances on Tuesday evenings or Wednesday mornings, even if a huge story breaks, no meetings, however urgent. George Osborne explains that David Cameron 'would try and avoid doing anything on Tuesday night, so even when there were things like state banquets, which all for some reason are always on Tuesday night, he would try and leave them the moment he possibly could'.

An account by G. W. Jones of the Prime Minister's PMQs preparation, written in 1973 during Edward Heath's premiership, shows a process that would be recognisable to those working on PMQs today, although some of the timings are different: the decisions in 1997 to move PMQs to Wednesdays and at the beginning of 2003 to move it from a mid-afternoon slot to noon had an obvious knock-on effect for preparation schedules. But in the age of closed questions, asked in a predictable order, Heath's team had the luxury of knowing not just what would come up and when but, even more importantly, what subjects were definitely not on the order paper:

> The Prime Minister settles down to the questions in the late evening [of the day before PMQs], concentrating on the main answers. He clears away the final ones over breakfast, so that when his staff arrive at 9 a.m. the folder awaits their attention. The Prime Minister initials those he agrees with, makes amendments and suggests further investigation on others. Departments are again contacted for extra information and to clear any major change in the answers. New material is inserted to take account of topical events or a changing situation, such as current

negotiations. The revised folder is back with the Prime Minister by 1.30 so that over lunch in his flat he can make a last intensive effort. The Prime Minister keeps free of lunch engagements on Tuesdays and Thursdays so as to be able to work on questions. He now concentrates on the supplementaries, underlining some points, noting others and inserting new ones. At 2.30 p.m. there is a briefing session at No. 10 of all his private secretaries, his PPS, the chief of the No. 10 press section, and his political secretary. They go through the questions and answers, suggesting changes or points to emphasise, or warning of pitfalls. At 3 p.m. they leave for the Commons so that the Prime Minister can be in his seat by 3.15 p.m.[143]

John Whittingdale, a former political secretary to Margaret Thatcher who joined her PMQs prep team in 1988, told us, 'The process went like this. The night before, the parliamentary secretary in the private office would assemble the briefing pack, which would be the briefing on the key topics from every government department which he'd call in. And he'd spend the week or the preceding few days looking out for topics which looked likely runners, and then he'd get the briefing in. And that would all go into the overnight box, she would do the box at six in the morning, and then at nine o'clock we would have the morning meeting.' That hour-long meeting would be used to identify likely topics, based on press secretary Bernard Ingham's press digest, and then more briefing would be commissioned. Whittingdale told us that 'Mrs T. hated newspapers, she always took the view that anything written about her in the newspaper was bound to be bad and therefore far better not to read it, so instead she had Bernard's compilation of what was in the newspaper.' The press digest 'was a slightly Bernard view of the world, and it was subject to some editing, so stressing things that Bernard thought were important or that she would want to read and sometimes leaving out other things, but for the purpose of PM's Questions, given that she wasn't going through the newspapers, it was essential'.

Thatcher's team would reconvene at about 12.30 and 'go through the briefs that Dominic [Morris, her parliamentary secretary] had prepared, so we'd go through each topic which we thought was most likely. I would try and think of attacking points, questions she might be asked, she would go through it, this would continue till approximately half past two when we would all get into the cars and go across to Parliament – bear in mind the IRA was active in those days so security was quite a big consideration, so we would sometimes take different routes. We would then go up to her office before she went into the Chamber, so from roughly 2.40 to 3.10 she would be there continuing to go through it, but by now not really absorbing new information, practising a few lines, just needing reassurance. She'd been Prime Minister for eight years and she got very nervous and actually you could see her leg shaking at the dispatch box sometimes.'

It all amounted to a significant amount of time out of the Prime Minister's diary. In total, Whittingdale told us, 'She will have spent probably an hour to two hours going through the briefing in the box from nine to ten, and then from half past twelve to quarter past three, it would be about four hours' preparation for fifteen minutes twice a week.'

PMQs prep is demanding enough for the Prime Minister on Tuesdays and Wednesdays, but for the Prime Minister's staff, and for the civil service, PMQs never really goes away. For the research and information team, the work starts on a Thursday, the day after the previous PMQs. Theo Bertram told us about No. 10's role as a pre-PMQs clearing house for information from across government: 'Most departments have a PMQs team, but in addition to that most private secretaries care about any issue that's going to come near their patch at PMQs, so that means that most of them are actively reaching out to give No. 10 information, to highlight where things have gone wrong and to say, "This is what the issue is," so that you could have the DWP saying, "We want to highlight this figure in this report which shows that this has gone up by 25 per cent when we've committed to it going down; the reason for this going up is because the way we've recorded the numbers has changed," or whatever it is, so you have someone giving you that information, and then you double-check it and boil it down to the shortest way of putting it, and then ideally you'd talk it through with the PM, even if it's a two-minute conversation like this where it's "This might come up, this is your response."'

The Prime Minister needs to know what she's likely to be attacked on. Just as in opposition PMQs prep we had to bring Ed Miliband all the most damaging stories for the Labour Party – the 'bucket of shit' – so in government the Prime Minister's advisers are often purveyors of bad news. It doesn't always help their relationship with the Prime Minister, as Bertram told us about his time preparing Gordon Brown: 'I would come and bring in not only what was the latest thing that the lobby or the Tories were saying about him, or [political gossip blog] Guido Fawkes, or anything that might randomly come up in Cameron's attack, because you have to have warned him, but I'd also have to bring him all the shitty stuff that his own side were saying. So we were just bringing him all this terrible stuff.'

Alongside all this is material about all of the opposition back-benchers on the order paper. No. 10 does not usually know what they will be asking about, but the Prime Minister can still be given information that will undermine their ability to attack the government: news of falling unemployment in their constituency, an embarrassing quote criticising their own party leader, details of donations they have received. John Bercow still remembers Tony Blair's response to his first ever PMQs question when he was a new Conservative backbencher in 1997: he made the mistake of asking a sleaze-related question about the ethics of the Labour Party's policy on accepting political dona-tions. Blair replied, 'I am intrigued that the honourable gentleman should ask such a question as I understand that his last employment was as special adviser to Jonathan Aitken'[144] – exactly the sort of fact that a Prime Minister's research team is asked to dig out. Bercow says that his former boss had 'either been by then sent to prison or he was on trial for perjury, so that was a very conclusive putdown'.

This political work isn't something for impartial civil servants, whose job it is to make sure that all the facts and non-political argu-ments are in place: it's done partly by the No. 10 special advisers and by staff in party HQ, and partly by the politicians themselves. Both David Cameron and George Osborne worked in the Conservative Research Department early in their careers, and produced material which eventually ended up in Margaret Thatcher's and John Major's PMQs folders.

Nowadays, much of this research work can be done using the internet, but in the 1990s, as Osborne told us, 'It involved tracking speeches by shadow Cabinet members and the Leader of the Opposition, getting subscriptions to a whole load of left-wing newspapers like the *Morning Star*, and literally having an enormous library of, you know, what has Donald Dewar said, what did Robin Cook tell the TUC, and in those days it was actually quite difficult to get these things because they only existed on paper, and unless you actually went to the Durham Miners' Gala and got a leaflet, it wasn't like you could tap in to the internet, "What did Robin Cook say to the Durham Miners' Gala?"'

Good advance work pays dividends. In 1984 Margaret Thatcher managed to outwit Tony Blair, then a backbencher early in his parliamentary career, by finding out exactly what he was going to ask her from the back benches and having an obscure prop ready in response. Blair asked about a contradiction between a recent statement by her Chancellor and her earlier 'endorsement at her party conference of the 1944 employment White Paper'. Thatcher was ready for him: 'I have a copy in my handbag,'[145] she said. Blair was stunned. 'She gets up at the dispatch box, brings her handbag out, puts it on the dispatch box, opens it, takes out this government White Paper from 1944, and proceeds to read a passage and completely wipes the floor with me,' he told us. 'Afterwards we worked out that someone must have overheard me doing the research in the Commons library.' John Whittingdale is not so sure: 'Well, she did use to keep extraordinary things in her handbag.'

As well as following the news, using their political judgement and – possibly – hiding around corners in the House of Commons library, the No. 10 advisers are helped to predict the questions by government departments which are identifying problematic issues in their area where the Prime Minister might be vulnerable, and helping to suggest answers. Indeed, one of the ways in which government can be prompted to make decisions is by the Prime Minister's team recognising that a possible PMQs question has an unsatisfactory answer, or no answer at all. It's not the job of the PMQs team to make the decision, but it is their job to flag that a PMQs risk exists and a decision is needed. It's not unusual for a concession, or a U-turn, or even a resignation, to take place on a Wednesday morning to undercut a likely line of PMQs questioning. During Theresa May's premiership, the Budget U-turn on national insurance contributions came on a Wednesday morning, just before PMQs. So did an announcement that the 55p-per-minute universal credit helpline – the subject of difficult questions from Jeremy Corbyn at PMQs the previous week – was to be made free.

Identifying the risky areas is mostly a straightforward process in which everyone is on the same side, but occasionally, Theo Bertram says, ministers try to use PMQs to resolve their own disputes – or to force No. 10 to do so. If a controversial decision hasn't yet been made, the risk that the Prime Minister might be asked about it can bring it to a head; but that risk may not be anything like as great as the department in question is claiming, in which case there's no real need to make the quick decision it's demanding: 'Let's say two ministers have been arguing about who's going to get more spending or who's going to be responsible for something, and the Prime Minister has pushed back on that, or has not given an adequate answer, and then one of them, in order to force it to a point where the PM has to decide, uses the PMQs process as a way to do it, so that this cannot be ducked or dived, this must now be brought up, so it's almost like the department are pushing something up the PMQs agenda, "Oh, this may come up," which you then have to work out, is it *really* going to come up, is it possible that the Cabinet minister ... may he have briefed someone?'

In the 1970s, as now, the quality of briefing for PMQs from different departments varied:

> Since they are not used to thinking in terms of the political situation faced by the Prime Minister, their material sometimes lacks political imagination. Their supplementaries may not reflect the Prime Minister's 'flavour' or 'tone', or his 'tactical sense'; the wording of the supplementaries may be so hedged with qualifications that the sentences are nearly impossible for him to utter. They may waste space on the blindingly obvious, yet miss the crucial point or neglect a difficult issue. Often they may reflect a narrow departmental, or even divisional, view, unaware of how other departments or divisions may be affected by their replies, and they sometimes fail to appreciate that the Prime Minister has not a detailed knowledge of the work of the department.[146]

It is the job of the civil servants and special advisers in No. 10 to take these briefings from across government and turn them into something the Prime Minister can use in the House of Commons. Not all Prime Ministers leave this job to their civil servants and special advisers, as John Whittingdale told us: 'I can't remember which department it was, I think it was Education, had sent in some brief about some attack story in the press, a defensive line, to which [Margaret Thatcher] said, "This is absolutely hopeless, absolutely *useless*. John, go and tell them that this *just won't do*." So I go across the study, pick up the telephone, the Downing Street switchboard say, "Yes, Prime Minister," I say, "No, it's John, can you get me the Principal Private Secretary in the Department for Education?" "Oh, yes, sir." On comes this poor chap who says, "Hello," and I say, "It's John Whittingdale and I'm with the Prime Minister now, she's seen the brief on this, she's not very happy," at which point she comes striding across the study and grabs the phone and starts haranguing this poor civil servant at the other end of the phone, "It's *just not good enough*," and I had this vision on Tuesdays and Thursdays between one and half past two, all over Whitehall people looking at their telephones terrified it was going to ring.'

Whittingdale says that there was more to PMQs prep for Thatcher than simply making sure she could get through each session: 'She used it to run the government. Because her view was: I have to be able to defend my government on anything that is going to be thrown at me at the dispatch box. Therefore she had to be up to speed on what every department was doing, and if she didn't like it she told them. I would always say that although it sounds ridiculous to spend four hours preparing for fifteen minutes, it was such an integral part of her very hands-on approach. She was not someone who delegated much, she liked to know what every department was doing, to be satisfied that it was doing the right thing and if it wasn't to go and tell them so. And she had also assembled the most extraordinary body of knowledge, you know, she did it twice a week for eleven years; by the end she just knew *everything*.'

David Cameron told us that as Prime Minister he used PMQs to spot weaknesses in policies and lines to take and to insist on changes:

'It's a forcing mechanism, because people always overestimate the power of No. 10 – it's tiny next to the departments – but it's that one time where your reach is everywhere and you can determine and make changes and observations, because you're saying, "Well, I don't care if the line to take is *x*, it doesn't make any sense and I'm not going to defend it," you know, and the pressure's on. So there's this great Whitehall battle taking place between No. 10 wanting to get the right answer to the boss, and the departments trying to hang on to the existing policy.'

PMQs is the place where a policy can unravel if it's not good enough, and if it does unravel it's the Prime Minister who will look stupid: 'You're there thinking, "Right, what are the answers to all these difficult questions?" And often that would link to a policy that you weren't quite happy with, or an answer you weren't quite happy with, and at that moment a battle between No. 10 and the department would take place,' says Cameron. 'And eventually you are supreme in that, because what you say at twelve o'clock is law. It was very personal because you'd look through the file and you'd see the answer to a question about this policy or that policy and you'd say, "Well, I'm not happy with that, why is that the case?" And then I would always try, I'm a collegiate chap, I would try and listen to the argument about why the answer was what the answer was. But sometimes it was just totally unsatisfactory, so you have to say, "I'm sorry, this won't survive. It won't survive scrutiny and it's not right."' And in the end, if the Prime Minister is unhappy, the Prime Minister can change a policy just by saying publicly what the policy is: 'You change it. It creates a fact on the ground. It often was the way that a change would come about.' Cameron cites energy prices, on which he unexpectedly announced a new policy in October 2012, as 'a good example of where I was sort of fed up with the way the department was handling a policy, where you just lay it down and then say, "Suck it up. You've got to make it work."' Alastair Campbell told us that Tony Blair 'got very, very angry, particularly in government, if he didn't have the facts. He couldn't stand it if you said to the Home Office, "We're doing this now," and he just got all the lines to take, as opposed to "These are the facts." That's when he got really pissed off.'

All of the material the Prime Minister might need in the Chamber goes into a folder, organised by subject area, with tabs or labels identifying which page she needs to go to when a particular question is asked. The briefing and information team in No. 10 is responsible for putting this together, but the Prime Minister will spend time making sure that she knows her way around it. Tony Blair's folder, Theo Bertram explained to us, 'was physical, just a thick, plain A4 binder, which then had a series of sheets of facts in, they could be basic economy facts, and most pages would have, as you'd expect, your key points, and then at the bottom, your key attacks, and we would keep all of that updated, so there's a section in his folder which is there every week which is just "this is your key facts, this is your key attacks". Most of those things he knows by heart but he might want to flip over just to remind himself while he's sitting and waiting for the question to finish. He relied on the folder, he felt confident in the work, he also felt confident he could go in and just basically knock down arguments.'

Each Prime Minister will have the folder, and the pages within it, drafted and organised in a particular way; George Osborne told us that David Cameron would spend some time alone on Wednesday mornings getting the folder into shape and the shape of the folder into his head, a job that nobody else could possibly do for him: 'He would have an hour between about ten and eleven just by himself, going through it and constructing his folder, so ripping things out, and so he would build his own folder.'

The pages inside the PMQs folder need to be produced in a format that the Prime Minister can read, which leads to an inevitable trade-off between the font size and the level of detail that can be included. Her biographer John Campbell says that Margaret Thatcher, who turned sixty in 1985, 'needed reading glasses, but did not like to be seen wearing them in public, so her briefs for Prime Minister's Questions and speech scripts had to be printed in large type. She would never admit to any hint of weakness.'[147] Tony Blair and David Cameron both found, entering middle age during their time as Prime Minister, that they needed to use reading glasses to consult their notes during PMQs and other events; the first time each appeared in public with glasses on it became a news story. Gordon Brown, who had lost the sight in one eye in a school rugby injury, and whose other eye, by the time he became Prime Minister, was deteriorating too, used to have his briefs typed up in large-size bold sans serif block capitals, which he would annotate with a thick black marker.

A civil servant who wrote PMQs briefs for both Brown and Cameron told us that Brown was particularly hard to write for, because he needed a large font and wanted plenty of numbers and supportive quotes: 'That tension between him wanting to know so much about everything, and the physical space restrictions, was really difficult.' Cameron – at least early in his premiership – demanded briefs that were much less defensive and more positive, more about the vision, although this partly reflects the difference between a government that has been in power for over a decade, and one which is just starting out. Different ministers, not just different Prime Ministers, want different things from their civil service briefs: Oliver Letwin, who was responsible for policy co-ordination across government under Cameron, 'was easier to write for because he was the same type of intellect as Gordon Brown, with the advantage you could write in smaller text'.

So the Prime Minister's briefing folder needs material to attack the opposition as well as the facts about each policy area. Some of this material will be topical, but much of it will be standard lines that change little from month to month or even year to year. Margaret Thatcher 'always liked to have the headlines from the winter of discontent', says John Whittingdale. 'Her comfort blankets were certain bits of paper, key quotes or facts, and she probably would never use them but she just liked to know they were there, and I used to have to have fifteen copies of these, because each time I'd give her one it would disappear and I'd never see it again, so I had to keep another one for the next time.'

Occasionally the Prime Minister's briefing papers for PMQs can come from other sources too. Anna Soubry told us that when she was parliamentary private secretary to health minister Simon Burns in 2012, she took it upon herself to reduce the controversial Health and Social Care Bill down to half a side of A4, 'one Sunday night in front of the telly on the laptop'. She also pulled together turnout figures for the various surveys of medical professionals which were showing huge opposition to the government's plans: 'I was dead proud of this obviously, and it was on one side of A4 and then all the quotes, and

I sent it through. I did that on the Sunday, and on the Wednesday Des Swayne was still [Cameron's] PPS, and I was in the Aye lobby, and Des came up to me and said, "Where's that paper? Where is it? Oh my God, where is it, where is it?" And I went, "I've got a copy in my handbag." "Give it to me now!" So I rushed over to my handbag and brought it out, and he just tore off down the corridor with this piece of paper. This is government, so this is the Prime Minister, with all the spads, with all the everything, and there's my piece of paper from the home computer, and a question comes in, and I saw it. There was the piece of paper. And it just made me laugh so much that this middle-aged woman had stayed at home on the Sunday on her laptop in front of the telly and done it, and there it was in PMQs.'

Here is the exchange between Ed Miliband and David Cameron, featuring the piece of paper from Anna Soubry's handbag:

ED MILIBAND: And 98 per cent of those in the Royal College of General Practitioners oppose the Bill. I have to say that it is hard to keep track of opposition to this Bill, because in the past seven days alone the Royal College of Physicians has called the first emergency general meeting in its history about the Bill, and the Prime Minister has lost the support of the British Geriatrics Society and the Royal College of Paediatrics and Child Health. So every week that goes by more and more health care organisations come out against this Bill. I have a simple question for the Prime Minister: can he now give the House a list of significant health organisations that are still wholehearted supporters of the Bill?

[...]

DAVID CAMERON: He said that 98 per cent of GPs oppose
the reforms – that was the figure. Let me give him the actual
figures. There are 44,000 members of the Royal College of
General Practitioners. Out of a total of 44,000, just 7 per cent
responded opposing the Bill. What about the Royal College
of Physiotherapists? Of the 50,000 in the Royal College of
Physiotherapists, 2 per cent. I know that that is enough for
the unions to elect him leader of the Labour Party, but that is
about as far as it will go.[148]

'And then', Soubry says, 'I was made a minister not long after that on
the basis that I was the only person in Britain who understood the
Health and Social Care Act.'

One of the most important jobs the Prime Minister is trying to
do at PMQs is to elevate the occasion from a focus on whatever
particular issues are going badly this week, which the Leader of the
Opposition and other MPs are likely to be asking about, to a much
bigger political argument about why the government is doing what
it's doing, and why its overall approach and philosophy are better
than the opposition's. Few members of the public, and indeed few
MPs, are truly animated by the minutiae of unemployment figures or
NHS waiting lists or local government workforce numbers or housing
starts or corporation tax levels, but the decisions the government
makes on each, and the impact of those decisions, point to bigger
truths about the government's programme, and about its success or
failure. As Theo Bertram told us about Tony Blair, 'The thing that
Tony also understood was that each PMQs is not about "do you
win this week, do you win next week". It was about "what is the arc

of your argument over a term?" And it can't be any longer than that because each time you get to a holiday everything resets and you get to start again afresh after everyone's had a break, including the lobby.' Each answer, or each sequence of answers, needs to find a way to move from the facts to the winning political argument.

The way to present the government's case, and to attack the opposition, is a political decision, made by politicians. In the end, the Prime Minister is the most important political strategist for any government, just as the Leader of the Opposition is for any opposition, and any half-decent leader will spend time working out themselves what the best political argument is. Ed Miliband says, 'I don't think there's any substitute. Part of being a decent politician is you can spot something that maybe other people aren't going to spot. I think I learned this from Gordon actually, he would find a thing that had a kind of resonance that maybe other people wouldn't spot.' We would joke about Ed's slightly nerdy tendency to go home after PMQs prep and do his own research in his 'Statcave' – few things are more demoralising for a political party's head of research than to discover that your own leader has personally dug out some fact you've missed – but it was an important part of getting his head around the arguments.

Tony Blair told us about how he thought through the different kinds of issue he knew he could expect to be asked about, and not just the factual answers he needed but the bigger strategic questions that were raised by each one: 'You have various categories, you have scandal, you have crisis, you have big politics and you have everyday life. And so in each one, on the scandal, the crisis, you have to work out, what's the big point that you're going to make? And on the

politics you're "where are you, where's your opponent's weakness?"
And then on the everyday it's got to be consistent, how do you guide
it to be consistent with your overall narrative?' Alastair Campbell says,
'Once we decided what they were probably going to go on we would
retreat, and in a way not worry what the questions were going to be,
but just absolutely boil down on the issue and really drill down and get
the facts. And then we would think, "Well, if this was us, what would
we be asking the questions on?"'

Blair would devote significant amounts of time to thinking through
how he wanted to characterise his opponents. 'The thing you always
have to do is work out what your opponent's weakness is,' he told us.
With William Hague, for example, whose use of humour at PMQs
was highly effective, 'once I had alighted on his strength I was also
able to alight on his weakness, which was that the jokes were often
all that he could do. And once you did that you kind of defanged the
attack, because every time he made a joke then it was confirmation in
a way.' 'That was a good response,' Hague concedes, 'but it still doesn't
mean you should stay off humour. But probably as we got towards
the general election he got that line, and with the general election
everything had to become more serious and my advantage got a bit
less in the parliamentary sense.' Campbell says, 'Hague was easily the
funniest and in some ways the best. And when we did the bit about
jokes not judgement, he stopped being funny, he really did.'

George Osborne told us that David Cameron tried to do the same
thing, carving out time to think properly about the argument he wanted
to prosecute at PMQs. It's easy to miss the extent to which PMQs
was central to Cameron's political life, and to which his confidence
handling PMQs in the Chamber was a product of years of experience

thinking about that specific discipline even before being elected Conservative leader. After working with John Major in government, he assisted Iain Duncan Smith and Michael Howard on their PMQs prep in opposition, before spending four and a half years asking the questions as Leader of the Opposition, and then seven years answering them as Prime Minister – a PMQs career spanning just over a quarter of a century, albeit with interruptions. We think that only the Labour MP Bruce Grocott, later Lord Grocott, who took part in PMQs prep for most Labour leaders from Neil Kinnock in the mid-1980s until Harriet Harman's second interim leadership spell in 2015, can claim to be a longer-serving PMQs veteran – and unlike Cameron, Grocott never actually had to ask or answer the questions.

Cameron's first experience of working on PMQs came in the early summer of 1991, when as a young Conservative Research Department staffer he was called in to assist John Major's PMQs preparation: 'I was summoned to No. 10 to work for John Major, and his political secretary Judith Chaplin, who I knew anyway, but I was sort of tolerated, they didn't really like having this fresh-faced youngster trying to sharpen up and put in barbs and jokes and whatever.' Working for Major on PMQs provided Cameron with a political apprenticeship he could not have acquired anywhere else.

Cameron says that his experience with Major helped him, much later, to think about how he wanted to use his own prep time as Prime Minister: 'It took up far too much time in Major's diary, I mean it was *insane*. Because it was 3.15 in the afternoon, you went over there in the morning and did a prep session, and then I'd sit in Judith's office and write up the stuff, and then he'd have a sandwich lunch upstairs in the study and you'd do it all over again. My impression was he liked having very long briefing sessions with lots of people in the room, and I didn't really do that. I liked having the briefing session but then I used to go off with my folder and sort of sit there.'

George Osborne told us that on Wednesdays Cameron would 'start in the morning with a big meeting, I always thought personally there were too many people but he liked that, he would have a lot of people, maybe ten people'. After Cameron's morning briefing session, 'I tried to get to the House early. All the others tended to get there at the last minute; I liked to get there at 10.30. I particularly liked walking there, which I did a lot for the first few years. I used to like walking. And my ritual was just to spend time thinking it through. Quite a bit of it alone.' Both in the No. 10 briefing and for the last half-hour before PMQs started, he and his team would hold run-throughs which paralleled the run-throughs being held by our team in the Leader of the Opposition's office: 'Often Michael Gove, or George, would start throwing out the questions as they thought they'd come, and then I'd tend to do it right next to Prime Minister's Questions, just before, again, and that was very helpful because you'd see the potential run of play, sometimes you could see the weakness or the strength of a position, that was the way you tested it, and I think this does have a wider bearing on British politics, in a good way, which is that positions get tested.'

Any long-serving Prime Minister gets better at PMQs as they go along. There is no substitute, as with any skill worth mastering, for practice. Tony Blair told us: 'The funny thing is it got objectively harder as I went on, but subjectively I was much better at doing it. So by the end of my time I'd kind of mastered how to do it, which you should be able to do after ten years of doing it, but it was tougher, because obviously the opposition had also learned how to be a better opposition. But you know, we kept more or less upright during my time, I guess.' By the time Theo Bertram moved from Labour HQ into No. 10 to join the team briefing Blair for PMQs, Blair had been doing it for years. 'You could see he just oozed confidence, he'd seen it all, done it all, he'd taken so many questions, what's new that's going to come up that he hasn't had before? What thing could come up that's going to catch him off guard, given that he's already had this kind of experience so many times?'

When a government changes, the civil service is still there but the accumulated knowledge in the outgoing Prime Minister's head is suddenly gone. That's one reason why it's easier at PMQs to be a Prime Minister who takes office at the head of a new government following an election victory, as Thatcher, Blair and Cameron did, than to come in mid-term without a public mandate like Major, Brown or May. For a start, as George Osborne says, 'Generally speaking Prime Ministers who've been Leaders of the Opposition are much better prepared for the job in all sorts of ways, managing their party, being exposed to the publicity, the pressure of having to lead your party every week and every day.' And of course, they will have experienced PMQs before, albeit while asking rather than answering the questions – they know intimately how the whole thing works. For another thing, a Prime Minister leading a new government has no record to defend and can deflect difficult questions either by pointing at the future (we haven't done it yet but we will) or the past (it's a mess because they left it that way). And to make it even easier, their opponents are enfeebled, having suffered the trauma of an election defeat and, often, with a few months of a leadership contest to get through and perhaps an interim leader in place while the new Prime Minister is finding her feet and getting used to the system. It's only as time goes on that, in Osborne's words, 'you start to accumulate more things that you've said, and you've contradicted yourself' – and most of those contradictions will be inherited and owned, whether they like it or not, by any successor from the outgoing Prime Minister's own party if she steps down when her party is still in government.

New Prime Ministers promoted from within the governing party, as in the case of both Brown and May, will often not have experienced PMQs preparation before. They go suddenly from being a relatively small fish in a big pond to being a big fish in a very small barrel. The learning curve is steep. And they will almost invariably face a Leader of the Opposition who is more used to PMQs than they are.

Theo Bertram stayed in post at No. 10 and joined Gordon Brown's PMQs prep team. He told us, 'Gordon almost used the process as a way of understanding, it was like a PhD project really, a PhD for three weeks, "I want to know everything about how it works, I want to know in as much detail about everything else as I do about the Treasury." The first PMQs was just awful, it started the minute he arrived and went on all week, and you couldn't get a seat at the Cabinet table, so many people, partly really excited about being in No. 10, you've got Ed Balls, Ed Miliband, Douglas Alexander and everyone jumping up and down with excitement. And they were Tiggerishly excited, and then by the time it got to the period after the election that never was, it was me, James Bowler and Nicholas Howard [civil servants] in the room with Gordon, we were the only people that were consistently there, and it was a quiet, miserable place.'

Despite the work Gordon Brown and his team put in in that first week, he did not know the answers to all of the questions at his first PMQs. When David Cameron complained that the government had not yet banned the extremist group Hizb ut-Tahrir, saying, 'We think it should be banned – why has it not happened?' Brown answered, irritated, 'The Leader of the Opposition forgets that I have been in this job for five days.'[149] In Brown's defence, in Cameron's six years as Prime Minister he didn't get around to banning Hizb ut-Tahrir either.

Confidence is central not just to any politician's public performance but to their private behaviour. After Brown decided against calling an early election in the autumn of 2007 and was criticised for indecisiveness, Labour slipped behind in the opinion polls. Bertram says, 'I think he felt very lonely and there would be times when we would sit in the Cabinet Room, and there are two clocks in the Cabinet Room, one either side of the table, one of the clocks was put in by the PM so that he could see the clock. So what you'd have there was the sound of two clocks ticking, and there would be times when the Cabinet Room was silent for five, ten minutes at a time, when we were sitting there with Gordon and you'd just hear the sound of the clocks.' It took the global financial crisis of 2008 to give Brown, who had spent ten years as Chancellor before becoming Prime Minister, his confidence and sense of purpose back, and it came through at PMQs: 'When we had the financial crisis he knew deep down, without any doubt in his mind, that "I know what I'm doing on this, I don't care who's asking the questions, I know what I'm doing," and he just would bat people away, he was funny, he was humorous.'

Ducking out of an early election can lead to a loss of prime ministerial confidence, but so can choosing to call one and then losing your majority, as Theresa May did in 2017. One member of her team told us that they felt that Jeremy Corbyn's poor PMQs performances before the election had not given her enough opportunity to sharpen, and that her own loss of confidence afterwards had made it difficult for her to deal with what they recognised was a significant improvement on his part (an improvement, incidentally, that can partly be put down to Corbyn's own increased confidence after his impressive election campaign and result). They decided that part of the problem was that they were throwing too much information at her – 'It's very easy to sit round a table being clever.' But by the autumn of 2017 her team felt that they had settled on a way of preparing her for PMQs that suited her.

Instead of having 'streams of consciousness coming at her – "Ooh, this idea, why don't you say x, why don't you say z?"' – May's team worked to identify eight to ten items she should mug up on, while allowing her to rest on her knowledge of the big policy areas which she knew about in any case through the rest of her work as Prime Minister. They also worked on a series of generic 'ends of answers' – attacks, lines, jokes, general contrasts of the Labour and Conservative positions – which could be deployed at any time. And then they found time in the diary on Tuesdays and Wednesdays for May to work on it on her own: half an hour with her advisers followed by an hour alone, rather than having long briefing sessions with a big group of people.

Another current Conservative adviser told us that although May's PMQs performances have been criticised as flat, 'I think Theresa May is good at certain aspects of Prime Minister's Questions which shouldn't be overlooked. One is that she has a tremendous grasp of her brief. She really knows in depth a lot about the subjects she's been asked about, and so actually if you were to look at who gives a substantial response to the questions she does very well at that. It's not a theatrical performance.' John Bercow told us that David Cameron 'could sometimes give quite full answers, but actually answers now are longer, Prime Minister May is taking longer'. Bercow says that he has not complained to May about this, but gives it as one of the reasons why he so often allows PMQs to go on beyond its allocated half-hour: 'You can say that Prime Minister May is genuinely seeking to get more information across, and she's not giving flippant, soundbite-type replies, but equally you could say that they are very, very long replies and I want backbenchers to have a chance to get in.'

All Prime Ministers are under huge pressure, trying to fit the time they need to prepare for PMQs into a diary already packed with meetings with ministerial colleagues and officials, public meetings and visits, speeches, media interviews, summits and parliamentary appearances, and preparation for all of these, as well as all the official papers they have to read and make decisions about. They may have huge, ongoing, government-defining policy challenges to manage: a war, a global financial crisis, Brexit. And they have to deal with sudden shorter-term but no less challenging crises: natural disasters or terrorist attacks, leaks, scandals, resignations – all of which are liable to be topics at PMQs, as well as issues that have to be addressed in their own right. As one of Theresa May's team puts it, 'Bandwidth is a very, very serious issue.'

PMQs cannot be postponed or dodged, whatever else is happening. John Whittingdale told us how Margaret Thatcher prepared for PMQs while one of the biggest crises of her premiership rumbled on in the background. As the split between her Chancellor, Nigel Lawson, and her economic adviser, Sir Alan Walters, became increasingly public throughout 1989, it was inevitable that the question of which of them was in charge of economic policy would come up repeatedly at PMQs: 'Basically the old chestnut, you know, do you have confidence in your Chancellor, straight, do you, yes, no? And we said to her, "You are going to get this question." And she'd say, "I will say, the economy is *really strong*, we are enjoying *record growth*." And I and the PPS, who I think by then was Peter Morrison, one of us said, "That is absolutely hopeless, you have *got* to say you have confidence in the Chancellor and if you say anything else at all it will be taken that you don't." And she absolutely said, "No, I shall say the economy is *really strong*." And we were all going, "Oh, God, this is horrendous." And she went in and sure enough the question came up and she said, "Yes, he is a good Chancellor, and the economy is *really strong*." But she wouldn't tell us she was going to take our advice. But in her heart she knew we were right and she did.'

Neil Kinnock kept the pressure up, asking about the split between Walters and Lawson over and over again, which 'eventually, both in her refusal to provide conclusive answers on television interviews, and her refusal twice a week to give me a clear answer, saying whether she supported Alan Walters or Nigel Lawson, made the position of the Chancellor unsustainable'. On 26 October 1989 Kinnock devoted all three of his questions to the matter:

NEIL KINNOCK: Has it come to the Prime Minister's notice that since she was last at the dispatch box in July, Britain's balance of payments has moved a further £5.9 billion in the red, that Britain's home buyers and businesses have been hit again by higher interest rates and that in the meanwhile the number of Chancellors has doubled? In the interests of team spirit, will she get rid of the part-time one?

MARGARET THATCHER: Interest rates will stay as high as is necessary for as long as is necessary to get inflation down. With regard to interest rates and mortgage rates, the right honourable gentleman must be very glad that we do not have a socialist government, because in Australia mortgage rates are 18 per cent.

NEIL KINNOCK: I understand the Prime Minister's reluctance to answer the question about Sir Alan, or indeed any other Chancellor of the Exchequer. It would be wholly inappropriate for her to dismiss Sir Alan when she so completely concurs with everything he says, and everybody knows it. Is she aware that the confusion that is at the heart of government policy will remain as long as Sir Alan does?

MARGARET THATCHER: Advisers advise and ministers decide. Ministers in this government have a very sound economic policy, which is more than the opposition have.

NEIL KINNOCK: Does the report that the Prime Minister concurs with the view of her adviser faithfully represent her position?

MARGARET THATCHER: Had the right honourable gentleman listened to previous replies, he could not have asked that supplementary question. Advisers advise and Ministers decide. Ministers have decided, and we have an excellent economic policy.[150]

What you can't tell reading this exchange, and what Kinnock and the watching MPs on either side didn't know either, is the vital fact that only Thatcher knew when she gave these answers: Lawson had already resigned. As he wrote in his memoirs,

> When I returned to Margaret's first-floor study at Number 10 shortly after two o'clock, I told her straight away that I had reflected on our earlier discussion, and had not changed my mind. I handed her my resignation letter, telling her that I proposed to publish it as soon as practicable. At first she refused to take it; but then she took it and popped it into her handbag, unopened, saying that she did not wish to read it. She begged me not to resign, heaping extravagant praise and flattery on me … She then said that she had no time to discuss the matter any further as she had to prepare for Prime Minister's Questions.[151]

John Whittingdale marvelled to us that 'she did a PM's Questions having just literally an hour before accepted his resignation, and went ahead and did it, knowing something appalling had happened in her government like Lawson going. I mean the principal private secretary knew and that was literally about it. And she was as robust as she ever was.' Nothing can get in the way of PMQs. Whatever else is going on, whatever the pressures on a Prime Minister, she has to be able to compartmentalise it and get on with the job.

6

THE JOUST

The questions and answers are the point of the leaders' exchanges at PMQs, and the whole won't work without them. But the event isn't a dispassionate question-and-answer session: whether you like it or not, as Tony Blair says, it's a joust. It's all very well complaining about the noise, and the jokes, and the evasions, and the insults, but in the end, both sides are trying to win. And the really memorable material, the stuff that defines which side wins and which side loses, is often not in the questions and answers themselves but in the rejoinders and jokes that go alongside them. PMQs without rejoinders and jokes is like a Christmas tree without the baubles, tinsel, coloured lights, stars or whatever you like to hang on a Christmas tree. Puritans might find the decorations gaudy and insufficiently serious, but for the rest of us they're what makes the whole thing worth looking at. And anyway, if you're a puritan, what are you doing with a Christmas tree – even an undecorated one – in the first place?

On Ed Miliband's prep team we spent significant amounts of time, as most leaders' PMQs prep teams do, thinking about how best to respond to the other side's attacks, and how best to go on the offensive. It takes work. David Cameron told us: 'I think the skill of Prime Minister's Questions, whether you're in opposition or in government, is to think through the subjects, and then think through the questions you're going to get asked, think through your answers, think through the comeback to your answers, and think through the answer to that answer, and that's where I thought both Miliband and I were quite skilled, is that you could tell sometimes that he had a good comeback to my comeback, and I had a good comeback to his comeback, even though we couldn't both have known exactly, we'd guessed, we'd thought ahead, and that's why it was quite good theatre because it was a mixture of genuine spontaneity and sort of predicted spontaneity, possible predicted spontaneity. I think you're only really effective at it if you can genuinely think on your feet, sometimes it has to be rapid fire, and it's something you've thought of on your feet, because you can't pre-think everything. The thing that works is when there's a question, an answer, a rejoinder and a rejoinder to the rejoinder. It's the latter bits that really fizz because everyone knows the first question and probably the first answer are quite rehearsed. Nobody really knows what's happening after that.'

As Ed Miliband says, 'It's slightly like an optical illusion, which is that the rejoinders work because it looks like a spontaneous response to somebody's attack on you, when in fact it's not a spontaneous response at all, it's a pre-planned response, because you knew he was going to say that, because you've done the work.' Danny Finkelstein makes a similar point: 'One of the things you learn about PMQs is it's a bit like game theory, which is that the important point is not what you say, but what you say given that you know what they're going to say in response, so the whole game is "How do I get them to say something, how do I cope with the fact that they're going to go there?" and then you often think of iterations until you finally find one where the issue is difficult for them.'

In one of Ed's early PMQs in December 2010, it was only by anticipating a potential weakness – the fact that David Cameron was likely to make a connection between the subject, tuition fees, and Ed's past involvement in student politics – that we were able to come up with a response about Cameron's own time at university and his membership of the Bullingdon Club:

DAVID CAMERON: He is just demonstrating complete political opportunism— [*Interruption*] Yes, total opportunism. He is behaving like a student politician and, frankly, that is all he will ever be.
ED MILIBAND: Mr Speaker, I was a student politician, but I was not hanging around with people who were throwing bread rolls and wrecking restaurants.[152]

This part of the exchange is not directly about university funding: Cameron moves away from it to attack Ed; Ed stays away from it to hit back. It's a good example of how at PMQs, as Ed said to us, 'the gap between triumph and disaster is so small. The bread rolls one where I did well: if I hadn't had the bread rolls line, Cameron's student politician line would have been the stand-out line and it would have been "Oh my God, Ed's been characterised as a student politician, that's a real problem," but because I then went back to him on the Bullingdon Club it became about him.'

Every question the Leader of the Opposition asks, apart from the first one, has two parts. The second part is the actual question. The first part is the rejoinder to the Prime Minister's previous answer. The rejoinder is crucial, and it can do a number of different jobs. Most obviously, and often crucially to the structure of a whole set, it can provide the answer to the previous question – 'I notice the Prime Minister didn't answer the question, so let me tell her...' – demonstrating the Prime Minister's evasiveness or ignorance, taking into account the fact that the Prime Minister will very often reply with a standard subject script that does not directly address a specific question, and bringing the focus back to whatever it was that the Leader of the Opposition started with. So: 'How many young people are unemployed?' 'Today's unemployment figures show that unemployment has fallen to x.' 'The Prime Minister has tried to gloss over the fact that while *overall* unemployment is down, *youth* unemployment has risen to y.'

In this example from June 2013, in which David Cameron does indeed reply with a standard subject script that does not directly address the specific question, the rejoinder is the whole point of asking the question in the first place:

ED MILIBAND: Last May, the Education Secretary said that 'work will begin immediately' on 261 projects under the Priority

School Building programme. Can the Prime Minister tell the
House how many have begun?

DAVID CAMERON: What I can tell the right honourable gentleman is that infrastructure spending under this government has
been higher than it was under Labour, and we have about
£14 billion reserved for capital spending on our schools. But
we have had to clear up the appalling mess left by the Building
Schools for the Future programme.

ED MILIBAND: I do not think the right honourable gentleman knows the answer. I will tell him the answer: 261 schools
were promised, only one has started. Now perhaps he can
explain why.[153]

That is a factual response, which pivots instantly into a tight second
question which puts the Prime Minister on the rack.

One of the most important uses of rejoinders is to deliver rebuttal.
Again, this is easier to do when you know roughly what the Prime
Minister will say. 'The Prime Minister said x, but the truth is y' takes
back the initiative, invariably gets a cheer from your backbenchers,
makes the Leader of the Opposition look quick on his feet, and gives
the Prime Minister a difficult choice between arguing back at the
start of the next answer, which will make the whole of PMQs messy,
or letting it go – effectively conceding the point.

(Rebuttal is often misunderstood in politics. Employing rebuttal
doesn't necessarily destroy an opponent's point – it can't always,
because inconvenient facts are still facts – but it creates the impression
that there are two sides to the story. And just like in a relationship,
escalating something irritating into a row rather than letting it go

isn't always the best strategy. This is why rebuttal's fetishisation by some politicians and some parts of the media – a product of New Labour's much-mythologised 1997 'Rapid Rebuttal Unit' – is so irritating. Unless your rebuttal can conclusively close a story down, going into battle by attempting to rebut a particular argument draws attention to that argument, which may or may not be wise. And it gives journalists a new angle, and a reason to write more stories about it, which may or may not be something you want. Sometimes it's better just to sit quietly and wait for a story to go away. Sometimes your opponent's argument is just better than yours.)

Preparing rejoinders is the flip-side of the bombproofing discussed in Chapter 3 – looking for things your opponent might say that will be good prompts for a comeback. Sometimes one of the leaders will have a rejoinder waiting in their back pocket, hoping desperately that their opponent will deliver the line that sets it up. Here's David Cameron in March 2009 with a killer rejoinder that he knows will work just as soon as Gordon Brown uses a quotation – any quotation at all – in one of his replies. Eventually, on question five (Cameron must have been sweating by this point, worried that the set-up would never come), Brown produces two contradictory quotes by George Osborne and Ken Clarke, showing that they disagree on the cost of a Conservative proposal – in normal circumstances a powerful attack. Cameron pounces:

GORDON BROWN: On the right honourable gentleman's great £50 billion scheme, the shadow Chancellor said that it 'does not add to public expenditure'. However, the shadow shadow Chancellor [a reference to Clarke, then shadow Business

Secretary – it made sense at the time] has said that 'the tax-payer will take some of the hit'. The Conservatives do not know whether the scheme that they are proposing will cost money or not cost money: that is how bereft they are of ideas for the economy. The Leader of the Opposition does not understand that this is an unprecedented global banking crisis. Unprecedented means without precedent. Global means that it affects the whole of the world. The sooner that he wakes up to the fact that we need global action to deal with it, the better for our country.

DAVID CAMERON: I am glad that the Prime Minister is back to reading out quotations, because we now know how long a pledge from him lasts. Yesterday, he said in *The Guardian*: 'I personally have always said that modern politics, with its focus on who said what, when, how and why, is far too divisive for the problems that a country's got to meet.' What a complete phoney![154]

The Speaker made Cameron withdraw the word 'phoney' as unpar-liamentary language. It was worth it.

We had a similar experience in May 2011 of hoping that David Cameron would use a line we were expecting so that we could hit him with a prepared rejoinder. We had noticed that Cameron's standard NHS script consistently referred to the fact that the number of doctors was rising. Since he had only been Prime Minister for a year, this seemed a bit much, so we got him to say it again (Ed Miliband asked, 'A year into his government, how would the Prime Minister rate his handling of the NHS?'), got the reply we were looking for ('The number of doctors is growing very quickly') and Ed rolled out the planned comeback: 'In case the Prime Minister did not realise, it takes seven years to train a doctor, so I would like to thank him for his congratulations on our record on the NHS.'[155]

One of the biggest jobs done by leaders in their supporting material in PMQs is to highlight damaging and politically embarrassing topical stories for the other side which aren't directly relevant to the line of questioning. As Harriet Harman told us, 'If there's anybody who's been putting the boot into the Prime Minister behind the Prime Minister's back, it will get raised in PMQs, the Prime Minister will know it's true and have panic in his or her eyes; we'll all know it's true, and it's a point at which the coherence of the team gets tested as well, and exposed. That's what happened with John Major. Everybody knew that he was calling them bastards and they weren't supporting him, and that made PMQs torture for him.' PMQs is often the biggest opportunity of the week for the leaders to comment publicly on their opponents – but the biggest current political embarrassments for the other side are often not suitable topics to ask the Prime Minister about. And of course, the biggest current political embarrassment for the opposition will *never* be the Leader of the Opposition's chosen PMQs topic.

So each side will be looking for ways to shoehorn the other's misfortunes into its questions and answers. Some of this will be in the wrap, on question six (the easy, bog-standard and very dull way of doing this would be something like 'The Prime Minister has no answers to my questions on the housing crisis. In a week in which we learned that the minister for something other than housing has done something bad that's completely unrelated to housing, doesn't this show that the government has run out of ideas and it's time they called an election?' – we hope we never quite sank to this level). Jeremy Corbyn did this well in his final question at a PMQs in October 2017, starting with universal credit, which had been the main subject of his set, before introducing other government divisions which he had not previously mentioned to give a wider sense of Tory weakness:

> The Conservative Party and the government say they have full confidence in universal credit, but will not vote for it. They say they will end the NHS pay cap, but will not allocate any money to pay for it. The Communities Secretary backs £50 billion of borrowing for housing, but the Chancellor says it is not policy. The Brexit Secretary says they are planning for a no-deal Brexit. The Chancellor says they are not … Isn't it the case that this government are weak, incompetent and divided, and unable to take the essential decisions necessary for the good of the people of this country?[156]

Incidentally, this was the end of a six-question set in which Corbyn did not include any crowdsourced questions – a good example of a growing flexibility and of his and his team's recognition that being bound by a particular strategy could get in the way of being as effective as possible.

Here is an example of David Cameron, in opposition, pulling together a litany of unhelpful quotes about Gordon Brown's leadership by Labour politicians:

> This is what Labour MPs are saying about their Prime Minister: he is losing touch; he does not know what fairness is; he needs

to see the world through the eyes of voters; he is like a scared rabbit in the headlights. The Labour peer Lord Desai said that the Prime Minister's leadership style is like porridge. Another week like this and it will be Cheerios. Is it not the case that the Labour Party has finally worked out that it has a loser, not a leader?[157]

That was not Lord Desai's first appearance as a PMQs attack line for the Conservatives, incidentally: he had a role in 1993 as John Major's only defence against John Smith, when Smith was attacking him relentlessly for breaking an election promise by extending the scope of VAT. Desai, as a Labour economic spokesperson in the Lords, had publicly called for the same thing, giving a relieved John Major something to say.

Here's Cameron again, finding a way to mention the amazing and, to Labour, embarrassing story of the Reverend Paul Flowers. Flowers was a Methodist minister, non-executive chairman of the Co-Operative Bank and very occasional Labour adviser who, in 2013, was caught buying drugs in a scandal which led to the press rather brilliantly nicknaming him 'the Crystal Methodist'. Of course Ed Miliband was never going to ask a question remotely relevant to the story, but Cameron found a neat way of sliding a reference into a more conventional attack on Labour's spending plans: 'Labour has already spent the bank levy ten times over. The youth jobs guarantee, VAT cuts, more capital spending – Mr Speaker, that is not a policy; it is a night out with Reverend Flowers.'[158] It's a good line, but we had failed to predict quite how hard Cameron would go on the story, as Ed remembers: 'We just went in and got absolutely smacked in the head, and most of the time you knew you were about to be smacked in the head, but we just had no idea it was coming. "Oh, you know, there's that Paul Flowers thing, well OK, spend five minutes on the rejoinder": he spent *six questions* going on about Paul Flowers as if I was his flatmate or something, and I'd met the guy like two times in my life. He was totally shameless, Cameron, about it.'

What both sides are really trying to do, but fail to achieve most weeks, is to create a moment that can cut through beyond the immediate PMQs joust, and beyond Parliament itself, and even beyond that day's television news, to say something deeper and more memorable. A characterisation of a policy, an opponent or a government. A line that encapsulates where a leader stands and who he or she is, or sums up the state of politics. It might be a joke, but more often its power is not that it's funny but that it's true – or perceived to be true, which in politics is more important. These moments are rare. Most PMQs are ephemeral, despite the work that goes into them and the attention they get at the time: important while they're happening but forgotten by the end of the day.

In January 1997, months before a landslide election victory that would sweep Labour to power and the Tories out of office, Tony Blair created one such moment at PMQs. The ostensible subject was John Major's difficulty in persuading his Eurosceptic MPs to support the government's policy on the single currency. The whole exchange between the two leaders took six minutes. But the only thing anyone remembers from it is three words, delivered by Blair in three seconds: 'Weak, weak, weak'. Blair confirmed to us that this moment was not spontaneous but planned in advance. We're going to quote the entire exchange, so you can see the moment in context: what both leaders are doing, the tactics each uses, and the role of the 'Weak, weak, weak' moment – the one line this PMQs is remembered for – within the whole.

TONY BLAIR: A few weeks ago, the Prime Minister said that it was essential in the national interest that our options remained open on a single currency and that he expected Conservative candidates to stand on that national manifesto. Is that still his expectation of Conservative candidates?

JOHN MAJOR: I think that, before taking me to task on this, the right honourable gentleman should perhaps talk to the scores of his own members of Parliament that the right honourable member for Bethnal Green & Stepney [Peter Shore] said would oppose his stance. As the right honourable member for Bethnal Green & Stepney said, 'I think it almost an obligation to be honest with my own electorate.' But the right honourable member for Sedgefield [Blair] would not understand that. He entered the House on an election address that demanded Britain's withdrawal from the Community, even though he said later, 'I wasn't actually opposed to membership of the EC ... I said within the closed doors of the Labour Party that I disagreed with that policy.' Behind closed doors he says one thing, in public another: not the politics of conviction, but convenience, saying anything to get a vote – and that is what he advocates to his candidates.

TONY BLAIR: The Labour Party put its manifesto to its membership and got 95 per cent support – I doubt that the Prime Minister could put his manifesto to his Cabinet and get 95 per cent support. After all, I was only asking him to agree with what he himself said a few weeks ago. If he cannot say that he now expects Conservative candidates to do that, has he still the vestige of authority and courage left to stand at that dispatch box and say now that at least he strongly urges and seeks to persuade Conservative candidates to stand on his and the government's position?

JOHN MAJOR: The right honourable gentleman is just being plain silly. Is he telling the House that the right honourable member for Bethnal Green & Stepney, the honourable member for Bolsover [Dennis Skinner], the right honourable member for Chesterfield [Tony Benn] and the honourable member for Newham South [Nigel Spearing] are actually going to support his policy on Europe at the general election? He raises it on this day of all days – the first two Labour questioners on the order paper are among the fifty who say that we should not join a single currency. The right honourable gentleman may ask his candidates to fib to the electorate – our candidates will set out their views, we will follow the policy that the government have set out and people know our policy. What he is trying to do is to censor and smother what his party stands for.

TONY BLAIR: I asked the Prime Minister two questions. I said, as he himself said a few weeks ago, 'Does he expect them to stand on the same manifesto?' I answer, 'Yes.' I then asked him, 'Will he at least seek to persuade people to stand on the same manifesto?' I answer, 'Yes.' He is so weak and powerless, he cannot even say. He cannot even get to that— [*Interruption*] Is it not extraordinary— [*Interruption*]

MADAM SPEAKER: Order. The House must come to order.

TONY BLAIR: Is it not extraordinary that the Prime Minister of our country cannot even urge his party to support his own position? Weak, weak, weak, weak. I tell him that his weakness and his failure of leadership are the reason his government are the incompetent mess they are.

JOHN MAJOR: Whenever the right honourable gentleman gets abusive, we know that he is losing. If he is concerned about strength, will he today sack the honourable member for Oldham West [Michael Meacher], who yesterday contradicted what he said about tax? Will he today sack the deputy Chief Whip of the Labour Party [Nick Brown], who yesterday contradicted what was said about tax? All the right honourable gentleman does is heckle and waft his arms around in a hopeless gesture. Yes or no – will he sack them or not? It is his policy, they are members of his shadow Cabinet, and they have denied his policy. We have set out consistently what our policy is. I have said that it is important to keep the options – all the options – open. The right honourable gentleman sniggers – I am quoting his words, not mine. He has followed in grandmother's footsteps in following policy after policy of ours. He says that we should keep the options open. We keep the options open, but his policy apparently means something quite different, because he dare not admit what his policy is.[159]

Blair is forensic, using a simple, logical structure: two questions about the Prime Minister's position, and a third and final question which is not really a question at all, summing up Major's answers and contrasting them with the answers he says he can give, as Labour leader, to the same two questions. One simple question on one. A prepared rejoinder and another simple question on two. A summary of the exchange and a political attack on three. The words 'Weak, weak, weak' at the heart of the final intervention (Hansard has a fourth 'weak': that was later, quieter, after a long pause). It's focused, brutal stuff.

Major's answers don't do a lot wrong. In response to a basic Labour attack that he has no authority over his own MPs on the issue of Europe, he points out, with evidence, a) that there are Labour MPs who do not agree with Blair's stance on the issue, and b) that Blair himself had disagreed with his party's European policy in 1983. Quite simply, says Major, Blair's attack on the Conservatives applies equally well to Labour.

It doesn't work. And the reason it doesn't work, as so often at PMQs, has less to do with PMQs itself and more to do with the wider political context. Major, by this point, was widely seen as a weak leader who could not control his party. Blair was widely seen as a strong leader, exerting authority over his. If those public perceptions had been reversed but the same questions and answers given, Blair's attack would have fallen flat and Major's response would have resonated. The power of Blair's line of questioning derives from this pre-existing dominant narrative, but it also dramatises it, in a concise form that can be replayed again and again on television and radio, in just three words.

(You could boil down the whole of the run-up to the 1997 election to two Blair soundbites, each consisting of one word repeated three times. On the positive side, dramatising Labour's agenda for government contrasted with the Tories' neglect of public services, 'education,

education, education'; on the attack side, dramatising the Tories' unfitness for office contrasted with Blair's firm leadership of a united party, 'weak, weak, weak'.)

Blair's other biggest PMQs moment in opposition, almost two years earlier in April 1995, was also based on the contrast between his and Major's leadership, as Alastair Campbell recounted in his diary:

> I had worked out a line of attack which TB improved by watching the news for once and said why aren't the interviewers asking if the Tory rebels have given a guarantee that they will support the government in future votes on Europe. That became the question and then we rehearsed a line to use if Major came back at him with our own divisions – I lead my party, he follows his – which turned out to be the biggest blow TB had yet landed at PMQs, which produced a massive cheer on our side and a look of real pain on theirs. The PMQs hit was gigantic ... it was a good day.[160]

'The Labour benches went berserk,' the Conservative MP Gyles Brandreth wrote in his own diary. 'We sat sullenly, knowing it was true.'[161] The pattern was the same: Blair asking Major about divisions over Europe within the Conservative Party, Major pointing out divisions over Europe within the Labour Party, but the combination of a memorable line and the wider political narrative making it a clear Blair win.[162]

Theresa May's first PMQs, in July 2016, included a highly effective scripted moment, in a response to a question from Jeremy Corbyn about insecure work:

I am interested that the right honourable gentleman referred to the situation of some workers who might have job insecurity and potentially unscrupulous bosses. I suspect that many members on the opposition benches might be familiar with an unscrupulous boss – a boss who does not listen to his workers, a boss who requires some of his workers to double their workload and maybe even a boss who exploits the rules to further his own career. Remind him of anybody?[163]

The line 'Remind him of anybody?' was delivered in a way that was unmistakably reminiscent of Margaret Thatcher, as nobody watching could fail to spot. The reason May's set-up and punchline worked so well was that at the time Corbyn's leadership was under pressure following what many thought was an underwhelming performance for the losing side during the EU referendum campaign. Several shadow ministers had resigned, and a leadership challenge by Owen Smith was just getting underway. In this context, job insecurity was a risky topic for Corbyn to raise, since the jokes wrote themselves. More or less exactly a year later, after losing her majority in a general election she had been under no pressure to call, it was Theresa May who was the subject of exactly the same obvious gag as she launched the Taylor report into insecure work. Perhaps it was a poor choice of event to relaunch her premiership.

Just as May's first PMQs as Conservative Party leader included a scripted moment designed to symbolise who she was and show what change she was bringing to her party – even if it was a backward-looking change – so did David Cameron's, in December 2005. In fact, Cameron had two scripted moments, as well as a theme which demonstrated his new approach. The theme was the Conservative Party's willingness to back Tony Blair's public service reform agenda, providing enough votes to overcome any Labour backbench rebellion: 'The first issue that the Prime Minister and I are going to have to work together on is getting the good bits of his education reforms through the House of Commons and into law,'[164] Cameron began. This was aimed at making the Conservative Party look reasonable as well as at drawing a dividing line between Blair and his backbenchers, who would know that rebelling on an issue where government and opposition agreed was a safe option, carrying less risk of a government defeat. Cameron asked three questions on education and another two emphasising his party's willingness to work consensually towards an international climate change treaty – another symbol of change in the Conservative Party.

These lines of questioning helped to dramatise the purpose of Cameron's leadership, but even more important were two moments perfectly designed to be clipped for broadcast. The first was in his very first question, where he broke from what he was saying about education to respond to the heckling by Labour's Chief Whip, Hilary Armstrong, heckling which he and his team would have predicted would come from someone on the government benches: 'That is the problem with these exchanges – the Labour Chief Whip shouting like a child. Is the right honourable lady finished?'[165] George Osborne confirmed to us that this apparently spontaneous moment was planned in advance. Pointing out rowdy behaviour by your opponents is nothing new – in opposition Tony Blair repeatedly referred to 'the Tory yobbos' when interrupted at PMQs[166] – but it creates the impression of a distinction between you (high-minded, constructive, taking the serious business of politics seriously) and them (loutish, unruly, uninterested in serious discussion). In reality, of course, both sides are as bad as each other, although MPs on the government side can usually generate more noise because by definition there are more of them.

Cameron's second moment was the most memorable of all. Criticising Blair's unwillingness to allow schools to control their own admissions – but as with all the best PMQs moments, the soundbite transcends the specific policy at issue – Cameron said, 'This approach is stuck in the past, and I want to talk about the future. He was the future once.'[167] 'He was the future once' was a great line, casting Cameron as the 'heir to Blair' (young, dynamic, changing his party), acknowledging the qualities Blair possessed that Cameron now wanted to emulate, but emphasising that Blair's time was passing. Ed Miliband tried to repeat the line, and the trick, at a PMQs in June 2012. It didn't really work. 'He just wants to talk about the past – he was the future once,' said Ed; 'Imitation is the sincerest form of flattery,' replied Cameron.[168]

The line was an important part of the long-term Cameron strategy of preparing for an election against Gordon Brown, not the current incumbent. George Osborne says: 'We'd always thought Brown was our most likely opponent, so Brown was always anyway the focus. We'd started splitting them, and praising Blair, or pointing out Blair was trying to do the right thing and being stopped by his Chancellor, because we knew Brown was going to be the opponent at the election.' Alastair Campbell told us: 'I kept bumping into Osborne, on Hampstead Heath and at parties and just round and about, and he was telling me very, very openly what their strategy was. And it

was "Vote Blair, get Brown; this guy's a proper leader, he's not; he was
the future but the other guy's the past," and actually that was part
of the thinking of "You were the future once," to say, "You were the
future, but your next guy's the past, and I'm the future."' By praising
Blair in 2005, the Conservatives were consciously preparing for a
post-Blair world.

Cameron's first PMQs impressed Blair, as well as Alastair Campbell:
'I don't think Tony would have done "You were the future once" to
an older Prime Minister. I think he thought that showed real nerve.
There was a risk in that. It was quite clever. But it was a risk. I can't
remember what Tony's top line was in his first PMQs. I think the
aim would have been to show he could do it, get through it. Cameron
clearly set himself a bigger objective. He decided he was going to
really make a mark. And when he did that, part of me thought, "Oh,
I'm not sure the public are going to like that." And maybe they did and
maybe they didn't, but what it did show was he had real confidence.
And his people liked it. That's important.'

George Osborne told us that Cameron's strong opening performance at PMQs, along with other decisions which helped to define
him in the eyes of the public, such as being filmed cycling to work,
was crucial to the early success of his leadership. It was all carefully
plotted out: 'We put a lot of thought into those first couple of weeks,
the grid of the first couple of weeks, which most Leaders of the
Opposition don't, mostly because they're so focused on trying to win
the campaign, they haven't really thought about what to do next.
Whereas we had the luxury of knowing by then, because we'd beaten
[David] Davis and the ballot in the country was a sort of foregone
conclusion.'

Michael Howard's most memorable line in two years as Leader of the Opposition was a prepared rejoinder to Tony Blair in December 2003, during a PMQs discussion about the proposed introduction of university top-up fees. After Blair had spent his first answer defending the policy, Howard came back with, 'Let me make it clear: this grammar school boy will take no lessons from that public school boy on the importance of children from less privileged backgrounds gaining access to university.'[169] The line cleverly pointed up the vaguely counterintuitive fact that the Labour leader was more 'posh' than the Conservative leader – something Howard and his advisers would have been keen to highlight – while asserting the Conservatives' commitment to helping the less well off (in fact George Osborne, another public school boy, had a hand in it, 'which was ironic', he told us). One way we can tell it was prepared, and not a spontaneous response to what Blair had said, is that Blair had not actually mentioned the importance of children from less privileged backgrounds gaining access to university in his answer at all, so the rejoinder was not strictly relevant.

Of course, the next time the Conservatives actually got into government they didn't just fail to abolish university tuition fees; they trebled them from £3,000 to £9,000. Not only that, they defended this increase partly on the basis that the alternative would restrict access to university for those from underprivileged backgrounds – precisely the argument Howard had taken issue with at his most successful PMQs. Not only that, Michael Howard, by now ennobled as Lord Howard of Lympne, voted in December 2010 for tuition fees to be trebled. Still, PMQs moments are created to win in the moment, not to be checked years later for policy consistency. It was a good line.

Many of the most memorable PMQs moments over the years – but also many of the most cringe-inducing – have been jokes. The frequency of jokes at PMQs rises and falls with the leaders' willingness, and perceived need, to deploy them. Neil Kinnock told us that he didn't spend much time thinking of jokes, 'because Thatcher had no sense of humour, you see'. ('It wasn't her strength,' agrees John Whittingdale, understatedly.) But most politicians do demand jokes: as Vince Cable told us, you need humour 'unless you get a May–Corbyn situation where they both neutralise each other'.

People can be quite sniffy about the jokes at PMQs, which isn't just a complaint about their quality but also sometimes a slightly high-minded disdain for something as frivolous as humour when serious issues are at stake. This is a mistake. There's nothing wrong with making something that's important funny. Alastair Campbell quoted to us T. S. Eliot's characterisation of wit as the 'alliance of levity and seriousness (by which the seriousness is intensified)'. William Hague, one of the most effective deployers of parliamentary humour, told us about the uses of jokes: 'You're trying to make it memorable first of all, because this is true of speeches in general, that people remember things much more if they've either laughed or been in tears, and since you don't want to make them all cry every week, humour is the main way for things to stick in their minds. Secondly it raises morale on your own side, because you need all those MPs, particularly in those days, utterly downcast a lot of the time, to go to the tearoom and say, "Oh, didn't our leader give us a good outing today?"' Angela Eagle agrees: 'Jokes are an important part of making a political point, and I think that a lot of people will remember a joke, or some jibe, far more than they'll remember some boring peroration about policy.

And so you can actually sum stuff up quite well with jokes. Or you can sometimes get your opponent a bit rattled and see how they react and whether they can be witty back.'

People do remember jokes. David Cameron still remembers Tony Blair's complaint in December 1997 that the Liberal Democrats 'call for more money for health, education, local government, the coal industry, transport and the environment, and all that is to come out of 1p extra on the standard rate of tax. They also want the programme for the young unemployed, but they do not want the windfall tax. All I can say is that it must be the longest "p" in history.'[170] Cameron describes this as 'brilliant because it was a political insult that was toilet humour in a way, but it was genuinely funny and insulting, while making a very strong political point'.

Hague makes another point about humour, which he says he learned from John Smith: 'It's quite effective to make the other side laugh at themselves, to make their backbenchers laugh at their leaders. It's quite undermining over time, it's not going to bring the government down but it does get to them, and John Smith was very good at doing that.' He remembers one particular parliamentary speech by Smith as shadow Chancellor in June 1989, during the long dispute over economic policy between Nigel Lawson and Sir Alan Walters referred to in Chapter 5. Smith quoted Margaret Thatcher saying 'Nigel is a very good neighbour of mine' and then recited, teasingly and at length, the theme song to the then-popular Australian soap opera *Neighbours* ('Neighbours – everybody needs good neighbours. Just a friendly wave each morning helps to make a better day. Neighbours need to get to know each other. Next door is only a footstep away. Neighbours – everybody needs good neighbours.

With a little understanding, you can find a perfect blend. Neighbours should be there for one another. That's when good neighbours become good friends').[171] Hague, who was a new MP at the time, says: 'I sat there *really* appreciating that, and giggling along with the Tories at a Prime Minister you didn't normally giggle at, very effective. So quite often the way I was thinking about my own jokes was, the humour was directed at *Labour* MPs, of what *they* will then laugh about, they'll go to the tearoom saying, "Yeah, he's right about Blair, that's spot on."'

Hague's PMQs prep team seems to have had more fun than anyone else's, ever. It was, he remembers, 'a very enjoyable atmosphere, which I encouraged strongly because I think it is generally in an atmosphere of good humour and lateral thinking that you get some bold and original thinking, and it was as much lateral as logical really, our preparation for Prime Minister's Questions. We were coming up with crazy ideas that could not possibly work but they led to some other idea, and the laughing about it and teasing each other about it led to good lines that I then deployed in the actual Chamber. That was perhaps rather unusual, to have that much levity and make fun of several hours doing it. Not every team has that chemistry, particularly on the government side I think, it's harder on the government side because you've got the civil servants briefing you, rather than as Leader of the Opposition when you've got your political soulmates there who were with you for the duration. It also depends on the working style of the principal.'

John Whittingdale, who was Hague's PPS, told us, 'I'm not as funny as the others, George [Osborne] and Danny [Finkelstein] were the great comedians, so William, George, Danny, with Seb [Coe] and me, would sit and talk about it, and I'd have tears rolling down my face, and for every line that William could use there would be three he couldn't use, usually about Peter Mandelson. And it would be just joke-telling.' 'It never would have happened that we'd have arrived at the end of that process without any jokes,' says Finkelstein. 'We'd usually have five or six, because it was constant, so I was totally spoiled. The problem is that it's never been like that again with any other politician, because he had a great sense of humour and he was really funny, you'd never have to labour to make jokes, they were just kind of flowing, everyone was joking away. It was my best thing, I really loved it.'

The Hague joke everyone recalled to us was not actually delivered at PMQs at all, but in the Queen's Speech debate in 1999, when Tony Blair was trying to ensure that Frank Dobson rather than Ken Livingstone would be selected as Labour's candidate for mayor of London: 'If the Prime Minister is finding the problem so difficult, I have a solution for him. Why does he not split the job of mayor of London? The former Health Secretary [Dobson] can run as his "day-mayor" and the honourable member for Brent East [Livingstone] can run as his "night-mayor".'[172]

David Cameron had joke-writing help from others, including Danny Finkelstein and Michael Gove: Gove, Cameron told us, was particularly good at linking contemporary cultural references with political points. Cameron says, 'PMQs is not unlike political cartoons. The best political cartoons juxtapose a political truth with a current image, but also with another cultural reference. And sometimes it just doesn't work because you couldn't make a cultural reference relating to a television programme that nobody had watched. Michael Gove was brilliant because he'd sometimes come up with very funny things which linked those things.' But Cameron came up with a lot of his jokes himself: 'Because you're thinking about it, because you're in the firing line, you would mull over jokes in your head.' When Cameron's jokes landed, they could be brutally effective. In February 2015 he capitalised on shadow Chancellor Ed Balls's failure in a TV interview to remember the name of Bill Thomas, a businessman who chaired Labour's Small Business Taskforce: 'His shadow Chancellor was asked on television whether he could think of one single business leader, do you know what he said, Mr Speaker? He said, "Bill Somebody"! Bill Somebody is not a person – Bill Somebody is Labour's policy.'[173]

When politicians are not naturally funny, their desire for jokes to deliver at PMQs and other set-piece events can be a dangerous distraction. Hague says, 'It's better not to try, and to do whatever else they're good at, than to try it and have it fall flat all the time, as with most things in life.' Gordon Brown always wanted more jokes, and often felt that jokes he was given were not good enough; Tony Blair would ask for a line, not a joke – something that summed up an argument or an attack, tightly, but without necessarily being funny. Anyone who has ever worked in a PMQs prep team will have received unsolicited joke suggestions from people who are desperate to have a gag used by the Prime Minister or Leader of the Opposition. There is an undeniable satisfaction to knowing that you came up with a joke that landed well at a high-profile political event like PMQs. But as Theo Bertram remembers about his time at No. 10, 'We'd often get input from comedians and people emailing in with their comments, "Oh, you should do this", and they'd get forwarded to you, just some *terrible*, hackneyed, *utterly* unhelpful contribution.'

Many – too many – PMQs jokes seem to be there because the leaders think there ought to be a joke there, rather than because they've thought of a joke too good to miss. Here's John Major's stand-in Tony Newton responding to John Smith in 1993 with a then-topical reference to the film *Jurassic Park*: 'The right honourable and learned gentleman's dealings with the trade unions makes *Jurassic Park* look like a tea party.'[174] The more you try to think about the logic of this joke, the more your head hurts, and the more you realise that you should stop trying to think about the logic of this joke. Norman Shrapnel recounts seeing Groucho Marx visiting the Commons at some point in the 1960s or 1970s, and being confronted with the reality that much parliamentary humour does not translate into anything the outside world can possibly find funny: 'Mr Heath was chuckling away, and at one point his shoulders went into the full heave; yet all the Leader of the House had said was that they hoped to finish the Finance Bill by Wednesday. Why should a line like that have them rolling in the aisles? The Marx spectacles shone with frozen incomprehension.'[175]

David Cameron in particular had a compulsion to try to shoehorn in topical, but terrible, gags. Topical gags about the Oscars: 'In this Oscar week, perhaps the best we can say is that Daniel Day-Lewis was utterly convincing as Abraham Lincoln, and the right honourable gentleman [i.e. Ed Miliband] is utterly convincing as Gordon Brown: more borrowing, more spending, more debt.'[176] Topical gags about Ed Miliband choosing the Robbie Williams song 'Angels' as one of his Desert Island Discs: 'I think it is fair to say he is no longer a follower of Marx; he is loving Engels instead.'[177] Topical gags about the Labour adviser Arnie Graf having the same first name as Arnold

Schwarzenegger: 'Their top adviser – get this, Mr Speaker – is called Arnie and he has gone to America, but unlike Arnie he has said, "I'm not coming back."'[178]

'You should see the ones that were left on the cutting room floor,' says Cameron. 'There were some absolute clunkers, and you can tell, funnily enough, sometimes ones that you thought were funny, they clunk in the House of Commons. And when a joke clunks in the House of Commons, boy does it clunk, it really sinks. But I thought that one bad joke wasn't a reason to stop telling jokes. You have to keep going.'

Ed Miliband reflected to us on the impact of David Cameron's jokes at PMQs, and the occasions when they worked and didn't work: 'I'm not sure it was the quality of the joke that defined whether it landed, because I think most of his lines were pretty good lines. It's if he was on the defensive on an issue and then he went to some old baloney line, if you have the joust without the substance, and you're weak on the substance, and the opposition leader skewers you on the substance, your joust lines just land like absolute tumbleweed, because you're like, "Well, why is he telling a joke about something that he read in the papers three days ago when he's got no answer on the NHS?" But if you're on the up and it ties in and so on ... you can't just treat it as a comic turn thing.'

One or two of Theresa May's gags after replacing David Cameron provided evidence that while the Prime Minister might have changed, the joke writers hadn't. Here's an exceptionally contrived joke from September 2016, which seems to be an allusion to Jeremy Corbyn's odd decision to allow himself to be filmed sitting on the floor of a 'ram-packed' train before subsequently going to a vacant seat:

'The train has left the station, the seats are all empty, and the leader is on the floor. Even on rolling stock, Labour is a laughing stock.'[179] The worst thing about this joke is that nobody stopped her saying it.

Jeremy Corbyn does not deploy jokes at PMQs very often, and this rare example of a Corbyn gag directed at Theresa May demonstrates just how sensible that is of him: 'Restoring parliamentary democracy while sidelining Parliament – it is not so much the Iron Lady as the Irony Lady.'[180] Perhaps, in Corbyn's defence, this looked better written down – but having just seen it written down, we don't think it does.

These jokes don't work. They are all examples of the leaders, and their teams, overstretching and failing in a desire to get a laugh. But that desire is not misplaced, and the jokes are not a distraction from the point of the event. Laughs at PMQs are worth reaching for. The leaders want good responses and lines and jokes because they know that they will be performing PMQs in front of a live audience – not just watching on TV but right there in the room with them. Winning round the audience in the room matters. As leader, you want to make the MPs on the other side laugh despite themselves, or grudgingly admit that you've scored a hit. You want to give your own MPs, whose own future prospects depend on you being a winner, heart and confidence that you are indeed a winner. To do that effectively, you need to understand not just your material, but the theatre where you're performing it: the Chamber of the House of Commons.

7

THE CHAMBER

The House of Commons Chamber is smaller than you might think. There isn't space for all 650 MPs, and those who want to be sure of a place collect 'prayer cards' before the start of business to reserve a seat. This isn't usually necessary except for big events like Budgets, major debates and, every week, PMQs. At Wednesday lunchtime, the Chamber is always full. MPs spill off the benches into the gangways or stand around the Speaker's chair at one end of the Chamber and at the Bar of the House at the other. In the confined space, the noise is enormous. 'It's a hideous thing, it's a baying mob,' says Tony Blair. Harriet Harman says, 'It's impossible to overstate how loud it is. It is a roar. You can't hear yourself think or speak, it is so, so noisy.' Ed Miliband says, 'Tory MPs shouting at you, baying at you, it is definitely off-putting.' Angela Eagle told us, 'My dad came in to see PMQs once, not while I was doing it, and he said he'd never heard such noise.

And I'd kind of forgotten how loud it was, he said it was just this wall of noise.' When the Speaker shouts, 'Questions to the Prime Minister!' at noon, the roar that erupts can be felt in your sternum.

On television, the noise of the Chamber doesn't come across in the same way it does in real life. Most misleadingly of all, the voices of the MPs asking and answering questions can be clearly heard on television, whereas in the Chamber itself it is often impossible to hear what is being said. In July 2013, two MPs took decibel readings at PMQs on behalf of the BBC's *Daily Politics* programme, and found noise levels of 89 decibels in one part of the Chamber, as loud as a food-blender, and of 97 decibels in another, as loud as Liverpool's football ground, which can hold 54,000 fans.[181] Some MPs, and especially the Prime Minister, who needs to hear the questions and know what they are about in order even to attempt to answer them, lean back to listen to small speakers built into the benches – when the House is in full voice, attempting to hear an MP from the other side of the Chamber without artificial amplification is futile.

The leaders are the centre of attention, and they can feel it. As Harriet Harman told us, 'There's something about being the one person standing up; you are the only person standing up. Everybody else is sitting down. And the centrality of that focus on you, together with the enormous noise, together with the fact that everybody's squashed in, because there aren't enough seats in the House of Commons for all the MPs, you are physically jammed shoulder to shoulder, thigh to thigh, all squashed in like sardines, and then you stand up. And that is a very exposed moment but it is a moment full of potential. And more or less every Prime Minister's Questions there is that air of anticipation. It is theatre.'

The front benches are as crowded as the rest of the Chamber, with the ministerial and shadow ministerial teams who have just taken part in departmental questions being shunted along to make way for the leaders and the most senior ministers and shadow ministers. Bodies are tightly packed, with the only gaps emerging when the leaders stand up. One of Gordon Brown's Cabinet ministers told us that he would spend the half-hour in terror that Brown, after standing up to answer each question, would accidentally sit back down on his lap.

Who sits closest to the leaders is the result of a complex mix of availability, precedence and usefulness: Ed Miliband would usually want Ed Balls nearby; Harriet Harman, as his deputy, needed to be seen to be close; and often he would ask the shadow Cabinet member with responsibility for whatever issue his questions covered to be next to him to prompt him with facts and rejoinders. But this carried with it the risk of giving away the subject of his questions before he stood up: bringing shadow Health Secretary Andy Burnham to sit next to him would be a big clue to David Cameron that Ed was about to ask about the NHS.

Ed says, 'Sometimes people would whisper answers to you. Or rejoinders. But the trouble is that those rejoinders that you just do on the spur of the moment, they're quite high risk because you don't have time to think them through and they could hit you in the face.' On the other side, George Osborne told us, 'I used to sit next to Cameron and feed him lines during PMQs. Sometimes Ed Miliband would call it out but it didn't really matter, because he'd go, "Yeah, I'm talking to my Chancellor, what's wrong with that? Not like the last lot." But I would always sit next to Cameron and think of answers and say, "Remember that fact," so I was there right next to him.'

The two front benches are close enough that, despite the noise, MPs on each side can make comments their opposite numbers can pick up, but which the TV microphones miss. Tony Blair remembers speaking at the dispatch box as Prime Minister on one occasion when 'someone from the Tory front bench says, "Does he know his flies are down?" And some person sitting there says, "Oh yeah!" So I'm thinking, "What do I do here?" It completely put me off, because I'm thinking, "If they really are that's a bit of a problem, on the other hand I can't start fondling myself to see and pull it up again, so what the hell do I do?" It was a bloody lie as well, because when I sat back down obviously I… but they were always shouting things like that. You know, "God, he looks ill today, is he ill?" So you'd get that, there'd be varying degrees of insulting banter.'

The leaders' parliamentary private secretaries (PPSs), MPs whose job it is to liaise between the leaders and their own party's MPs, usually sit just behind the front bench. The job is not without its perils. One of Ed Miliband's first PPSs, John Denham, who took part in PMQs prep with us and evidently had a talent for learning Ed's lines, was once caught on camera mouthing along to Ed's questions as he sat behind him, to his later embarrassment.[182] A subsequent PPS, Jonathan Reynolds, managed to leave a copy of Ed's script, including some planned rejoinders to possible attacks, in a House of Commons lavatory.[183] It leaked. The notes revealed the pretty obvious PMQs secret that not all of Ed's responses in the Chamber were spontaneous, and also showed which possible lines of attack we were most worried about. It wasn't as damaging or annoying as the time Ed left his notes on the lectern at the end of a TV debate during the 2015 general election campaign, from where they found their way onto the front page of *The Sun*, but it still wasn't all that helpful.

As William Hague's PPS, John Whittingdale played a vital role in one particular session in February 2000, on a day when Labour's First Secretary of the National Assembly for Wales, Alun Michael, was facing a no-confidence vote. After Tony Blair answered a question on the matter from a Tory backbencher by saying that 'I believe that the Welsh First Secretary is doing an excellent job and so does the Labour Party',[184] Whittingdale received a text message telling him that Michael had just resigned. He passed it forward to Hague, who had asked three questions earlier but still had another set of three questions left. Hague dumped his planned questions and, says Whittingdale, 'just went to town, and Blair clearly didn't know and was left floundering. And that, you see, was only because of the power of text messaging.' Hague repeatedly asked whether Michael had resigned, enjoying the obvious fact that Blair had no idea: 'Not only has the Prime Minister forgotten why he imposed the First Secretary – he does not even know whether the First Secretary is in office at this moment. Is the First Secretary still in office?'[185] Hague told us, 'I changed my questions, and Tony Blair was sufficiently good that he knew something was wrong here, but he managed to get through all these questions without saying yes or no, with such general blather, and actually that's the mark of someone who's good at it, at the answering in a sticky situation.'

The Prime Minister's PPSs have a continuing role throughout PMQs, carrying large additional files that supplement the Prime Minister's folder with briefings on unexpected topics and on the backbenchers who ask the questions; they can pull out relevant notes and pass them down to her while the questions are being asked. In October 2017 a member of the public wrote to Theresa May to complain about some distracting behaviour that was spoiling his experience of watching PMQs on television:

> Fairly recently, one of your blue-suited MPs has decided to sit behind you and do all his office work from a huge lever-arch file, often on his lap, with bright yellow index stickers which he annoyingly flicks through, opens and closes, makes notes etc., whenever you, as the PM, is making any urgent or important response to the likes of Citizen Corbyn! I find it almost impossible to concentrate on what you are saying, because of the 'scribe' carrying on his office work immediately behind your back. Would you kindly tell him to lay off the paperwork while you are busy with the vital exchanges during PM Questions. Maybe he feels his paperwork is more important than following the debate – in which case he should stay in his office!!!

George Hollingbery, Theresa May's blue-suited PPS, phoned the complainant up to explain what his job involved.

Most of the MPs on both sides at PMQs have no intention of asking a question, but they're not just a passive audience: they're the chorus. They are there to support and cheer on their leader, and there is a mutually reinforcing or mutually undermining relationship between how well their leader does and how much noise they make. MPs will find it hard to cheer enthusiastically for a dull or clumsily drafted set of questions, or for a leader who is clearly being beaten, and a leader whose MPs are deflated will find it difficult to animate even a good set. Angela Eagle compares it to 'being on a football terrace supporting your team: it's not actually yelling at people, it's like supporting your team, because you want your team to come out on top, and you're part of the team and you can actually stand up and contribute if you get called, you're on the pitch as well as on the terrace'.

Like football supporters, MPs may passionately want their side to win, but they know perfectly well that it hasn't when it hasn't. Harman says: 'Although your own side is predisposed to cheer and support you, it happens so often that if somebody's done badly at PMQs, however much their own side try and cheer, it's a feeble, artificial-sounding, unconvincing cheer. So nobody's ever in any doubt. And at the end of PMQs the person who's done best, all their side, their eyes are shining and they're smiling. And the other side just slope out feeling glum.' The House respects a good argument, or a good line, including from the other side, as Eagle told us: 'In general if somebody does well and they score a hit the other side will go "Well, yeah, yeah, I'll give you that one", so there's a kind of grudging "Yeah, fair enough."' Gyles Brandreth wrote in his diary, 'Energy, attack, humour – deploy all three at once and both sides of the House give you credit.'[186]

Some MPs have a particular seat they like to sit in. Dennis Skinner has sat in the same spot on the front row, halfway down the Chamber, since he was first elected in 1970: 'I went on that bench when I first came in. It was, without doubt, a left-wing bench, no question, they were all left-wingers on that bench, like Frank Allaun from Salford, and Russell Kerr, who used to drop to sleep, he had a sleep problem, he used to drop off and I used to sort of nudge him to keep him awake.' After the 2015 election, the huge new intake of Scottish Nationalist MPs tried to take the bench over. Skinner and his colleagues were having none of it: 'They were prepared after a row that they'd allow me a seat, and I said, "If you think I'm going to be happy sat amongst you you've another think coming." So then I encouraged Ian [Lavery], and Ronnie Campbell, and Grahame Morris, Ian Mearns, so that we occupied half the bench. We used to rush in in the morning. In the early days we'd rush in from the bottom end, they'd be at the top end, and we were actually running, and one Labour MP who was a whip, I think, she said, "Oh dear, there'll be trouble, I don't know what will happen," she came in to witness this thing. And so Ian said, "We're having half the bench, that's the agreement." And so in a way it was a good thing that the whip was there because I think it brought home to the Scot Nats that they'd have to do a deal.'

The Conservative MP Anna Soubry told us that she always sits in the same place at PMQs: in 'the noisy corner', near the back, alongside the Speaker, so that 'you're in Bercow's ear but not necessarily in his eye'. She and her colleagues yell heckles across the Chamber, taking advantage of pauses left by the Leader of the Opposition, 'like, "I've been thinking…" "That's a change! There's a surprise! Gosh! Finally got there!" You know, or things like, "That answer wasn't good enough…" "Well, try asking a proper question!" But cleverer than that.' They join in with feed lines, too, with a mock-shocked '*Aaaah!*' when the Prime Minister reveals a fact that undermines the opposition's case: 'That's another one, which is classic: the Prime Minister says, "Who said that? The *Labour Party!*" "*Aaaah!*" There's a lot of pantomime.' Some of the heckling from the noisy corner is directed at overly loyal questioners on her own side: 'When anybody said "long-term economic plan", because we don't like clichés, we used to do this, "*Ker-ching!* Five pounds for that man, give that man a fiver, *Ker-ching!*"' And, 'When somebody asks a very long question, you'll hear people like me shouting out "*Division!*" Or the other one is "Have an adjournment debate!" But "*Division!*" we love shouting that one. It's the same as "*Taxi!*"' Ann Treneman, former parliamentary sketch-writer for *The Times*, told us that some of what is shouted in the Chamber is 'slightly cruel humour where a really long-winded MP, people will start shouting at them and saying, "Keep going!" People think that's bullying, I mean technically it is bullying, but it's not *really* bullying because that person goes on forever. And it's a very limited amount of time at PMQs, and if you're going to take longer than thirty seconds to ask a question you really have to get a grip.'

Cabinet ministers don't generally sit on the back benches during PMQs; if they have not been found a space on the front bench they tend to arrive just as it starts, when the Chamber is already full, and find a place to stand or squat. 'By the time I got into Cabinet,' Anna Soubry says, 'I would sit in the same place at the feet of the Speaker, so whereas before I had been shouted at by the Speaker for making a racket, I was at his feet, I never got told off. I mean I could sometimes see the clerk, David [Natzler], flinch at the noise, but I never ever, ever got told off. And my eyeline was Cameron, and Cameron would look at me, and I would go "Yes! Yes!" like that [at this point, Soubry looks at us, grinning, two thumbs up]. And that would spur him on.' Dennis Skinner told us that he tries to pre-empt obvious cop-out answers: 'I do join in on questions, I sort of answer it, "Oh, this'll be a review, it'll be a review, in due course," things like that. "Come on, is it yes, is it no, come on." And sometimes [*singing*] "They're re-view-ing the sit-u-a-tion" – that's from *Oliver!*'

It's certainly true that the whips on both sides encourage their MPs to cheer their leaders and shout down the other side. Soubry says that David Cameron's PPS, Desmond Swayne, would send emails calling for lots of noise, and even suggesting particular words to be used. But, she told us, 'all these things were completely ignored by us. We never did that. I mean, I don't really remember even reading any of that, because we would tend to do our own thing.' It isn't that Soubry and her colleagues are disobeying their whips' instructions; it's that they are heckling on their own initiative. When the Speaker complains that the whips have orchestrated the heckling on the Tory benches, Soubry says, 'we all go, "No they haven't, I'm just being naturally unpleasant," or something like that'. John Bercow himself told us of a conversation he had had with a particular unnamed MP who was very loud: 'I rebuked her for excessive noise, and then I did say to her privately, "I know we don't know each other very well, but I cannot believe that you would behave like that at your dinner parties." To which she rather disarmingly replied, "Oh, Mr Speaker, I don't think you know what my dinner parties are like."'

Bercow believes that the noise could be stopped. 'If the whips instructed colleagues to behave they would,' he says. But earlier in his career – Bercow was a Conservative MP from 1997 until his election as Speaker in 2009 – he is happy to admit, 'I behaved badly on an industrial scale. I don't want you to get the wrong impression on this front. It's not a question of sort of modest and infrequent, or better still very occasional misconduct, it was remorseless, loud, in-your-face, bash-it-over-the-head misconduct. In no way did I do it under exhortation from the whips, in fact particularly in the later years but really for much of my time in Parliament, I had a relationship with the Conservative whips characterised by trust and understanding: I didn't trust them and they didn't understand me.' It's not clear why, if Bercow's own heckling was uninfluenced by his whips, he is so confident that the whips would be able to shut other MPs up. As he remembers, 'I regarded it as a bear pit and I rather relished the bear pit. I thought there was much to be said for it, not least in terms of sheer enjoyment from the vantage point of the participant.'

Neil Kinnock told us that although the House of Commons had always been noisy, orchestrated yelling was something that developed in the 1980s under Margaret Thatcher as part of a wider operation to ensure that she performed effectively at PMQs. 'It became gradually noticeable, but it isn't something that you instantly see. There would be some barracking from our side, but either through deference or proper respect or demoralisation or whatever else, our side never launched into the organised barracking which came to characterise the Tory back benches. And you could actually observe their whips scattered across the back benches, saying, "Come on, make some bloody noise," or words to that effect. So organised barracking became a feature. Consequently, Prime Minister's Questions changed noticeably by having a Prime Minister arriving with a script, that she would use regardless of the question, supported by backbenchers whose purpose was to give unrelenting and loud support to her, and to disrupt and shout down anybody from the other side, not just the Leader of the Opposition but anybody from the other side.'

Whether or not Margaret Thatcher started it, everybody tries to do it now. The noise is an integral part of the atmosphere and something all leaders have to contend with, or use to their advantage. William Hague says that 'you still have to keep going. It's counterintuitive. You had to keep going unless there was some advantage in stopping, some other advantage in reacting to something, some stupid thing that somebody had shouted or something, but otherwise you had to keep going.' Following the 1997 Labour landslide, Hague had to deal with an especially unbalanced House of Commons: on the Tory side 'there were plenty of seats. Now it looks as if both sides are full, but then the Labour MPs couldn't remotely all sit down, but they could make a heck of a noise if they wanted to, and I had to keep going over 420 hostile voices so I really needed to project my voice.'

Harold Macmillan described the House as being

> rather like those Italian lakes, one moment it's calm, the next moment there is suddenly a tremendous storm ... like a prep school, there are boys who are popular, whom you must *never* slap down, even if they are asking a silly question, on the other side ... then there are the unpopular, the tiresome, and the House rather enjoys their being slapped down ... You must remember that, like a school, on the whole it dislikes the front bench (the masters) ... often you can turn an enemy into a friend, by some slight recognition.[187]

One thing that always calms the storm is the two leaders' solemn tributes to the victims of terrorist attacks or natural disasters, or to soldiers killed in the line of duty. Most weeks, PMQs is the only appearance at the dispatch box for both the Prime Minister and the Leader of the Opposition, and therefore the only parliamentary opportunity for either of them to recognise such deaths. During our time working on PMQs, with British forces still deployed in Afghanistan, these tributes came frequently. The wall of noise would die down rapidly as David Cameron began his first answer in too many sessions with words along the lines of 'I am sure the whole House will wish to join me in paying tribute to those servicemen who have fallen since we last met for Prime Minister's Question Time.' Ed Miliband would follow with a similar form of words before starting to ask his first question, and with a similar effect on the volume. One journalist told us that the press gallery assumed that this was deliberate, and that the tributes were read out with the specific intention of creating a breathing space. They weren't: politics can be a cynical business, but it is not as cynical as journalism. Nevertheless, there is no point denying that reading out the names always had that effect. One of the jobs of the opposition PMQs prep team on a Wednesday morning is to call No. 10 to check whether there are any tributes to the fallen that day, and to be given a list of names and other details, including pronunciation.

Formal tributes will always create silence, but that silence evaporates as soon as the leaders return – sometimes, it has to be admitted, with a jarring change of tone – to the political meat of PMQs. So creating more space is a skill. Not just at the start, but throughout PMQs a good leader can work the Chamber, manipulating the noise levels, holding MPs' attention through the silences, giving MPs on their side no alternative but to insert a 'Hear, hear!' or a 'Shame!' in a pause they have left for exactly that response – in just the same way that a stand-up comedian can force a laugh just through the cadence of a sentence, or a politician on *Question Time* can vary the pace of an answer to produce a Pavlovian round of applause at the end of it.

As Angela Eagle says, 'Timing is really important in the House of Commons. Because that way you can almost conduct. And so saying nothing and having a space is really important. But not enough space for them to fill it with something else, not enough silence for a good rejoinder to be heard. They've got to be frightened of saying something because they're worried that you'll be able to respond quickly to it.' Eagle herself showed a brilliant command of pace in her first PMQs as stand-in for Jeremy Corbyn in December 2015, warning her opponent, George Osborne, that he should be worried about the leadership ambitions of 'somebody a few places down from him on the Treasury bench' and pausing for a full twenty-five seconds for MPs to ask who she was referring to, and shout suggestions, before letting the noise die down, pointing at Theresa May and saying with a smile, 'She knows who she is.'[188] She was right, too.

The most obvious way of leading MPs in the Chamber is with a call-and-response litany of your side's achievements or the other side's failings. Begin a list, and signal properly that that's what it is, and they'll soon join in. The deficit – *down!* Interest rates – *down!* Inflation – *down!* Taxes – *down!* Unemployment – *down!* We would regularly build these lists into Ed Miliband's wrap or into his rejoinders, knowing that it was a reliable way to get Labour MPs shouting behind him. 'It gives your side something to cheer about,' he says. 'You know, "The Labour government? I'll tell you about the Labour government, the highest patient satisfaction ever, more nurses than ever before, more doctors than ever before, blah blah blah."'

Here, for example, is John Major's last ever PMQs response as Prime Minister to Tony Blair, at the end of a Conservative government whose agenda was frequently derailed by 'sleaze' scandals, setting out a litany of what he saw as Labour's own hypocrisy on the issue, with his backbenchers roaring their support:

> The stain, if stain there will be, is upon a Labour front bench that has smeared and smeared and smeared again. The Labour leader has traded in double standards from the moment he took up office. This is the Labour leader who sells policy to the trade unions for cash [*'Hear, hear.'*]; who refuses to comply with the code of practice on party funding [*'Hear, hear.'*]; who calls for party openness but will not publish the secret funds of his own office [*'Hear, hear.'*]; who attacks share options but takes money from millionaires for his own party [*'Hear, hear.'*]; who attacks businessmen and asks them to fund things for him, who flew Concorde and failed to declare it [*'Hear, hear.'*]; who has a deputy leader who spends a weekend at a five-star hotel and does not declare it [*'Hear, hear.'*]; and who flies to the other side of the world to do newspaper deals and never admits to them [*'Hear, hear.'*]. If there are any double standards, they sit there – on the opposition benches.[189]

George Osborne proudly recalls this as one of his earliest contributions to PMQs as 'part of the supply chain of ammunition' in the Conservative Research Department, 'feeding up into the machine'. It created an effective performance in the Chamber, but as so often it's important not to overstate the impact of an effective performance in the Chamber. Hansard records the Conservative MP David Shaw delightedly shouting, 'Game, set and match,' as Major sat down. It wasn't. Shaw lost his seat in the Labour landslide a few weeks later.

A variant on the 'call and response' on your own side is the 'hands up' trick, where you ask the MPs opposite you to raise their hands if they agree with their leader's position on a difficult topic, or if they support a beleaguered minister, or if they will personally benefit from a recently announced tax cut. This generally works because MPs on the other side are not quite sure what to do: they want to say they back their leader, they don't want to put their hand up for the leader of the opposite party, they probably really are uncomfortable about the issue being raised; so there will always be a scattering – much worse than unanimity either way – who will raise their hands out of loyalty, while looking sheepish. The fact that some have put their hands up then makes it all the more obvious that most haven't, which is the impression the trick is designed to create in the first place.

David Cameron managed to pull exactly the same 'hands up' trick twice on the same issue, when in both 2010 and 2015 he asked Labour MPs to indicate whether they were going to put a picture of their leader on their election leaflets. In 2010, this was a prepared response to a predictable Gordon Brown attack on the Conservatives' much-mocked 'airbrushed' election posters of Cameron's face. When Brown said, 'He can have his posters; we will have the policies,' Cameron came back with 'The Prime Minister asks about pictures. Why don't we do a bit of market research? When it comes to Labour members' election addresses, hands up, who is going to put the Prime Minister's picture on the front? Come on, hands up.'[190] Cameron could come back to highlight how few of them there were. Five years later, again faced with an opponent whose personal opinion poll ratings were worse than his own, Cameron did the same thing to Ed Miliband: 'How many people will put the Leader of the Opposition on their leaflets? Come on! Hands up!'[191] Of course, 2017 saw a general election campaign in which the Tories put both Theresa May's *and* Jeremy Corbyn's photos on most of their leaflets, and Labour put neither on most of theirs – and we all know how that turned out.

The wall of noise that the leaders face, and sometimes manipulate, is made up of hundreds of individual voices. Sometimes a witty heckle can be heard over the cacophony, or finds a sudden, tiny silence in which to flourish. Heckles can even be mildly surreal. In October 2010 David Cameron was asked about the late president of the Patients Association, Claire Rayner, whose final words were 'a warning to the Prime Minister that if he screws up the NHS she is going to come back and haunt him'.[192] The end of the question, and much of the answer, was accompanied by a Labour MP – Chris Ruane, we think – delivering a long, ghostly 'Wooooooo!'

John Whittingdale, who told us he is not a heckler himself and dislikes the jeers at PMQs, acknowledges that 'a well-placed single line can completely disarm or unnerve somebody speaking, and that is a skill. You'll have seen if somebody gets up and says something which can be misconstrued, or is a slightly bad choice of words, they can be absolutely destroyed before they've ever got the question out. And it is terrifying. I'll always remember Seb Coe froze, I think it was his first ever Prime Minister's Questions and he literally froze, he got up and he couldn't speak. And all of us felt incredibly sympathetic to him because it is a terrifying experience and he was a new MP.' Dennis Skinner told us his technique for avoiding being put off by the noises coming from the other side: 'When you stand up at Question Time you've got a sea of angry faces. I don't look at them, I look at a panel. I don't see the point of looking at angry faces, or otherwise it might change your attitude. Cameron probably thought I was looking at him, I never was. Because there would always be, even on a good day, a growl by the enemy when I got up, so you don't encourage that.'

Slips of the tongue will be pounced on by the MPs opposite. In December 2008 Gordon Brown misspoke while trying to explain the purpose of recapitalising banks which were on the brink of failure. 'The first point of recapitalisation was to save banks that would otherwise have collapsed. We not only saved the world...' he said, before correcting himself to 'We not only saved the banks...'[193] But it was too late. Once Brown had inadvertently claimed to have saved the world, it was impossible to get back on track over the jeers and mocking laughter coming from the Conservative benches.

Some of the most effective parliamentary heckles take advantage of that most dangerous of rhetorical missteps, the ill-timed pause. In the noise of the House of Commons, where it can be difficult to hear your own words, it's tempting to pause to let the sound die down, or to repeat yourself. Labour's shadow Chancellor John McDonnell succumbed to this second temptation in October 2015 when, in the face of a wall of sound from Tory MPs, he described his own U-turn over whether he wanted Labour MPs to vote for or against the government's fiscal charter as 'embarrassing, embarrassing, embarrassing, embarrassing, embarrassing' (Hansard only records one 'embarrassing', presumably to spare his embarrassment).[194] Pausing mid-sentence, or repeating yourself to be heard in the Chamber, is almost always a mistake, because the broadcast microphones are picking up your voice perfectly well: even if they can't hear you on the other side of the room, they can hear you at home. The best advice is: plough on through the noise.

Jeremy Corbyn failed to take this advice when responding to a European Council statement by David Cameron in February 2016. He provided the perfect set-up: 'Last week, like him, I was in Brussels meeting heads of government and leaders of European socialist parties, one of whom said to me...' and then left a fatal pause, into which leapt a Conservative MP with the words 'Who are you?' Corbyn's qualities do not include an ability to take jokes at his own expense with good humour, and his irritated 'No. What they said... The Conservative Party might care to think for a moment about what is going on' only made things worse.[195] Margaret Thatcher made a similar mistake as Leader of the Opposition in a debate in 1977, when she intended to use the sentence '"The Prime Minister is an expert in political wheeling and dealing." However, after she uttered "The Prime Minister is an expert" she was loudly interrupted by government backbenchers screaming "hear, hear".'[196] It was too late to salvage the situation.

The atmosphere in the Commons Chamber when it is full partly reflects Parliament's gender balance, with the tone often being criticised for being masculine, macho and sexist. Even after the 2017 election, which increased the number of female MPs to a record 208, men outnumber women two to one. When Margaret Thatcher became Prime Minister in 1979, the Commons was 97 per cent male, and of course that shaped and defined the atmosphere, and the way she was perceived as well. The first question she ever received at PMQs, from the Labour MP Stanley Clinton Davis, concluded with the admonition, 'In replying to all questions will she please not be too strident?'[197]

Thatcher once used a strikingly maternal image to describe her

approach to defending her government at PMQs: 'One tends, particularly with the kind of atmosphere in the House of Commons at
Question Time, when you are always attacked, to defend yourself.
Most women defend themselves. It is the female of the species. It is
the tigress and lioness in you which tends to defend when attacked.'[198]
John Whittingdale told us that although she was 'intensely feminine',
Thatcher 'never thought of herself in political terms as a female
politician, she thought of herself as a politician. And she asked for
no special favours and didn't intend to give them to anybody else.'

Harriet Harman says: 'There is this feminist critique to be made
of PMQs which is that it's very focused on one person, it's very
combative, it's the moment when it is not the team, it is just you. And
that is the all-conquering leader mode, or vanquished victim mode.
So, it's high noon, and very focused on one person, and very noisy.
And it's as far away from deliberative, seeking consensus, that you
could possibly get. And for years the women's movement argued, and
in particular Labour women argued, that it was a very sort of macho
way of doing politics.' But when her turn came to answer questions
as Gordon Brown's deputy, and later to ask them as Leader of the
Opposition and as Ed Miliband's deputy, she knew she had to work
with the system as it was, rather than trying to change it and be
accused of weakness.

When Harman first entered Parliament in 1982, so-called 'women's
issues' were often not regarded as the proper stuff of politics. She told
us about the very first question she ever asked Margaret Thatcher at
PMQs as a backbencher: 'I asked a question which was not part of
the normal basket of political issues that get asked, which was about
holiday play schemes for the children of working women, and it was

really awful because not only did she sort of sneer at me, and they all sniggered because this was not regarded as what was political and what we should be asking at PMQs, but also all my own side was like, "Oh, how embarrassing, she's asked something which is not a proper political question."' *The Guardian*'s Norman Shrapnel, writing in the late 1970s when, as he put it, 'there are still far fewer women in the House than there are Etonians', observed that women MPs

> have to work harder, talk louder, run faster just to keep up – or, occasionally, to get away. If they are sexually attractive they face further aggravations in this male-clubbish atmosphere. I recall one young Labour MP raising the question of first-child allowances, and being infuriated by what she took to be the knowing looks on the benches across the Chamber. 'When I have an interest to declare,' she snarled at them with a mixture of parliamentary correctness and naked fury, 'I shall declare it.'[199]

Female MPs on both sides of the House have had to face juvenile, sexist heckles and jeers about their appearance. The Conservative MP Teresa Gorman, elected in 1987, was 'shaken by the sheer crudity and cruelty of some of the men in the House of Commons. "Shortly after I got into the House of Commons, Dennis Skinner would shout across the Chamber to me, 'Tell us your age! Where's your birth certificate? Here she comes, Harvey Proctor [her predecessor as MP for Billericay] in drag!' It was all quite intimidating."'[200] Labour's Barbara Follett, an MP from 1997 until 2010, said in 2004, 'I remember some Conservatives, whenever a Labour woman got up to speak they would take their breasts – their imaginary breasts – in their hands and wiggle them and say "melons" as we spoke.'[201] Anna Soubry is sceptical that this still goes on: 'That might have happened twenty years ago, but to suggest that happens now is absolutely not true. I feel very, very strongly, that does not happen. These are old bits of mythology.' Ann Treneman points out that 'women also attack each other, women also shout. It is a confrontational chamber, so people who don't like confrontation, whether they're men or women, are going to have difficulty with it.'

Nevertheless, there is some evidence that things have moved more slowly than they might have done, despite the shift in the overall gender balance of the House. In the 1980s, the Conservative MP Edwina Currie could comment on Labour's Dawn Primarolo 'sitting right at the top of the back benches with a short skirt, crossing her legs. Every time she crosses and uncrosses her legs all these lads on our side go "mmoooorre"! It's really very funny!'[202] In 2010 the Labour MP Lisa Nandy sat in the gangway between the benches to watch the Budget, wearing a long skirt, to find that 'Conservative MPs on the benches opposite were waving their white order papers and shouting "Knickers!"'[203] Now, thanks to social media, you can be publicly sexist about women MPs at PMQs from the privacy of your own home. In March 2012 the *Sun on Sunday* columnist Toby Young tweeted, 'Serious cleavage behind @Ed_Miliband's head. Anyone know who it belongs to?' before announcing to a grateful world that the cleavage in question belonged to one of the Commons' youngest MPs.[204]

Labour has led all the other parties on female representation and Ed Miliband was able to exploit the gender imbalance between the front benches at a PMQs in February 2014. An already-planned set on women in the Conservative Party was given additional resonance by the fact that, as it turned out when he got into the Chamber, there were no women at all sitting on the government front bench. We had taken the precaution of texting Labour's female shadow Cabinet members to make sure that as many of them as possible were sitting on our front bench, but the seating plan opposite was beyond our control. We were lucky: Theresa May was away. 'A picture tells a thousand words,' said Ed, pointing across the Chamber.[205] Slightly garbled phrase aside, he was right: nobody remembered anything else he or David Cameron said that week, but it was a clear win, because the image the Conservative front bench presented was the only proof we needed for the attack we were trying to make.

Sexist comments are still made in the Chamber, but now they are more likely than ever to backfire on those who make them. In April 2011, when David Cameron, infuriated by Angela Eagle's heckling, turned on her and snapped, 'Calm down, dear,'[206] she knew immediately it was a victory for her and a defeat for him: 'I was quite pleased that I'd got under his skin because he made a fool of himself really, and I thought also, because he was angry and he let rip a bit, it was very – and this is what PMQs can do – very truthful about him. He showed a side of himself by accident that nobody in his office would have wanted him to reveal. So I thought, "Ha! Got you!" and didn't think anything of it until everyone started saying, "Oh, calm down dear, calm down dear," and then the media started texting me.' Eagle was quite happy to exploit it. 'It was a sexist comment. I thought it was revealing of him. I mean that sort of stuff's water off a duck's back to me, I've been in politics long enough to have heard virtually everything there is to hear, but for him to do that with the whole nation watching... Immediately it was like, "Oh, she's got no sense of humour, blah blah blah," all that crap, and I just thought, "No, you're bang to rights, mate." I would not have gone on and said, "I'm really offended," you know, come on, I was shouting at him! Although I was right and he was wrong.'

Cameron still insists that the comment was not sexist, and indeed that it was probably not even aimed at Eagle: 'That was totally off the cuff. I watch a lot of television, I always have done, I used to work in television and I remember things from television, and that was an advert. And most people in the House of Commons don't watch television, and so they thought it was sexist, whereas what it actually was was a take on Michael Winner saying, "Calm down, dear." But it was bad, because it came from me, a man, and I don't think it was particularly at Angela Eagle actually, it might have been at Ed Balls, I'm not sure, I think I was referring to Ed Balls, but anyway the point is there was no *mens rea*, it was not sexist in intent, it was the funny line from Michael Winner.' *Mens rea* or not, the perception which the incident fed, that Cameron's instinct was to reach for a gendered insult when under pressure, meant that a few months later, when he responded to a question from Conservative backbencher Nadine Dorries by saying, 'I know that the honourable lady is extremely frustrated,'[207] nobody gave him the benefit of the doubt; he apologised to her later.

The 'Calm down, dear' incident was a manifestation of one of Cameron's biggest weaknesses at PMQs: he was easily provoked. Even when he was still Leader of the Opposition, Labour spotted that his face would go red when he was annoyed, and therefore tried to annoy him. Theo Bertram says, 'The good thing with Cameron was you'd know when you'd got him because he flushed, literally his face went red, you could see the colour in his cheeks, so Gordon could do it. Gordon knew it too, you could see, "We've got him". It's a pretty terrible thing to have as a Prime Minister, to have such a visible tell, but he would go red in the face.' Angela Eagle told us, 'The red used to go in a line all the way up, and you could see that he was losing it, and he would go bright red in a line, and so obviously you did your best to try to get him to do that.' Cameron admits, 'I'm easily wound up, and all politicians have a thick skin and I've got a thick skin, but in Prime Minister's Questions the barbs get to you, if someone had a good one against you, you could sort of feel it, but I think I probably showed it. Dennis Skinner sometimes used to shout the most appalling things across the floor. So I did sometimes have a go at him, and never really to much great effect actually. I think, on the whole, you do better to just ignore all the noises off. But I always found that hard, because I found it genuinely distracting.'

Ed Balls in particular, sitting in his usual place next to Ed Miliband, played a useful role with his irritating 'flat-lining' hand gestures and quiet under-the-microphone spoken commentary. 'Ed Balls really irritated the hell out of me,' says Cameron. Angela Eagle remembers, 'Me and Ed Balls used to both get in his eyesight and it used to put him off sometimes, so we did it deliberately to put him off.' Ed Miliband told us, 'Ed Balls was a very good sledger. It was Shane Warne-esque.' Balls himself recalled in his memoirs, 'Nothing annoyed [Cameron] more than the simple phrases: "You're supposed to be the Prime Minister. You're supposed to know these things. Why can't you answer the questions? Why are you floundering around? Are you sure you're up to this?"'[208] Cameron explains, 'I can't really do two things at once, so I find it very difficult to concentrate. Even though the general noise in the House of Commons doesn't really bother me, someone really close, the noise was frustrating.'

Eventually, he would snap. Balls wrote:

> I'm absolutely certain he never came into a session on Wednesday intending to say something nasty or patronising – you'd some-times see him visibly trying to calm down and control himself – but eventually his inner Flashman would win out. I always knew I'd got him when one of his own backbenchers was asking some patsy question he didn't even have to listen to, and he'd instead glance over at me and hiss: 'Why don't you just shut up?' or 'Stop waving your stupid hand'… Down the front bench, Sadiq Khan would look at his watch and say 'Well, it took him twenty-two minutes today' or 'Seven minutes! That's a new record!'[209]

See if you can spot the exact moment in this David Cameron answer to a question from a government backbencher when the heckling from Ed Balls finally gets too much:

> What we need to do, both in Britain and in Europe, is to com-bine the fiscal deficit reduction that has given us the low interest rates with an active monetary policy, structural reforms to make us competitive, and innovative ways of using our hard-won credibility … Which we would not have if we listened to the muttering idiot sitting opposite me.[210]

Cameron's own team recognised that it was a problem, even briefing in May 2011 that they were concerned that 'the characterisation of the

Prime Minister as the fictional schoolboy bully Flashman from *Tom Brown's Schooldays* is gaining resonance with the public. As a result Mr Cameron will try to give his Commons performances a "makeover" so they are "less aggressive" and "more prime ministerial".'[211] The problem with briefings like this is that the opposition can read them too, so at PMQs the day after the story was published, as soon as Cameron attempted to make a joke, Ed Miliband had the opening he was looking for to say, 'We read in the papers about a PMQs makeover, but I have to say that it did not last very long. Flashman is back.'[212] Cameron is phlegmatic about the Flashman charge: 'I think it was six of one, half a dozen of the other. You've got to be good in the way you can be good, and sometimes a flash turn of phrase… often in politics your strength is your weakness and your weakness is your strength, you know.'

In Cameron's case, the occasional loss of self-control was worth it because it went alongside the quality which makes the biggest difference to the effectiveness of a PMQs performance: self-confidence, ease, authority. Some have it, some don't. At their best, in their different ways, Macmillan, Wilson, Callaghan, Thatcher, Smith, Blair, Hague and Cameron all had it – even if some had to work hard to get it. Duncan Smith, Corbyn and May didn't or don't. Major had more of it than many people remember. Miliband knew he needed it, and did what he could to synthesise it. Brown had it when he was on ground where he felt confident, and when he wasn't, it left him.

Theo Bertram vividly described to us the sense that, too much of the time, Gordon Brown was trying just a little too hard at PMQs for the best of himself to come across: 'Authenticity comes from being relaxed, and from believing in yourself, but also sometimes being spontaneous, but there's also, you know, watch the flight of the ball as it comes towards you, adjust your position before you hit the ball back, you don't need to whack it back, you just need to get it back over the net, but look at the ball as it's coming towards you, move your feet, slightly adjust what you're doing, hit it back. That's all you do. All you need to do as Prime Minister is just get the ball back over the net, doesn't matter whether you've answered the question, just get the ball back over the net. What Gordon used to think about was "I need to hit the ball really hard." And you don't need to hit the ball hard. And he was, "Well, whereabouts on the ball do I need to hit it, I'm worried about my stroke, my stroke isn't…" No, no, no, relax your posture more, just be ready to move your feet, you just need to hit it over the net, you don't need to whack it back. And understanding that the balls that come from backbenchers, they're *backbenchers*, you don't even need to hit it back again, just make contact with the ball.'

David Cameron, who faced Brown at PMQs for the whole of Brown's premiership, told us, 'The whole point about Brown was he's a sort of great big dump truck of a politician who flattens his opponents, you had to kind of dance round him and stick a pin in the tyre. Brown had one gear, very much, and it was thump your opponent, and I learned from that a bit because I used to go and watch him in Treasury Questions when he was Chancellor, and I remember just thinking, "Oh God, we can't just do it like this," because even if you asked a question about, you know, "Shouldn't we work together to relieve the Angolan debt crisis?" it would be "Eighteen years of Tory misrule", thump thump thump, he only had one gear, and it was really tiresome, and I think that was one of the things that convinced me that you needed a more sort of conversational style and you needed to vary the pace and the length of the bowling.'

Cameron found Tony Blair, who he also faced at PMQs for two years, more impressive: 'Blair's ability to turn from praising a colleague to attacking a Tory to uniting the nation to talking about the grief of a mother who'd lost a soldier, he had a very good mix, I thought he was very good.' At its best, Cameron's style – particularly asking the questions in opposition, when he was less constrained by his briefing book – was natural and conversational, giving the impression that he had only just thought of whatever it was he was saying at any given moment, and that changes in tone, whether jokes or asides or sudden flashes of indignation, were spontaneous. It worked well. 'The thing is,' says Cameron, 'it's got to be you, it's got to be your own style, and then it's easier to bring the variety that you want to bring. If the whole thing was a performance and you were pretending to be something else it would be a disaster, because as soon as you went extemporary you'd fall off your perch.'

Self-confidence partly comes with the political climate, and partly creates it. A leader whose party is on top can behave like it at PMQs. A leader who behaves at PMQs as if their party is on top can convince people that it is – and if you convince people you're on top, you're halfway there (we've all, in all walks of life, met people who can do that). But a leader who comes across as pleading, or appears to defer to an opponent, is already losing, and so is their party. You have to look down on your opponent, not up at them. This matters: it's the first thing most viewers see, and may be the only thing they remember. John Smith's biographer, Andy McSmith, compared Smith's body language at PMQs with that of his predecessor, Neil Kinnock:

Kinnock, who had to endure years up against Margaret Thatcher, with her hundred-plus majorities, looked tight, grim and determined to get through with it, like a man walking head down into a storm; but the bulky figure of John Smith takes command of the few square feet of floor allocated to him, and he turns this way and that, with a finger raised to emphasize his point and a slightly pleased-with-himself look, just like someone who has waited a long time to be able to do what he is now doing.[213]

It's easy to write this kind of confidence off as the product of Eton, or the Oxford Union or the Glasgow University Union, or a career at the Bar – important points on the CVs of Cameron (Eton), Hague (the Oxford Union), Smith (both the GUU and the Bar) and Thatcher and Blair (the Bar). And it may well be the product of those places, in those cases. But using that to write it off, rather than to seek to replicate it and win, is a mistake. You can try to make a virtue of not having it, if you don't have it. But if you don't have it, unless you are very lucky in your opponent, you're not going to be winning at PMQs very often.

Self-confidence can manifest itself in an air of superiority, bordering on mockery, bordering on contempt for your opponent: not just in having a cutting gag, but in delivering it with just the right edge. John Smith confronting John Major over tax rises the Conservatives had enacted after promising in their manifesto to avoid them: 'Was the whole manifesto written on a wet night somewhere in Dudley?'[214] William Hague attacking Tony Blair for being insufficiently briefed on a tax on small information technology companies: 'We are talking about the knowledge economy, and judging by the Prime Minister's answer, he is not part of it.'[215] David Cameron incredulous at Gordon Brown's explanation for calling off a planned early election: 'He is the first Prime Minister in history to flunk an election because he thought that he was going to win it.'[216]

Margaret Thatcher's most famous PMQs moment was a glorious contemptuous snap, a self-confident pursuit of an opponent's heckle which, she instinctively saw, had given her an opening to assert her dominance. When Labour's deputy leader, Denis Healey, sitting on the front bench close to his leader, Michael Foot, suggested in April 1983 that she would 'cut and run' and call an election before the economy worsened, she turned on him. 'The right honourable gentleman is afraid of an election, is he? Afraid? Frightened? Frit? Could not take it? Cannot stand it? If I were going to cut and run, I should have gone after the Falklands. Frightened! Right now inflation is lower than it has been for thirteen years – a record which the right honourable gentleman could not begin to touch.'[217] This was a Prime Minister on top of her game.

Once the leaders' duel is over, the Prime Minister has to keep going, dealing with backbench questions from both sides. But the Leader of the Opposition's job is done. Ed Miliband told us that when he felt he'd done badly, it was painful having to sit there waiting for the next twenty minutes to pass, beaten but unable to do anything else. But 'sometimes you'd have a really successful one against Cameron and you'd be thinking, "Please, let no backbencher ask him a gift question which is going to allow him to get his troops going again," and I would whisper to Ed Balls, "There's only two more to go," because you'd know that the story out of it would be something bad for him, but if something went wrong and somebody asked him a question which allowed him to make news or rally his troops then the mood would be slightly different.' The second half of PMQs might not be the main attraction, but it can change the story.

8

BACKBENCHERS
AND SMALLER PARTIES

Asking six questions of the Prime Minister is hard, but asking just one is harder. With six, you can anticipate the answers and prepare responses to them, exposing weaknesses, narrowing or broadening the angle of attack. With one, you have no comeback at all. You ask your devastating question about the terrible state of, say, the education system, the Prime Minister reads out two lines about how good the education system is now and how terrible it was when your party was in power, and the session moves on. It doesn't matter if the answer ducks the key issue, or misrepresents the facts, or makes an unfair attack on you or your party. That's it. You're done.

That doesn't mean that backbench questions are pointless. In fact, they can achieve a lot. It isn't unusual for PMQs to generate several different news stories, and many of these will come from the backbench questions, not the leaders' exchanges.

There are too many backbenchers seeking to ask questions to be accommodated in one session – even when it is extended well beyond its allocated half-hour, as it has regularly been by Speaker John Bercow, as discussed in Chapter 1. The Speaker first calls the MPs whose names have been printed on the order paper, balancing them out and promoting people up the order if necessary so that the questions always alternate between government and opposition. Bercow told us, 'I try to get through all of that lot first and then I see how many real "free hits" there are with people who are standing who aren't on the order paper at all.'

He explains how he tries to make sure as many people get a chance as possible: 'Because of the competitivity at PMQs and the fact that so many people want to take part, there is a total list of how often somebody's asked a PMQ, and in broad terms, those who are on a zero have got a better chance of being called. However, there is one other factor that's quite important and that is the immediacy of the matter they want to raise if they've tipped me off. And they will ask in advance. Sometimes they will say, "Job losses in my constituency, a murder in my constituency, the threatened closure of a mental health unit in my constituency, and it's terribly urgent because the decision's being made next week or the week after." I would try to help.'

Bercow also tries to ensure as much balance as possible, making sure that the third largest party – which since 2015 has been the SNP – has three questions including the two allocated to their Westminster leader, Ian Blackford, and that the Liberal Democrats are not left out. He tries to ensure diversity of questioners too: 'I like to get a mix,

I wouldn't want to call six men and no women, and frankly if I'm honest about it, if there are fifteen people standing, and twelve of them are white and three of them are BME, I would try to ensure that the diversity principle was respected. Now of course there will be critics who say, "Politically correct nonsense, that doesn't matter at all"; well, I think "political correctness" is used as a term of abuse, so I reject that.'

Backbenchers have few opportunities to speak to a full House of Commons Chamber. It can be a nerve-racking experience, with in some ways higher stakes than for the leaders, who get to come back again and again. William Hague told us, 'You're going to live with it for the next few weeks as a backbencher whether it's a good question or not, and you've only got a few sentences and you can see them, some who memorise it and then get it wrong, some who try and read it, which doesn't go down well.' Reading a question from a piece of paper, which might seem like a completely unremarkable and even sensible thing to do, is frowned upon and can provoke disgruntled heckles and shouts of 'Reading!'

The Labour MP Kevin Brennan told us that he tries to follow the guidance set out by his colleague Paul Flynn in his book *How to Be an MP*: seize the attention of the House, make a powerful new point, and pose an unanswerable question.[218] This is most obviously a technique for opposition MPs trying to catch out the Prime Minister, but Brennan used the formula as a new MP in 2002 in a skilfully constructed question directed to Tony Blair, but aimed at the Conservative Party:

> When will the Prime Minister do something about state subsidy junkies? Is he aware that one organisation has received a massive 300 per cent increase in handouts from the taxpayer since 1997

with no improvement whatsoever in its performance? Does
he agree that that shows that pouring money into unreformed
institutions is a waste of time? [*Interruption*] Yes, you've got it.
The answer of course is Short money, paid by the taxpayer to the
Conservative Party.[219]

Blair was impressed enough by this to send Brennan a personal note
praising the question: evidence that asking good backbench questions
at PMQs can do an MP's prospects plenty of good. It's also evidence
that part of good political leadership is making the people you lead
feel valued and noticed – Brennan still remembered the note fifteen
years later.

Two of the most successful PMQs practitioners as both Leader of
the Opposition and Prime Minister, Tony Blair and David Cameron,
thought deeply about how to ask questions at PMQs long before
they reached the front bench. Blair says he took Prime Minister's
Questions very seriously as a young MP: 'When I had a question to
ask I would spend the entire morning just on my one question just as
a backbencher, crafting it, recrafting it, thinking about it. And I often
saw MPs stand up and ask these questions which they obviously
hadn't thought through and I thought, "How on earth can you *do*
that? How can you be so *incompetent*? This is the biggest event of
the week, and you can't even be bothered to sculpt the question
in the right way." So I was a student of it before I ever did it and what
I learned was that you had to be really forensic.'

Cameron, writing as a backbencher in 2002, identified four types
of PMQs question: the unanswerable question, the 'teaser' which
might catch the Prime Minister off guard, the '*Daily Mail* special'

which focuses on whatever issue is making headlines this week, and the dull but effective local question.[220] This list isn't exhaustive – most notably, it completely misses out the sycophantic government whips' questions, which we'll discuss later, although at the time Cameron was writing, with Labour in government, none of these came from Conservative MPs – but it's a decent summary of MPs' options if they want to write their own question.

The 'unanswerable' question is usually much more answerable than it looks on paper, even if it sounds terribly clever at the time (and we're happy to admit we've attempted to write more than our fair share of them ourselves). 'Is the Prime Minister proud of [insert bad thing]?' will simply draw the response 'What I'm proud of is [insert good thing].' The game here is less to stump the Prime Minister than to make the evasion really obvious. It's also important to think about what the Prime Minister's answer is likely to be. The Labour MP Richard Burgon asked what he may have thought was an unanswerable question to David Cameron a few months before the EU referendum in 2016. In fact it was completely answerable, as witnessed by the fact that the Prime Minister had an instant answer:

> RICHARD BURGON: If the British people vote to leave the European Union, will the Prime Minister resign – yes or no?
> DAVID CAMERON: No.[221]

The fact that this answer was proved to be false some months later, when David Cameron lost the referendum and resigned, does not make it a good question. What are you going to do about the fact that he broke his word and resigned – call for his resignation?

The most effective unanswerable questions are straightforward gags, where the answer doesn't matter at all. Labour's Tom Blenkinsop, at a time when the phone-hacking scandal was still fresh in the memory, including the strange detail that David Cameron had ridden a former police horse owned by former *Sun* editor Rebekah Brooks, asked a question about Cameron's experience of fox-hunting, and 'whether he used his own horse or borrowed one from a friend'.[222] Another horse-related unanswerable question came in January 2013, when Ed Miliband's set of six questions on the economy just did not have space for a line he had come up with himself, which referred both to the ongoing horsemeat scandal and the rumoured – and somewhat implausible – challenge for the Tory leadership by the obscure Adam Afriyie. It seemed too good to waste, though, so the question – 'On the subject of food safety, can the Prime Minister confirm that traces of stalking horse have been found in the Conservative Party food chain?' – was passed on to Labour backbencher Alex Cunningham, who delivered it perfectly, with accompanying neighing noises from the Labour MPs around him. The question managed to stump Cameron rather more effectively than Ed's main questions did,[223] as well as stealing more of the post-PMQs headlines. If you're going to ask a question like this, you have to know how to land a gag. Standing in a crowded House of Commons Chamber when nobody is laughing at your joke can be at least as lonely as dying on stage at a comedy club.

'Teaser' questions are harder to answer than they look. They can often be kept very brief, giving the Prime Minister even less time to think than usual, and they are best delivered in a curious, innocent tone. As Labour MP Alison McGovern says, a question is good 'if you've sat down before the Prime Minister knows what the answer is'. The example Cameron gives in his 2002 article is of a notorious accidental killer question by Tony McWalter, a former philosophy lecturer turned Labour MP, who put this to Tony Blair: 'Will he provide the House with a brief characterisation of the political philosophy that he espouses and which underlies his policies?' To make it worse, this was the very first question of the session. The answer Blair eventually alighted upon might be described as many things, but it does not set out a philosophy:

> The best example that I can give is the rebuilding of the National Health Service today under this government – extra investment. For example, there is the appointment today of Sir Magdi Yacoub to head up the fellowship scheme that will allow internationally acclaimed surgeons and consultants from around the world to work in this country.[224]

As Harriet Harman says, 'If he'd had five minutes' notice he would have done it, but he was taken by surprise. And everybody then said, "Oh, Tony doesn't have a political philosophy." He did have, of course, it was partly about not being ideologically political, but that in itself is a political philosophy. It was just that he was taken by surprise. You cannot be taken by surprise at Prime Minister's Questions because then everybody extrapolates from it completely. And then you can't get away, it sticks around.'

Paul Flynn wrote about a series of effective 'teasers' to Gordon Brown by Tory MP Michael Spicer, 'strikes that left Gordon no thinking time to frame an answer. Spicer asked, "What is the economic theory behind an end to boom and bust?" Later he queried, "Now we face stagflation, what's he going to do about it?" As Brown's premiership drew to a close, Spicer asked, "Will the Prime Minister confirm that he will soldier on to the bitter end?" All three wounded.'[225]

The question Neil Kinnock told us was the most effective PMQs backbench question he ever heard counts as a 'teaser', and although Kinnock didn't ask it he claims the credit for it. A Labour MP came to his office on a PMQs day and asked if there was anything he wanted him to ask Margaret Thatcher and, distracted and busy, Kinnock dismissively replied, 'Oh, just ask her the price of a sliced white.' John Fraser took the suggestion more seriously than Kinnock had intended. 'If, during her busy day, the Prime Minister has time to go to the supermarket, how much would she pay for a large white and how would it compare with the price ten years ago?' he asked. Even written down in Hansard, Thatcher's discomfort is palpable: 'I am sorry, we do not buy large whites.'[226]

The topical 'Daily Mail special' question can be used, as David Cameron says, to 'pick the issue that the middle-ranking tabloids are having kittens about and give it some oomph', to the advantage of the questioner who gets to 'make it onto the front pages and enjoy fifteen seconds of fame'.[227] But it is at least equally useful, and probably more useful, to the government, who can get a prime ministerial quote on the story of the day onto the lunchtime news bulletins and into every newspaper without issuing a press release or holding a press conference – so government whips might well make it clear to a backbencher that a question about the latest tabloid scandal would be welcome. If the world is outraged about something, then the Prime

Minister can use PMQs to make it clear that she is just as outraged, and indicate that action will be taken.

Backbenchers can also use PMQs to highlight issues in their own constituencies, or to take up cases their constituents have raised with them, or highlight campaigns they are supporting. As Ann Treneman says, 'This is the moment that the *Gazette* back home can write saying they raised dog poo in the street, and the Prime Minister is demanding action on potholes. I mean, potholes, dog poo, railway stations, the list is endless, music licensing for village halls, roundabouts, parking...' Local stories with national significance can be raised too. Any MP representing a constituency where a high-profile serious crime or disaster has taken place in the previous week will usually be called by the Speaker to raise it with the Prime Minister at PMQs. But MPs are national as well as local politicians. Angela Eagle says, 'I've never been interested in the "I've got something going on in my constituency" question. I've always thought that the best use of PMQs, unless you've got something really important going on locally, is to ask the big political questions, not to do very parochial questions.'

The government can use backbenchers' questions to set up announcements they have already planned: signalling a change of policy, or ensuring that a positive story for the government will come out of PMQs whether or not the Leader of the Opposition has a good day. George Osborne told us that Gordon Brown's use of this technique early on in his time as Prime Minister 'rather threw us to begin with because it meant that the news was invariably "The Prime Minister's announced something," and those first couple of months were quite difficult.' But in government the Conservatives learned to adopt the same tactic. So for example, when Tory backbencher Oliver Colvile kicked off PMQs on 19 December 2012 by asking 'what progress Sir John Holmes has made in his review of medals, especially for those who served on the Arctic convoys with bravery and endeavour', there is absolutely zero chance that Colvile had not been in dialogue with 10 Downing Street beforehand. We know this because David Cameron was prepared for it, announcing that there would be a new Arctic Convoy Star to recognise veterans of those convoys, and winning positive headlines as a result.[228]

That was the first question of the session: a particularly important one for setting the tone. The government always has one backbench question immediately before the Leader of the Opposition stands up, and will often try to use this to cause as much trouble as possible. The most obvious way of doing this is by planting a question whose implications bleed into the Leader of the Opposition's opening question. If there is a good-news story for the government on the day of PMQs, such as a fall in unemployment, then a backbencher asking about it can set the Prime Minister up, not only to extol the government's virtues, but also to express a hope that the Leader of the Opposition will welcome the good news too. This is a no-win situation: if he does, then it takes momentum out of his opening question; if he doesn't, it's very noticeable that he doesn't want to talk about it, and the Prime Minister can return to it at the start of the next answer.

Even better is for a government backbencher to ask the Prime Minister about a story that's embarrassing for the opposition, so that the Prime Minister can ask the Leader of the Opposition to comment on it. Here's an example from 2013:

RICHARD DRAX: Does the Prime Minister agree that it is totally unacceptable for members or prospective members of this House to say anything that supports terrorism?

DAVID CAMERON: I absolutely agree with my honourable friend. Frankly, it is absolutely staggering that someone is standing for public office who has said this: 'In October 1984, when the Brighton bomb went off, I felt a surge of excitement at the nearness of Margaret Thatcher's demise. And yet disappointment that such a chance had been missed.' Those are the words of the Labour candidate in the Eastleigh by-election. They are a complete disgrace and I hope that the leader of the Labour Party will get up and condemn them right now.[229]

Cameron was able to read out the details of what John O'Farrell, Labour's by-election candidate, had written in his bestselling account of being a Labour activist in the 1980s, *Things Can Only Get Better*, which had evidently recently been read by someone in the Conservative Research Department. The fact that Cameron had the relevant quote to hand is definitive proof of the hardly earth-shattering fact that this was a co-ordinated effort between Richard Drax and No. 10. Cameron was also able to challenge Ed Miliband to condemn his own candidate – a challenge Ed ignored, asking the question he had already planned, on the economy. That meant that Cameron could come back after Ed's question, before answering on the economy, to ask, 'Is it not amazing that the Leader of the Opposition will not condemn someone who apparently speaks up for terrorists? Is that not absolutely disgraceful? He will have a second chance when he gets up again.'[230] Cameron was already on the offensive, on a subject of his own choosing, and was able to pursue it well into Ed's set – all thanks to a well-placed backbench question.

Many of the backbenchers on the government side will be asking questions which put the Prime Minister under no pressure at all. Every week, a backbencher will ask something along the following lines:

> This morning we received the news that in my constituency of Middleton-under-the-Wold, employment has risen and unemployment has fallen for the ninth consecutive month. Will the Prime Minister join with me in praising the many great businesses in Middleton-under-the-Wold which have played their part in helping more and more people have the security of a job and the ability to provide for their families, especially PJ & Duncan Tyres Ltd, which has recently taken on fifty new employees at its new regional distribution centre, and does she agree with me that this huge success is only possible thanks to the careful economic stewardship being offered by this government, and would be put at risk by the disastrous policies being offered by the party opposite?

This question, which we have just made up, might look on the face of it like an embarrassing, sycophantic waste of time. And of course it is. But it isn't just that. It does several important jobs at once. First, it marks out the backbencher as a loyal supporter of the Prime Minister who isn't seeking to make trouble and should be considered for a job in the next reshuffle, or perhaps a knighthood. Second, as in so many sports, time-wasting is an important tactic. This question takes up a chunk of time which the Prime Minister doesn't have to spend doing anything more difficult than finding a form of words with which to agree that yes, on reflection employment rising is a good thing, and now you come to mention it, businesses which give people jobs are really ace, and I'm glad you highlighted PJ & Duncan Tyres Ltd because they probably distribute really good tyres, regionally, and yes, we are rather a good government actually, and the opposition really wouldn't be a good government, in fact they would be a bad government. And third, it gives the backbencher an excuse to put out a press release to their local paper, headlined something like 'Prime Minister praises great Middleton-under-the-Wold business', which has a good chance of filling half a page with a story about how brilliant the government is and how you should totally vote for that MP again at the next election.

We don't say any of this to mock, except maybe a bit. All of these jobs really are important, which is why government whips approach their MPs before PMQs to find out what they want to ask about and encourage them to take a question that's been written for them. If you know what an MP is asking about, and you know what the answer is, that's one less thing to worry about, and goodness knows Prime Ministers have enough to worry about already.

So government whips spend time distributing lists of 'some suggested topics that the Prime Minister would be happy to receive a question on'[231] to their backbenchers, and trying to make sure they know as many of their side's planned questions as possible. As one former government special adviser told us, handing out softball questions means that PMQs is 'fifteen terrible minutes, not thirty'. This is nothing new: as early as the 1960s efforts were being made to ensure that the Prime Minister was not under constant attack at PMQs. In 1973 G. W. Jones wrote that

> under both Mr Wilson and Mr Heath the government's own backbenchers recognised that the government's standing might be injured if only hostile questions were put to the Prime Minister. Some champions of the Prime Minister, therefore, regularly arrange to table questions so that they can make friendly points in their supplementaries and he can display a favourable picture of his administration.[232]

But the use of whips' questions developed significantly during Margaret Thatcher's premiership, to the extent that a recent analysis of questions received in Parliament by successive Prime Ministers from Thatcher to Cameron found that Thatcher had the highest percentage of 'helpful questions', at 19 per cent of the total she received.[233]

That took work. Planting questions, as well as making sure that the Prime Minister knew what her own backbenchers were likely to ask, was an important part of John Whittingdale's job as Margaret Thatcher's political secretary, he told us: 'I would ring up the people on the order paper and I'd say, "The Prime Minister would be very interested to know what you're thinking of asking today," and they'd say, "I want her to say something nice about my new road scheme," or something, and I'd say, "Well, that's hugely important and I'm sure I can get her to give you something, but could we do that another time and maybe you'd like to do something different at Prime Minister's Questions, such as…" The best outcome would be that we would give them the question, the worst outcome would be that they would say,

"No, I'm absolutely adamant I'm going to ask this question," but at least we'd know it, so we would know exactly what all the people on the Conservative benches on the order paper were going to ask.' Planting questions was one of David Cameron's responsibilities when he worked on PMQs for John Major, too: 'It was rather exciting, in my twenties I was writing both the questions and the answers sometimes. I had my own little bit of political theatre I was responsible for writing very bad scripts for.'

If the Prime Minister's team is going to plant questions, the Prime Minister has to play along or else squander backbench goodwill. Major irritated his own side by failing to be sufficiently grateful to those who tried to be helpful to him, as Gyles Brandreth, a Conservative whip whose job included trying to plant questions, wrote in his diary in March 1994:

> Unfortunately, our leader doesn't make it any easier for us to recruit helpful questioners by the way in which he regularly appears to 'put down' those that have been 'put up' to ask him planted questions. Some poor sap – Olga [Maitland], Nick Hawkins, anyone, me – is given a question, gets up, asks it precisely as drafted and agreed with No. 10, and instead of getting a warm and winning reply, is given a sort of patronising brush-off by the boss who appears to snicker in collusion with the opposition implying 'Who are these children coming up with these creepy questions?'[234]

It's better and more graceful to welcome the softballs. In March 1998 Tony Blair responded to a spectacularly friendly question from backbencher Barry Jones – it concluded with the less than forensic 'Will he accept also that the Budget was magnificent?' – with an amused 'On balance, I would agree. Some people may not like some old-fashioned sycophancy – but not me.'[235]

In May 2014 Conservative backbencher Andrew Percy revealed to a BBC film crew – perhaps somewhat naively – a whips' pre-PMQs email to Tory MPs. The list of suggested questions included 'The OECD has joined the IMF in forecasting that the UK will be the fastest-growing economy in the world. Does the Prime Minister agree this proves our long-term economic plan is working?' – which does at least include a fact to make the question topical, unlike the next one: 'Does the Prime Minister agree with me that our long-term economic plan is giving more people who want to work hard the security of a regular pay packet?'[236] No Tory backbencher was quite shameless enough to ask either of these questions, although the session still had some pretty easy softballs. Speaking to the BBC, David Cameron defended the use of whips' questions: 'If you're saying it's appalling that Tory MPs should possibly use any of these phrases, I'd say politics is about the team putting across a team message and so people shouldn't be too worried about that happening in Prime Minister's Questions.'[237]

This was the very same David Cameron who in 2009 had mocked veteran Labour backbencher Gerald Kaufman for asking what looked like a whips' question of Gordon Brown, saying, 'When even the old-timers are reading out the whips' handout questions, we know things are really bad for the government.'[238] Being in government changes your view about many things.

While toadying questions serve a purpose, they have the significant downside that they look like toadying questions, provoking eye-rolling at best and heckling at worst. Opposition MPs will yell 'Give him a job!' at the compliant questioner. A better approach for loyal government backbenchers is to ask a question that challenges the government but gives the Prime Minister an opportunity to make a case: identifying a problem and asking what the government is going to do about it. And, of course, to make sure No. 10 has advance notice of the question, so that the Prime Minister knows what's coming. Anna Soubry told us, 'I have very rarely asked a question where I haven't given the courtesy of telling them what I'm going to ask. And I've *never* asked a question that I've been asked to ask.' It's more impressive to deal well with a question that looks hard than to deal well with a question that looks easy, and part of the job of a loyal government backbencher is to try to make the Prime Minister look impressive.

A lack of patsy questions can be telling too. Harriet Harman observed to us after one PMQs in October 2017, shortly after Theresa May's disastrous Conservative Party conference speech in which everything that could possibly have gone wrong did go wrong, and several things that could not possibly have gone wrong also went wrong, that the questions asked by government backbenchers really revealed the mood: 'Last week, there was not, until past half past twelve, one non-hostile question to Theresa May, including from her own side. All her own side were putting the boot in: all their questions, HS2, Brexit, BAE Systems, God, this was *her own side*. It's almost like they were thinking, "Well, I'm going to get my oar in for what I care about because it's not as if there's anything worth supporting here." So it's the moment where it can be seen by us whether the Tory backbenchers are really onside for the Prime Minister, and vice versa.

And we could all see that they've all gone rogue basically. There's no discipline any more.'

It's not just the government that plants questions. Opposition whips, too, try to make sure they know what their backbenchers are asking, and suggest questions their MPs might want to use. Again, this is partly so that backbenchers are supporting their party's main message – sometimes by trying to encourage a number of questions on the topic the leader is asking about, sometimes to make sure that a range of subjects are being covered. Occasionally the whips will attempt to discourage an opposition MP with the first question on the order paper, who will speak before the Leader of the Opposition, from stealing their leader's thunder by raising the topic which they are planning to ask about. The whips are also attempting to provide some quality control, to try to stop questions being asked that are politically unhelpful, or boringly apolitical, or, much more commonly, less problematic for the Prime Minister than the MP asking it thinks. It wasn't unusual in our experience for Labour MPs to come up with questions they thought were brilliant, only for David Cameron to bat them aside using exactly the script he had been using, and we had been watching him using, for months.

As Labour advisers, we spent time drafting backbench questions for the whips to distribute, both to the Labour MPs on the order paper and to the 'bobbers': members who were not listed but who would spend PMQs bobbing up and down, trying to catch the Speaker's attention. These often included questions discarded from Ed Miliband's prep session – if he had changed topics, or decided that a particular question didn't fit into the planned sequence or, on at least one occasion, thought of a really good joke he couldn't use.

Sometimes, we wanted to make sure that a particular question on a particular subject was put to David Cameron even if there was no case for Ed doing it. Where possible, we tried to suggest additional questions on the topic Ed was already asking about. This had several benefits: we had already researched the topic, so there would usually be extra unused material which it was easy to draft questions on; David Cameron would often have used up most or all of his script on that topic when responding to Ed, and so would be running out of relevant material; and it made Labour look like a competent operation which was able to co-ordinate its PMQs attacks. Of course, this last benefit would have been achieved more often if we could get more than two or three backbenchers to take a question, which we rarely could. MPs are difficult creatures to herd.

If you're asking a backbench question on the same topic as your leader you have to be good, but not too good, as Harriet Harman says: 'It doesn't do for a backbencher who comes in after the Leader of the Opposition to make the case better than the Leader of the Opposition, and that sometimes happens. And that's a bit of a bittersweet moment if, say, the Leader of the Opposition's chosen to go on housing and actually the killer question comes not from their one, two, three, four, five, six, but the one question from the backbencher. And that sometimes does happen, that a backbencher can capture it with one question, and outshine the front bench, and I don't think that's welcome at all.'

While it's hard to get backbenchers to co-ordinate a series of questions, a quick-thinking MP can sometimes follow up a poor answer from the Prime Minister to an earlier question. As a fairly new MP in February 1994 Angela Eagle was preparing to ask a question to John Major about a foreign aid scandal involving the Pergau Dam in Malaysia, but changed her plans: 'Lynne Jones got up and asked about Rover, which had just been sold to a foreign buyer, and Major got up and said, "It's not a matter for me." And you could hear there was an audible intake of breath all around the House, and I just thought, "That's outrageous." And his own side were shocked. And so I just thought, "No, I'm going to follow this up." And I didn't do the Pergau Dam question, I got up and said, "If the sale of the last British-owned car-maker isn't a matter for the Prime Minister, then can he tell us what is a matter for him?"' The question impressed John Smith, and Eagle told us that 'there was some coverage that decided that that had all been planned, but it couldn't have been because nobody knew that he was going to respond to the initial question by saying, "What's it got to do with me?" Nobody knew he was going to say that so it couldn't possibly have been planned.'

One person is given the right to ask two questions from the back benches every week: the leader of the third largest party in the House of Commons, who faces a very different kind of challenge from that facing the other leaders. Unlike the Leader of the Opposition, the leader of the third party – the Liberal Democrats until 2010, and the Scottish National Party since 2015 – asks questions without the benefit of a dispatch box to rest their notes on or to lean against: a useful prop, a sign of authority and of parity with the Prime Minister. But more importantly, by definition they only have a small number of MPs to cheer them on – even the peak of sixty-two achieved under Charles Kennedy's leadership in 2005 left the Liberal Democrats with fewer than 10 per cent of all MPs. Whereas the Leader of the Opposition can generally expect at least a couple of hundred of his own MPs to listen in respectful silence and then cheer when required, the Liberal Democrat leader regularly had to make himself heard over the jeers of over 500 people on both sides of the House. Sir Menzies Campbell wrote in his memoirs that Paddy Ashdown 'told me of one occasion where the baying cries from the massed government and opposition benches were so loud his voice could not be picked up by the microphones'.[239]

It didn't help that neither of the two main parties had any love for the Liberal Democrats, both being used to fighting elections against them. As John Bercow says, 'They do sometimes like to bully the third party. It's an old phenomenon that everybody in the Conservative and Labour parties loves to hate the Liberal Democrats.' It does come across at PMQs. Angus Robertson of the SNP was heard with rather more respect at PMQs between 2015, when he became the Westminster leader of the third largest party and was granted the right to ask two questions a week, and 2017, when he lost his seat to the Conservatives.

The most obvious explanation for the different levels of respect shown to SNP and Liberal Democrat leaders is that the SNP had been so successful that they had removed from Parliament almost everyone who felt any personal animosity towards them. Their dominance in Scotland in the 2015 election, where they won all but three seats, meant that there were almost no MPs anywhere else in the House who had any experience of fighting the SNP in elections, or who held any particular grudge against them – so it was harder for them to muster the enthusiasm to jeer. The Scottish Labour Party and Scottish Conservative Party both contain plenty of people who would happily heckle an SNP leader, of course, but between 2015 and 2017, they weren't in the room.

Robertson's calm, measured, forensic approach to both David Cameron and Theresa May at PMQs won many admirers. Alastair Campbell says, 'Angus Robertson developed a reputation, quite quickly actually, as a very effective questioner of Theresa May. Partly because Corbyn wasn't asking about Brexit so he could fill the gap. But he had two questions and you could tell he was really doing the work.' Liberal Democrat leaders had their PMQs moments too, despite the hostility from both sides. Charles Kennedy saw it as an important way of carving out a distinctive position for his party – especially over Iraq, where his party's position really was distinctive. He wrote:

> What may seem flat or drowned out in the Chamber can come over as the sole, sane voice in the asylum to the real world outside watching on television. Iraq gave me my opportunity. We were asking the awkward questions of Tony Blair that the Tories could not. And the House wanted to hear his answers. At one stage I felt dispirited, until a senior Cabinet minister approached me and encouraged me to persist. 'You're asking the questions half the Cabinet would love to ask – but can't.'[240]

The third-party leader often has to forgo asking questions on the biggest political story of the week. As Miranda Green, who worked for Paddy Ashdown, told us, 'Other party leaders have got an extra dimension of difficulty preparing for PMQs because you've got to pick a subject that the Leader of the Opposition's not going to go on, so you've got to have back-up, a plan B as well, and the plan B can be, if the Leader of the Opposition has asked the obvious questions on the burning issue of the day, as it were, what's your other angle that's also in line with your party line, party positioning? Or it can just be, "Oh God, well, if he's gone on the NHS waiting lists or whatever, should we just do something completely different as a plan B?" So there's a lot of trying to work out how to game it, if your best line gets taken already.' Of course, the third-party leader doesn't know what the main opposition party leader is going on, so it's impossible to plan with total confidence. But there will always be topics – like Iraq for Charles Kennedy – where the two main opposition parties have different policies or, even better, where the government and the official opposition are in agreement. These are usually foolproof places to go.

Sir Menzies Campbell was frequently the butt of ridicule during his short spell as Liberal Democrat leader, and didn't help himself with his choice of questions at PMQs. A decision to ask Tony Blair about head teacher shortages at his very first PMQs as leader, for example, left a perfect opening for Blair to respond with 'As the right honourable and learned gentleman knows, it can be difficult to find the head of an organisation when the post is vacant, particularly if it is a failing organisation.'[241] 'I was angry with myself for having taken too little time to think about any bear traps in my questions,' Campbell wrote.[242]

MPs of all parties can be unforgiving of a bad performance, and Campbell found himself under pressure after one particularly weak effort in May 2006. It was, to be fair to the disgruntled Liberal Democrat parliamentary party, exceptionally poor: he ended his second question with 'When will the Prime Minister do something about the NHS, about DEFRA and about the Home Office?'[243]

which is really quite special. When Campbell attempted to explain himself to his MPs, it got worse, as he wrote in his memoirs:

> Much to my fury, my comments were leaked to the *Daily Telegraph* under the heading: 'I'm sorry for my poor showing, says Sir Menzies.' It went on to report: 'The failures at Prime Minister's Questions … have bemused friends and foes alike given his background as a barrister and QC. At Wednesday night's private weekly meeting of the Lib Dem parliamentary party, he surprised MPs by confessing that his court experience was no preparation for the cut-and-thrust of Prime Minister's Questions. According to one person present, Sir Menzies lamented: "Juries don't normally answer back."' It was an attempt at humour on my part which was deliberately misrepresented.[244]

Not all Liberal Democrat jokes backfire. It was a Liberal Democrat leader – at the time, an acting leader, although almost a decade later he took on the job on a permanent basis – who contributed one of the all-time great PMQs put-downs. In the preamble to a question to Gordon Brown that everyone has since forgotten (it was about the safety and security of the armed forces – we looked it up) Vince Cable said, 'The House has noticed the Prime Minister's remarkable transformation in the past few weeks from Stalin to Mr Bean.'[245] Nothing else Cable said in his two questions, and nothing Brown said in his answers, and nothing anyone else said in that whole PMQs session, was anything like as memorable. It summed up in one line the state of politics at that particular moment.

Cable himself insisted to us that the joke came to him very quickly and that it was the next part of the sentence, which he struggled to get right – 'creating chaos out of order, rather than order out of chaos' – that made the whole thing work. We disagree, and not only because we'd forgotten it ourselves until he reminded us of it. Watch the clip back, and it's the 'Stalin to Mr Bean' line that brings the House down, forcing Cable to pause for several seconds before continuing the sentence. Everyone already gets the joke, which is perfectly complete in itself, and the 'chaos out of order' line gets merely a polite murmur.

While the third-party leader can only use PMQs to ask questions of the Prime Minister, their party is trying to define itself against, and win votes from, the main opposition party as well. There isn't usually much that can be done about this, but Cable decided that 'simply going after Labour the whole time was not where I or we ought to be politically', and used a couple of his PMQs in 2009 and 2010 as stand-in Liberal Democrat leader, in Nick Clegg's absence, to ask about the controversial Tory donor Lord Ashcroft. As he said, the Tories 'weren't expecting it because they just assumed that I was there to heap scorn on the government'. He made it up to them later, serving for five years as Business Secretary under David Cameron.

As Liberal Democrat leader Cable, like Tim Farron before him, is at the time of writing the leader of only the fourth largest party in the Commons, and therefore has no special rights at PMQs, although the Speaker is likely to call him to ask a question more frequently than the average MP. When he wants to ask a question, he is reduced to bobbing like other hopeful backbenchers; Farron had a noticeably plaintive, frantic manner while doing so during the 2015–17 parliament, a discontented symbol of the reduced status of a party which had gone, literally overnight, from vital coalition partner to one with just eight MPs, and was coming to terms with a sudden loss of relevance.

It's difficult to say what the worst backbench question ever asked was, because there are bad ones every single week. But perhaps the prize should go to one which wasn't, on its own merits, a notably poor question. It was asked by the Conservative Ann Winterton, who on 6 January 2010 asked Gordon Brown about what she considered to be wasteful spending on wind farms. The reason this question was so terrible lies in the political context of the moment it was asked, not in the question itself. Shortly before she stood up, the former Labour Cabinet ministers Patricia Hewitt and Geoff Hoon launched a coup against Brown's leadership. The attempted coup became public while PMQs was taking place, but after David Cameron had finished asking his questions. Brown was completely oblivious. Theo Bertram, sitting in the civil servants' and advisers' box at the side of the Chamber, considered whether to pass a note down the front bench to warn him, but decided against it, because 'we'd have had to pass it down the front row, and every time you pass a note down everyone opens it and looks at it, and then what would happen when he picks it up? So we decided not to pass the note.'

The Conservatives had found out via their mobile phones what was going on, and the news was gradually filtering across the opposition benches. 'The Tories were desperately trying to work out who was left on the order paper that could still ask a question at PMQs, and could they rush to them and get them to ask a question to Gordon that would be deadly. And they managed to get hold of Ann Winterton, who was the last person on the list, and they were determined that she should ask the question, you could see them persuading her. And I was living in fear, hoping that the Speaker would rule it out. And he didn't rule it out and he came to her. She obviously knew that the coup was taking place but instead she asked a question that was designed to make out that climate change wasn't happening, it was something about wind turbines, it was just wonderful, I could kiss her, it was just fantastic, this terrifying moment, and yet the Tories were so obsessed with their own little things that they didn't take the opportunity that was in front of them.'[246]

Winterton's decision to stick to her prepared script rather than adapt to the needs of her party let a beleaguered Prime Minister off the hook and helped him to survive one of his most perilous days. Backbenchers may not be the star attractions at PMQs, but they have a vital supporting role: they can choose to be team players, or they can try to do their own thing.

9

THE SPINNERS
AND THE LOBBY

When the Speaker calls time on Prime Minister's Questions, MPs rush out of the Chamber to get their lunch – a slightly demoralising sight for whichever MP is leading on the next item of business. The leaders try not to spend much time thinking about what has gone well and what has gone badly. Ed Miliband told us that if he had a good PMQs there would be a sense of 'relief and people would have a spring in their step'; if he had a bad one, 'unless I felt it was going to be a running-sore issue, I wasn't bad at compartmentalising it and thinking, "Well OK, that was a bad one but let's just move on."' David Cameron would try to stop thinking about it too, but told us: 'The really annoying thing was, although I was always quite firm in saying, "Right, PMQs is over, got to get on with the rest of the job," I would always at about five o'clock in the afternoon think, "Oh my

God, that's what I should have said." The comeback that would have ended it all.'

The principals can switch off – often, in Cameron's case, with lunch with some of his MPs in his parliamentary office – but the work is just starting for the press advisers and spokespeople on both sides and for the journalists they have to speak to. A group of journalists known collectively as 'the lobby'– the name derives from the fact that they are given special access to certain parts of Parliament, including the members' lobby, to talk to MPs – report on the events in the Chamber. They pronounce on who has won and lost, pursue lines of questioning left hanging by the leaders' exchanges, and have a huge influence on how PMQs, and politics more widely, is consumed by the public. And if they can influence the public, then it's worth the parties trying to influence them. The lobby now consists of almost 400 journalists, covering national broadcasters and newspapers, regional media, specialist media and in recent years several digital media outlets. Lobby journalists are allowed to sit in the press gallery, a special area of the House of Commons Chamber, on a mezzanine level above the Speaker's chair, which is dedicated to them.

Getting into the press gallery is a serious business. There are uni-formed doorkeepers who guard entry fiercely, keeping out anyone who does not have the right pass. You are not allowed to bring in any bags and until June 2017, men had to wear a jacket and tie – there was a hat stand with spare ones on it just outside. Until 2011, you couldn't bring in tablets or smartphones and you are still not allowed to bring in a laptop computer, so the mobile phone is the device which does most of the work along with the good old-fashioned notebook, pen and shorthand. From a purely practical point of view, in many ways, the Chamber is the worst place for journalists to be if major news breaks.

The public gallery, directly opposite the press gallery, was walled off behind a vast sheet of glass in 2004. The new security measure did not prevent an incident just months later, when self-described fathers' rights protesters threw condoms filled with purple powder down from the public gallery into the Chamber during PMQs, one of them catching Tony Blair on the back. The sitting had to be suspended, and security measures reviewed. The protesters had managed to get into part of the gallery not shielded by glass to throw their condoms – barrier methods do not always work. There is no glass wall in front of the press gallery, and journalists are separated from MPs only by elevation. They are trusted not to chuck things into the Chamber, although in 2016 *The Sun*'s political editor, Tom Newton Dunn, accidentally dropped his mobile phone over the balcony, and only narrowly missed taking out a couple of MPs, Cheryl Gillan and Margaret Beckett, standing directly below him. 'A little to the left and you would have killed two birds with one phone,' said Gillan.[247]

Before television and radio, the journalists in the press gallery had to write down the politicians' words as they were delivered, with no way of playing them back to listen to them again. The official more-or-less verbatim record, Hansard, would not be published until the following day – far too late to be useful to reporters. So shorthand was a vital skill. Chris Moncrieff, who started work as a parliamentary reporter in the 1960s and was political editor of the Press Association from 1980 until his retirement in 1994, wrote:

For reporters, one of the most difficult periods was the 1970s when Harold Wilson and Edward Heath set about each other. Wilson's delivery, in particular, was a shorthand writer's nightmare. He spoke like a machine gun. Immediately after these furious exchanges, a lot of us piled out of the press gallery and got into a huddle outside, going through our notes. Usually, between us, we managed to get everything [he] said, but occasionally there was a word that eluded us all. In that case, I am ashamed to say, someone would shout: 'Let's make him say…' And we would choose a word to replace it which seemed most appropriate in the context. We all inserted it in our notes. We did this scores of times, and yet we had not a single complaint. In those days, there were no tapes to check the words.

PMQs was, Moncrieff wrote, 'exciting but nerve-racking, too. The object, especially for an agency reporter, was to do, say, five minutes in the gallery, rush out and dictate, without delay, straight from your notebook to a copytaker on one of the phones outside.'[248]

Paddy Hennessy was a lobby journalist for the *Evening Standard* before anyone had mobile phones. 'You would often rush out of the press gallery and get straight on one of the now defunct phones to dictate your copy for the final edition. You had to trust your own judgement as you often didn't have much time to confer with colleagues. You may have been able to have a quick chat but you were caught in the drama of getting your copy in as quickly as possible.'

At PMQs the gallery is normally packed. Media organisations have specific numbered seats allocated to them and location matters, because it affects which part of the Chamber, and which MPs, you can see. Ann Treneman, who was *The Times'* parliamentary sketch-writer from 2003 to 2015, told us: 'We've got two seats next to Hansard and then we've also got another seat on the side which is traditionally the sketch-writing seat, but when I came in as sketch-writer I bagged one of the other ones because I like seeing both sides. Otherwise, in the other seat you get a great view of the Prime Minister and the government but it's not so easy to tell what's going on with the opposition.'

The government and opposition press advisers each have a row of seats assigned to them at opposite sides of the Chamber, facing each other so they can see their boss and the MPs on their own side. Ed Miliband would often give us a fleeting glance as he sat down at the end of his questions: sometimes triumphant, sometimes apologetic, sometimes questioning. We would always know whether he thought he had done well or badly.

Press advisers are very much on show during PMQs. The lobby will look not just down at the leaders and MPs below them, but across at advisers' facial expressions, trying to judge their reactions: do they think their boss has won or do they know full well that this week was a stinker? Gabby Bertin, David Cameron's press spokesperson in both opposition and government, developed a poker face, where she 'tried not to look at anyone and look serenely in control' – even if she didn't feel that way. It's good advice. New press advisers can be giddy with excitement at making it into the press gallery for PMQs, and are instructed by their more experienced bosses to stop grinning like Cheshire cats when their boss lands a punch, or looking crestfallen when they get a beating. Ed Miliband has a noticeably expressive face; so, sometimes, did his advisers in the Labour box; we tried to avoid giving anything away.

Lobby journalists will often contact key opposition spinners in advance of PMQs, either asking for information about the planned line of questioning or suggesting topics or stories that they or their paper have been pushing or championing. But the Leader of the Opposition's spokesperson rarely gives out precious information about what the boss will ask: why risk that information getting straight back to the Prime Minister's team and giving them advance warning? Press advisers and lobby journalists have to have relationships based on trust, but Westminster is all about trading information. Bertin told us that when she was in No. 10, occasionally journalists would try and feed her information about what the Labour leader was going to go on at PMQs: 'There would be a bit of trying to horse-trade information, which I took with a little pinch of salt because I knew that they wouldn't know.' Her instincts were right: we didn't leak. Of course, she had experience from her own time in opposition that told her leaking from the other side was unlikely: 'We were so tight and quite disciplined on that front, not least because we often used to change our mind at the last minute. So you could end up looking stupid if you briefed anything in advance.'

The exception, sometimes, is the *Evening Standard*, which operates on a different set of deadlines from anyone else, and can be read on the way home from work by hundreds of thousands of London commuters – an audience the political parties want to hit. Both sides have sometimes found it worthwhile to try to give the *Standard*'s reporters notice of stories which would break at PMQs. Paddy Hennessy told us that sometimes when he was at the paper No. 10 would give him material in advance about solid mid-level stories that they knew would be announced at PMQs, which on a quiet news day could get a decent showing in the paper or even splash the front page. In opposition, Alastair Campbell says, it was not uncommon for a *Standard* journalist to be 'absolutely begging because he was on a deadline, so you'd just give him a line, but I don't think I'd ever say to him, "This is the question," because it might not be. You might change, or Tony might decide to do something completely different.'

Press advisers have a role to play both in the run-up to PMQs and in the aftermath. They talk to the lobby on an hour-by-hour basis and get a sense of the big stories which are about to break as well as the political temperature – who's up and who's down; who's vulnerable or who's been speaking ill of their party leader and could therefore be ripe for a joke or attack line. They will be part of the preparation so they can feed in any intelligence. Ed Miliband's head of press, Bob Roberts, would frequently pop into our PMQs prep sessions to advise on whether the topic we had chosen would work from a media point of view: would PMQs help to carry a story into the evening news bulletins, or was the story we wanted to focus on already running out of steam? Did we have a memorable line or soundbite that stood a chance of getting clipped? Jeremy Corbyn's director of communications, Seumas Milne, has been known to write the questions himself. Spinners will always want their boss to make some news.

The spokespeople will also need to understand the arguments their boss is making and have all the facts, figures and rebuttal material to hand. They will often need to do some mopping up after PMQs and answer any additional questions. On the opposition side this is mostly a predictable task: towards the end of prep on a Wednesday morning one of us would write a quick note for the press team giving

all the background on Ed's questions, explaining where facts or figures came from and sourcing any third-party quotes he was using.
The Prime Minister's official spokesperson has a tougher job. Just
like the Prime Minister, the spokesperson needs to be across all of the
answers to every question from every MP during the whole session
because afterwards they have to face the lobby for what is known as
the 'huddle'.

The huddle is an important part of the PMQs architecture but,
like the preparation on both sides, it's hidden from public view. David
Cameron, 25-year veteran of PMQs both behind the scenes and as
a participant, told us that it's 'the only bit of PMQs I've never seen'.
Gabby Bertin, who represented him in the huddle, says, 'When you're
sitting in that Chamber and the roar would go up of him having done
it and the order papers would be waving, I'd think, "God, I want to
be sick into my hand now because it's my turn."' In the Chamber, she
would frantically text colleagues to ask them for more information
about answers Cameron had given – or failed to give – to unexpected
questions: 'All the special advisers in my time knew to have their
phones on and be responding bloody quick, because I'd be texting,
saying, "What's the line on this?" and "Why has he said that?"'

The huddle is important for the spinners from both sides. It's their
chance to perform and flex their own muscles. Bob Roberts told us,
'It was important for your boss to win in the Chamber and for you to
win in the press gallery.' Alastair Campbell recalls that in opposition
he would rush out to start the post-match briefing as soon as he could
against his opposite number at the time, the Prime Minister's press
secretary, Gus O'Donnell, who later went on to be Cabinet Secretary
in the final years of Tony Blair's time as Prime Minister.

The post-PMQs huddle takes place just outside the press gallery, and all the journalists swarm first around the Prime Minister's press team: a civil service press spokesperson alongside the political spokesperson, a special adviser. The civil service spokesperson usually briefs the lobby twice a day ('We would try to neuter those Downing Street press briefings,' says Bertin. 'We wanted to make them as uninteresting as possible'), but on PMQs days the huddle is led by the political spokesperson, as PMQs is dominated by partisan material and attacks on the opposition which it is not appropriate for a politically neutral civil servant to discuss – they can still join in to make factual comments and explanations of government policy.

There is a long table which everyone gathers around; spokespeople either sit on the table or stand behind it depending on how confident they feel. Bertin used to sit on the table: she says that the journalists would sometimes push up close to her and she would be very aware of how much smaller than them she was. Rob Hutton of *Bloomberg News* told us that the huddle is 'a great forum for tall men, not so great for small women' – Hutton, as it happens, is a very tall man. Journalists shout out questions. There are no formal rules of precedence but it tends to be the big national newspapers or broadcasters who jump in first. The huddle is an important opportunity for journalists to get more detail on what was said in the Chamber by the Prime Minister and question any facts or figures. One long-serving former lobby journalist says: 'What you're trying to do is to get a story, or a twist on a story, that has emerged from PMQs. So you're looking to not necessarily trip up the spokesperson, although that sometimes can happen, but get them to go further than they maybe want or get them to go further than the Prime Minister has, or the Leader of the Opposition has, in what they've said.' It is technically not on the record, but it is not off the record either – anything the spokesperson says can be quoted as being from 'a source', and it's pretty easy to work out where it came from.

The huddle can be tough for spokespeople. Bertin recalls seeing one of Gordon Brown's press spokespeople, when the Conservatives were still in opposition, being 'absolutely taken down by the lobby, and it always slightly stayed with me, and it taught me that these lobby briefings were quite dangerous. This was before I was ever surrounded to the extent that I used to be in government.' She says, 'You had to tread the line between being confident in your answers but equally not being afraid to say, "Let me get back to you."' Journalists try to unravel the answers and catch the spokespeople out on something their boss has just said. Spinners try to say as little as possible that's new and interesting. It's a less structured format than PMQs itself, says Alastair Campbell: 'Journalists can be much more forensic than MPs, they can come back at you more.' Sometimes if the Prime Minister has had a rough time from the Leader of the Opposition, a good performance from an aide in the huddle can, as Bertin puts it, 'knock the edges off a bad PMQs'. Although a huddle after a tricky PMQs is not exactly something to look forward to, 'if things went badly in the Chamber but you then had the time to get better follow-up material, you felt OK because you had a purpose'.

The worst huddles are where the subject matter is complicated. David Cameron's language on Conservative energy price policy unravelled in a post-PMQs briefing in October 2012. In response to a question from a Labour backbencher, David Cameron had unexpectedly announced that the government would be legislating to make energy companies give the lowest tariff to their customers.[249] Nobody knew what he was talking about, and neither his own spokespeople nor officials at the Department for Energy and Climate Change could explain what he meant, leading to a feeding frenzy in the lobby. It got worse later that day. Rob Hutton told us, 'Cameron's spokesman Steve Field did a manful job of defending a policy that he didn't understand and didn't think could possibly work, and then, as he was walking down the winding stairs from the press gallery, remarked cheerily to a colleague that things hadn't gone too badly, given that the policy hadn't been the policy at noon. Sadly he was unaware that I was walking behind him, and overheard the whole conversation, enabling me to confront him at the afternoon lobby briefing with an anonymised story about how Cameron's own office had been blindsided by the policy. I'm not sure if he knew he was the source for that.'

Sometimes the only person who knows what an answer was supposed to mean is the person who gave the answer, and there is no alternative for the spokesperson but to ask the Prime Minister: as David Cameron told us, 'I'd often get calls from Gabby Bertin saying, "What did you mean by this?" There was often a post-match analysis there.'

Even if the Prime Minister's spokesperson gets a hard time in the huddle, it won't usually undermine a good PMQs performance. And if a journalist has a killer question arising from PMQs that looks good enough to create a big problem for the government and a great story for their news organisation, it's not something to ask in front of their competition in the lobby. They will raise it privately with the spokesperson later on and try and keep it exclusive – always the holy grail for journalists, and their editors.

Joe Murphy, now political editor of the *Evening Standard* and a lobby journalist since 1989, has seen a lot of press briefings. He told us that the Prime Minister's spokespeople are 'brilliant at what they do. By the time you get to the huddle, they are well informed and have a line. They are alert to bear traps and they won't wing it. They are smart enough to be cautious and know when sometimes, it's best to say nothing.' There is sometimes an advantage in letting the Prime Minister's words in the Chamber speak for themselves.

Once the No. 10 team is finished, the huddle will move on to the opposition press team, although the interest of the lobby does start to wane and people start drifting off for lunch unless the opposition can give them something juicy and fresh. Paddy Hennessy remembers thinking it must have been dispiriting for the opposition spinners to see a scrum of easily two dozen people around the No. 10 team and then finding that only about half a dozen hacks would wander over to them. Rob Hutton would always be kind and ask a question, he says. Bertin remembers the early days working for David Cameron, when 'no one wanted to talk to us in opposition so the huddle was often me and Tim Montgomerie [then editor of ConservativeHome] or whoever it was doing the Tory beat'.

The wider political climate makes a big difference. In the run-up to the 1997 election, when Labour was on the path to power, Alastair Campbell recalls the opposition huddles being busy. It was a different story for the party when it lost in 2010. Bob Roberts told us how he worked hard to make the Labour huddle relevant again by trying to use it to create news in some way: 'We needed it as it became a way to engage with the big story that came out of PMQs.' It was a key opportunity for him to react quickly and aggressively to a story, knowing that speed was of the essence because journalists would tweet lines immediately. 'Sometimes there just wasn't time to go back to the office, wait to sit down with Ed and clear a line, so I had to do it then and there,' he says. 'Sometimes we would use the huddle to give out an extra fact or figure, or say we would be writing to No. 10 or assert that we were outraged by something that the Prime Minister had said and demand an apology.' This was part of the reason David Cameron telling Angela Eagle to 'Calm down, dear' became such a big story. Roberts helped it to escalate quickly by framing Cameron's language and tone as sexist in the huddle (as we saw in Chapter 7, Cameron maintains that he was actually talking to Ed Balls) and giving the lobby strong quotes. Under Jeremy Corbyn, one journalist told us, Labour's post-PMQs huddle was pretty lacklustre until after the snap general election in 2017, after which Seumas Milne's briefings started to attract a much larger turnout and be taken more seriously.

The huddle is a key opportunity for all sides to engage. It's a way to build and strengthen vital relationships between the press and the party advisers. Effective press officers will take the opportunity to do a 'lobby round' later in the afternoon, walking around every media office, checking whether the journalists need any more information and getting a sense of what stories they are writing and what angle they are taking. Many of the newspapers' offices are located on a long corridor known for reasons lost to history as the 'Burma Road', and the best spinners will try and visit them a few times a week, if not every day, to take the political temperature and get the gossip. The relationships between journalists and spinners are very important. The media should not be allowed to run the show, but people consume politics through them, and so any professional contact which helps to make sure that a story reflects a party's viewpoint as much as possible is worthwhile.

The huddle helps to shape the post-PMQs narrative, but most important of all is what actually happens in the Chamber. The lobby's broad impression of how any given PMQs has gone tends to be pretty consistent, partly because they are all watching the same event and attending the same huddle but also because they are talking to each other – it is easier to go with the herd. One former Downing Street adviser told us that as recently as the early 2000s it would take several hours for political journalists to form a consensus about PMQs: who had won and who had lost. Now it happens even before PMQs has finished, with journalists tweeting and reading each other's tweets.

Before Twitter, the first published newspaper verdict was provided by a little box in Wednesday's final edition of the *Evening Standard* called 'Match of the Day'. It gave a mock match report ('*Match of the Day:* Gordon Brown *v* David Cameron; *Ground:* PMQs; *Kick off:* noon; *Score:* Brown 1, Cameron 2') with a couple of paragraphs of commentary and a brief 'Quote of the day'. It should not have been as big a deal to both sides as it was. Gabby Bertin says, 'It was a little thing in the *Standard* and it really mattered to us, we got very competitive about it and got very upset when it was a 3–0 loss. Joe [Murphy] was the first person I would hound.' Murphy says that David Cameron once told him that if he didn't win 'Match of the Day', there would be trouble at home. On occasion Andy Coulson, David Cameron's director of communications from 2007 until 2011, would call Murphy up to complain that Cameron had performed way better than he had scored him. The problem, says Murphy, 'was that Coulson was watching it on the telly and yes, Cameron may have looked good on the telly. But I was watching it from the press gallery, and in the bear pit the atmosphere was totally different. It was noisy and aggressive so Cameron would keep on the mic to make sure that he could be heard on telly, but sometimes that didn't work so well when you were watching in the Chamber, and you couldn't hear him properly.' Other newspapers followed the football score format, sometimes slightly unrealistically insisting on allocating the two leaders six goals between them, one for each question, so that scores could range from a 6–0 thrashing through an exciting-sounding 4–2 win to a 3–3 draw.

'Match of the Day' was decommissioned in 2012, partly because Twitter took over. That is now where instant reaction to PMQs takes place, both among journalists and among at least some of the wider viewing public. Twitter is more of a niche interest in real life than it can appear to those who exist simultaneously in both a Westminster bubble and a Twitter bubble. But few journalists, these days, are not on Twitter, and few journalists who watch PMQs are not keeping an eye on Twitter at the same time. So the parties' media teams try to influence the immediate Twitter reaction, tweeting the leaders' lines as they are delivered and encouraging their MPs and supporters to do the same. Labour emails its MPs with suggested tweets, containing key messages and some of the facts and figures that back up what Jeremy Corbyn is saying, before PMQs is over, and sometimes before it has even started – a practice that began under Ed Miliband. We would use the background note we had prepared for Labour's press team to take round the lobby as the basis for tweets containing instant rebuttal to lines David Cameron had used.

As social media has developed, and particularly as the ease of creating video clips has grown, it has changed the way in which many politically engaged people consume PMQs, but it has also transformed the way political parties – especially Labour under Corbyn – approach it. When the leaders' exchanges at PMQs are covered in TV news bulletins, even when one side has decisively won, viewers will still see clips of both leaders, providing some context, showing both sides' key messages and fulfilling the broadcasters' regulatory requirements for political balance (although TV journalists will still sometimes suggest that one side got the better of the exchanges). PMQs is shown, admittedly in heavily edited form, as the two-sided clash that it is. As Ed Miliband says, 'Sometimes a PMQs could go really well and it will look even-stevens on the news, and sometimes it will go badly and also look even-stevens on the news. Unless it's an absolute hide-behind-the-sofa situation, it can be quite a leveller actually.' But on social media, especially on Facebook, it's possible for a political party or politician to gain a huge audience for a PMQs clip that is entirely one-sided and unbalanced.

Labour can now reach a huge audience with a clip of Jeremy Corbyn at PMQs. And at any PMQs, no matter how well or badly any Leader of the Opposition has done overall, it will always be possible to clip a section of video in which he is attacking the Prime Minister, standing up for the people he represents, speaking truth to power, looking good. The context – which may well be that his argument was taken apart by the Prime Minister moments later, or even that the clip had little to do with the line of questioning – can be stripped away. It's easy to make almost anyone look effective at PMQs if you only show their best bits and don't show their opponent at all.

This helps to lower the stakes enormously, and for Corbyn the stakes were already unusually low. Corbyn's lack of dependence on the Parliamentary Labour Party – demonstrated after the EU referendum in 2016, when he comfortably won a leadership election among the membership despite having overwhelmingly lost a no-confidence vote among MPs – means that poor PMQs and other parliamentary performances are less consequential for him than for any leader of a major political party in decades. And his ability to present his best PMQs moments out of context via social media means that he doesn't even have to do well against the Prime Minister to look good to his supporters. Selective editing and social media help to turn a boxing ring into a pulpit.

Of course, this is something the Conservatives are capable of doing too, even if they have at the time of writing been less successful at reaching a wide audience through social media. They have tried to do the same thing, with short clips of Theresa May's PMQs attacks on Jeremy Corbyn or recitations of the highlights of the Conservatives' record in government being put out on Twitter and Facebook. As Jo Coburn, one of the presenters of the BBC's *Daily Politics*, puts it, 'They're playing full monologues without the other half on both sides and that plays beautifully to their own supporters.' At worst, this reduces PMQs to nothing more than an opportunity for both sides to trot out messages which barely make contact with each other, with victory depending not on the facts or the quality of the argument or the ability to respond effectively to the other side's attacks, but on whose Facebook page has the bigger audience.

Parliamentary coverage has changed, as Alastair Campbell told us: 'The media just don't cover politics in the same way now. When I was a journalist, we had two guys whose job, full-time, was to cover Parliament. Not politics, Parliament. *The Times* had a whole bloody army of them. Now they've got a sketch-writer.' This isn't quite fair to *The Times*, whose political journalists can regularly be seen wandering the corridors of the Palace of Westminster, but they are covering more than just what happens in the Chamber and the committee rooms, and it's certainly true that there is less coverage of parliamentary business than there used to be. Most of the broadsheets still have a political sketch, though, which plays its own part in shaping the narrative and the way in which MPs, and especially the leaders, are perceived.

Sketches are not news reports but the printed-word version of the political cartoon: at their best, both funny and capable of finding deeper truths than a simple factual news report can uncover: as John Crace, the sketch-writer of *The Guardian*, puts it, 'One of the jobs of the sketch is to make the subtext of politics the text.' Crace, who coined the brutal nickname 'the Maybot' to describe Theresa May's unfortunate tendency to repeat the same stock phrases again and again, told us, 'For some it's just a little light-hearted look at the politics of the day through the prism of 600 light-hearted words. I've always tended to look on it as something a bit more substantial, as a piece of political commentary, as a piece of political satire. I feel that the sketch is a place where you can hold the politicians to account in some kind of way.'

Some weeks, in some papers, at least in the print edition, the sketch is the only coverage of PMQs – and for some readers, as Crace says, 'if they read one political thing a day it might be the sketch'. A good sketch-writer will have an equal-opportunity approach: they will be scathing to both sides. They can provoke squeals of joy or shrieks of horror from politicians and their advisers – and either way, if they are good, nods of recognition.

Ann Treneman eventually moved on from sketch-writing, appropriately enough, to be *The Times'* chief theatre critic – like many sketch-writers she thrived on the theatre of PMQs. She says, 'People think that funny things just happen all the time to sketch-writers, but in general things are not very funny and they're rather worryingly dull. So the one thing about PMQs is that you have it as a fixed point in your week when you know you're going to see a clash between the most powerful person in the British government and the Leader of the Opposition. Everyone goes on about Punch and Judy politics, but you take away the Punch, or the Judy, and everyone gets rather bored. People like the fact that it's confrontational. And I actually think that's quite British. Anyone who's watched the American Senate deliberate will know that it's just Dull Central.'

Sketch-writers are focusing not just on the leaders but on other interesting characters in the Chamber, trying to convey the atmosphere: as Treneman says, 'There's so much more you hear when you're in the press gallery than you would see or hear at home.' She would keep an eye on what she called the 'naughty step' on the Tory side – the bench occupied by Anna Soubry and others, discussed in Chapter 7 – where 'they often were having their own little party', as well as the people sitting on the very back bench on the Labour side. A sketch is almost as likely to focus on a question or intervention from a backbencher as on the leaders' exchanges: Treneman says that although she was not a big fan of Dennis Skinner's class-based insults, 'I have to say he saved many a sketch'.

Strict broadcasting rules mean that much of what happens on the back benches is invisible to television viewers: MPs who are not speaking, or sitting in shot just behind a member who is speaking, will generally not be seen. So some of the most vicious hecklers, and some of the most unruly behaviour, go unnoticed by the public but not by the journalists in the press gallery.

Television is still the biggest way for both sides to get their PMQs messages seen by as many people as possible, both live and in bulletins later in the day. The audience for the BBC's *Daily Politics* is not huge – it is, after all, a daytime show – but its viewership has risen over the last couple of years and Wednesday's programme, when it shows PMQs live, gives it its best figures of the week. As presenter Jo Coburn told us, unlike almost all other parliamentary events, PMQs is something you can build a weekly television programme around: 'We know when it's going to happen and we know it's going to involve the Prime Minister and the Leader of the Opposition, and it is the forum that gets both sides quite excited, so it should be a good piece of broadcasting.'

It has had some unexpected fans. In 2008, Bruce Forsyth told *Radio Times*,

> Prime Minister's Questions, that's two guys getting it on there. At times it's pure variety, pure vaudeville, it's all the people I used to work with, Frankie Howerd and Les Dawson. I love it, that's why I tape it. Last week I forgot, and I was furious for the rest of the day.[250]

Former Oasis singer Liam Gallagher also said he watched it, in a 2016 interview with *Q* magazine:

'I am partial to Prime Minister's Questions though. I'm not bothered about politics, Theresa May and that other c**t can get on with it, but I like that geezer, the Speaker of the House. Check this shit out.' He pulls out his mobile. 'I nailed him calling some c**t out. [*Plays a file of Liam imitating the Rt Hon. John Bercow MP*] "Sir Edward Leeeeeigh!" Sent that to my kid. Who talks like that?! Funny as fuck.'[251]

Daily Politics' running order has been disrupted by John Bercow's tendency, as Speaker, to let the session run on well beyond 12.30. The longer PMQs goes on, the less time there is for post-match analysis. If anything, this makes life easier for the prep teams on both sides, for whom briefing spokespeople for *Daily Politics* on all the background to PMQs is vital but can be an irritating afterthought. When PMQs has finished, at the same time as the leaders' spokespeople are tackling the lobby in the huddle, a senior politician will be answering similar questions live on air, usually without having spent the morning in PMQs prep and therefore with the disadvantage of having had much less briefing than either the leaders or their spokespeople. As Jo Coburn says, 'What we're really trying to do is surprise them afterwards with the questions we can ask them, particularly detailed policy questions after PMQs, and that works less well these days because we haven't got as much time.' Increasing the amount of time spent on one kind of scrutiny reduces the time available for another.

This has reportedly irritated Andrew Neil, another *Daily Politics* presenter, but Bercow is indifferent. He told us, 'It may come as the most extraordinary revelation, an almost inexcusable surprise to Andrew Neil, but the timing of what he probably regards as an important programme, not least his starring role in it, which is important to him, is not a material factor in my thinking. Now I'm sure he's absolutely shocked by that, not that he's hermetically sealed, or considers himself an important political actor, or a frustrated would-be politician who never got here and would like to rant at us all from the side-lines from his position of presumed superiority, but to be honest, to put it very bluntly, I couldn't give a flying flamingo about the opinions of A. Neil Esquire.'

Coburn points out that PMQs is 'the set piece of the week, it's the theatre of Parliament, it's known around the world for that and we have a longer programme as a result, we get a government minister and a shadow Cabinet member, so we're talking about high-profile guests who we want to put on the spot over the questions and the issues that we think viewers will be interested in, and reflect what has happened in the House and the Chamber, and we now have far less time to do that. And John Bercow may say, "Well, that doesn't matter, that's television for you," but for us from our perspective we've lost out to a certain extent. And if that is going to be a permanent state of affairs we may have to rethink how we do things.' Formally lengthening PMQs to a regular one-hour session, as Bercow told us he would like to do, would at least make it easier for the broadcasters to predict how much time they have left to fill.

It is not the Speaker's job to care about TV schedules, but it is in Parliament's interest to be interesting. And at its best, PMQs can be the most interesting, and certainly the most accessible, parliamentary event. It is still an opportunity for both sides, especially the opposition, to get its messages on television – but it is not newsworthy automatically, simply by virtue of being PMQs. Its newsworthiness depends on what happens in the Chamber, on the choice of topic, the intensity of the debate, the quality of the joust and the leaders' performances. A line of questioning at PMQs that has nothing to do with any of the day's top stories, and does not break a story itself, is just not going to make the evening bulletins. A set of PMQs questions and answers which contains no interesting, pithy phrases, even if it is topical, may quite reasonably be left out of a television news bulletin in favour of other voices who can speak on the same topic using interesting, pithy phrases. If broadcasters choose to leave PMQs off the news, we should blame the politicians before we blame the news editors. Alastair Campbell told us, 'I would have been very disappointed if any Tuesday and Thursday in opposition we were not in the news. Very disappointed. Contrary to the mythology, I did not phone up and shout. We would get in the news not by shouting at people to put us in the news, but by what Tony did. So that was far more important. And likewise in government, my sense was PMQs seemed to be more high-profile back then than it is now.'

Jo Coburn told us that from a television point of view, 'The idea used to be from both teams, the political teams, to create the news story that would make the evening bulletins. Now that's changed a little bit with Jeremy Corbyn and Theresa May, because he has diverged from that idea of "Let's hit the Prime Minister with the story of the day and that will ensure that we make the evening bulletins." We get the impression now that the aim is to deliver on the subjects that are sincerely held to be good topics for Labour supporters and Jeremy Corbyn's core vote, and so he picks subjects that we don't always manage to anticipate.' Coburn thinks Labour is not even trying to get on the news: 'I just don't think they care as much about it. If it does get onto the news then that's fine, but what it does do is it really appeals to core voters, to grassroots and to their own side. And actually as a result Theresa May is responding in a similar sort of way to gee up her side, so that has slightly changed the nature of the questions that the opposition is asking.' If you don't try to get onto the news at PMQs, then you probably won't.

It's easy for politicians to resent the fact that so much of what the public sees of them is mediated by the press and broadcasters. Politicians and political parties can subvert an unfriendly media to an extent, by creating their own media and finding channels which will allow them to push their preferred messages in their own way – fighting a biased mainstream media with an even more biased, albeit openly biased, alternative. But in the end, much of what the public sees of politicians will come from what journalists choose to tell them, so it's worthwhile for politicians to try to encourage journalists to have a positive opinion of them. Overwhelmingly the best way of doing this is to perform well, and PMQs is one of the most important stages on which leaders perform. The spinners in the huddle and the ministers and shadow ministers in the studio for the *Daily Politics* post-match analysis have a role to play in shaping the way journalists cover politics, and therefore the prism through which the public sees the leaders. But the most important role is played by the leaders themselves, both in their performance and in their strategy. When a leader wins well at PMQs, even journalists on papers which support a rival party will say so. When a leader has been beaten, the spinners know it and the journalists know it. When a leader has ducked the biggest news story of the day, it tells the lobby something important. PMQs matters to the lobby, and to the political broadcasters, because more than any other event it gives them the opportunity to see how the leaders are performing, what their instincts are, what decisions they make under pressure and whether they have the support of their backbenchers. The best way to win over the lobby at PMQs is to win.

10

STAND-INS
AND DEPUTIES

PMQs is normally about the Prime Minister, and in particular the duel with the main rival for her job. But the PM can't always be there – usually because of international engagements – and in that case a substitute comes in for her. Usually the Leader of the Opposition also sits out the session, although Neil Kinnock sometimes asked questions to Margaret Thatcher's substitute when she was absent, as did John Smith to John Major's and William Hague to Tony Blair's. Both sides can nominate the person who will stand in – on the government side usually the Deputy Prime Minister, when there is one, or failing that the Leader of the House of Commons, although other ministers have stood in too. Of recent Prime Ministers, Tony Blair missed the smallest proportion of his PMQs, and John Major and Gordon Brown the largest, both missing more than one in nine of the sessions they were scheduled to attend.[252]

Occasionally the Leader of the Opposition has to miss a session even though the Prime Minister is present. William Hague stood in against Tony Blair in February 2006 while David Cameron was on paternity leave, at a time when there was also a Liberal Democrat leadership election going on. He opened with a subtle gag about the infighting between Tony Blair and Gordon Brown: 'For the first time in history at Question Time, all three parties are represented by a stand-in for the real leader.'[253] In 1983, at the height of the Labour Party's fight against Militant infiltration, both Neil Kinnock and his deputy, Roy Hattersley, missed a PMQs session because they could not risk leaving Labour's National Executive Committee. It was considered more important for them to vote in hearings against various Liverpool Labour Party members than it was for either of them to hold Margaret Thatcher to account. Denis Healey stood in.[254]

Kinnock almost missed another session through unforeseen circumstances but, as he told us, he had some help from the police: 'There was one wonderful occasion: I'd been speaking up north, I remember it involved coming through Preston, might have been a local government conference or something, and I got back to Euston at about ten to three. And Charles [Clarke] was with me, and he did a very sensible thing: he got on to the Metropolitan Police and said, "The Leader of the Opposition's on the train, the train's been held up" – which was absolutely true – "he's not going to be in Euston a lot before three o'clock, is there any way you can get him to the House of Commons by three o'clock or thereabouts?" And they said, "Yes, we'll see what we can do, Mr Clarke." So we came out of the train, we got into a squad car, and we got to the House of Commons in eight minutes. It was bloody wonderful. It was absolutely bloody wonderful. And I said to Charles afterwards, "Shit, I never thought about it, I should have got on the back of a bike, we could have been even faster." And he said, "As it is now, I'm still collecting my stomach from Euston," because we went like hell, and we were here, we walked into the House at three o'clock, into the Chamber at three o'clock.' This was perhaps the closest Neil Kinnock got to prime ministerial treatment in his whole nine years as Leader of the Opposition.

We thought Ed Miliband might have to miss PMQs on one occasion when a throat infection meant that he had completely lost his voice by the Tuesday evening. A friendly doctor prescribed some very strong drugs, collected by Ed's long-suffering diary secretary, Jill Cuthbertson, in the middle of the night, to be taken in the early hours of Wednesday morning. The drugs were, we were told, more commonly provided to opera singers who simply could not miss a performance. PMQs prep was conducted with occasional interruptions for Ed to stick his head under a towel over a bowl of hot water, and Harriet Harman was put on standby and briefed on the planned set of questions. His voice gradually returned over the course of Wednesday morning until he could just about stagger through, prefacing his first question with 'I should say at the outset that I am speaking through a sore throat, but I would not have missed this meeting with the Prime Minister for the world.'[255] He ended up putting in a strong performance against the odds.

When substitutes do come in, they do more than simply represent their missing leader: they are subject to different expectations, and it is their own reputation that is on the line. A PMQs session with stand-ins may generally have a lower profile, but the pressure on the stand-in is high: this is not part of their normal routine, but a rare moment in which they are at the centre of Westminster attention. If they do well, it can raise their stock in the long term and spark gossip that they might be a potential leader; if they do badly, they will not be able to come back and repair the damage the following week – but they might inadvertently make their boss look good in comparison. Theo Bertram told us that '[John] Prescott and Harriet [Harman] both understood that the way that they were going to do PMQs was different. And they were both great at it.'

John Prescott stood in for Tony Blair at PMQs on fourteen occasions, which Blair wrote put his deputy 'in genuine dread. Threatening to have a meeting abroad on a Wednesday was the only way I knew of terrorising him; he would palpitate with the horror of the approaching encounter, but he got up and did it, with a kind of swaggering blunderbuss approach that the House quite liked.'[256] His performances particularly entertained the sketch-writers – or 'screenwriters' as he once referred to them during a PMQs performance[257] – as he grappled with the English language. Ann Treneman describes him as 'the gift that keeps on giving'. Simon Hoggart wrote of one Prescott appearance in 2001:

> Like a tanned if somewhat overweight Australian lifesaver he stood on the shore, took an enormous breath, dived into the waves, and I swear did not breathe again until the whole half hour was up.
>
> On he plunged through the thundering breakers. Trick questions swept and spumed over his head. Rip tides tugged him

from below, dragging him toward the jagged rocks. But nothing could stop him as he stormed onward through the briny deep.

We watchers on the beach peered into the foam, desperate to catch a glimpse to show us he was still afloat. For whole minutes we would think he had gone under, but then we could see an arm or a strand of hair, and we knew that hope was not lost. It was an exhibition of superb courage and resilience.[258]

Harriet Harman, as deputy leader to Gordon Brown and Ed Miliband, was their designated stand-in when David Cameron was absent. She is the only Labour politician since Tony Blair with experience of both asking and answering the questions at PMQs, and was the first woman to answer at PMQs since Margaret Thatcher. She took her first ever PMQs appearance, in April 2008 against William Hague, seriously because she knew she had to: 'The conventional wisdom was I was going to be useless. The first time I was doing it I didn't feel I could allow all my detractors to be right in their prediction, so there was a lot riding on it for me. And the other thing about that is that I had only narrowly been elected deputy leader by 0.43 per cent or something, and this was the moment that those people who didn't vote for me but who wished standing in that place was Alan Johnson would be confirmed in their view, or those people who backed me would feel vindicated. And actually because it went so well a lot of the people who backed Alan Johnson, and who still massively supported him, said, "I didn't support you because I didn't think you were up to the job, and I think I was wrong and good on you." So it was a moment for people to change their minds about whether I could do the job. It's that fundamental and that important.'

Harman's first PMQs performance showed the importance, in being seen to do well, of not just being able to answer the questions competently but of finding a memorable line. She had recently been ridiculed for wearing a stabproof vest on a tour of her Peckham constituency with the local police, on which William Hague had prepared a decent joke: 'She has had a difficult week. She had to explain yesterday that she dresses in accordance with wherever she is going: she wears a helmet on a building site, she wears Indian clothes in the parts of her constituency with a large representation of Indian people, so when she goes to a Cabinet meeting, she presumably dresses as a clown.'[259] As Harman told us, 'He was counting on me being absolutely hopeless and he was calling me a clown, so that was my moment of greatest peril; if he was right, I was a clown, I would have been completely humiliated.' Fortunately, she and her team had predicted the prospect that Hague might make a clothing-related jibe, and she had an answer ready: 'If I were looking for advice on what to wear or what not to wear, the very last person I would look to is the man in the baseball cap.'[260] Her team debated whether they should do a joke at all: a woman at the dispatch box was a big deal; making a joke, which might fall flat, would raise the stakes even higher.

It was a significant moment for her: 'After my first PMQs when I went around Labour Party dinners and things like that, they would always introduce me as Harriet Harman who's deputy leader and who's just slayed William Hague at Prime Minister's Questions. That was always the most important thing I seemed to have done, having been an MP for God knows how many years.' It is rare for deputies to make news, but the evening bulletins carried it and hostile papers ran grudgingly positive headlines which amounted to little more than 'Harman makes joke'.

William Hague felt slightly differently about the pressure of that particular PMQs and, having asked questions both as a Leader of the Opposition and as a stand-in, about which was harder. Tackling Harman 'was harder than tackling Blair actually, because the higher they are the harder they fall really. Against a deputy Prime Minister it's actually harder and the stakes are lower, and they can just engage you in the undergrowth, as it were, and it doesn't matter really if it doesn't go very well for them. It's always better to be asking questions of a Prime Minister, they're more vulnerable than the people underneath them, there's more at stake.'

As well as deputising, Harman led the Labour Party for two spells after election defeats in 2010 and 2015, taking on David Cameron as Leader of the Opposition and achieving some success in changing government policy. Ann Treneman, who watched their exchanges from the press gallery, observed to us that 'it really helps if you've got people who have a bit of chemistry between them. Very weirdly, I think that Harriet had a bit of chemistry with David Cameron.' Cameron says: 'I thought she was very good actually. Because she had that mixture of conversational and also highly political. They were slightly lower-octane sessions, but I thought she was effective, and there were one or two issues where you definitely thought, "Oh, we've got to go and sort that out a bit." The anonymity in rape cases – which, weirdly, was one of those policies that popped out in coalition negotiations. I think it was partly the Conservative Party, partly the Lib Dems, and it became a policy without enough thought going into it. And it was quite interesting, then being attacked on it so vigorously by someone who otherwise would have seen the civil rights case. So you suddenly realise you have nothing left to defend it with. So that was a good example of Prime Minister's Questions seeing off something that hadn't been properly thought through.'

As Ed Miliband's deputy at PMQs in opposition after 2010 Harman continued to take the role seriously – albeit with significantly less preparation time and a much more relaxed atmosphere. Harman – the only person we know of who consistently refers to PMQs as 'PMsQs', with an extra 's' – generally needed a couple of hours on a Tuesday afternoon, followed by a civilised 9 a.m. start on a Wednesday with a break for bacon sandwiches from the Portcullis House canteen.

Harman's usual PMQs opponent during the coalition years was deputy Prime Minister Nick Clegg, who stood in for David Cameron on nine occasions, although William Hague also did it twice when Clegg was indisposed. Clegg presented Labour with a completely different kind of target from Cameron. As the leader of the smaller of the two coalition parties, he had chosen to enter government with the Conservatives and therefore had to defend Conservative policies which he had voted for but which he and his party had not previously supported. His decision to go into government meant that the Liberal Democrats lost the right, allocated to them as the third largest party by the Speaker since 1997, for their leader to ask two questions at PMQs, which Clegg had been doing for two and a half years.

Clegg's first PMQs as Cameron's deputy, in July 2010, was the first ever Liberal or Liberal Democrat response to PMQs since its formalisation in 1961. Clegg discovered that being a minister at the dispatch box, speaking on behalf of the government, is a very different thing from being an opposition politician in a TV discussion: there's a gulf between Question Time and *Question Time*. Responding to Jack Straw, making his first and only PMQs appearance standing in for a Labour leader, Clegg said something which was a boilerplate Liberal Democrat campaign slogan but which potentially had serious international legal implications for the UK government. Attacking Straw, who had been Foreign Secretary in 2003, Clegg said, 'We may have to wait for his memoirs, but perhaps one day he will account for his role in the most disastrous decision of all: the illegal invasion of Iraq.'[261]

The view that the invasion of Iraq was illegal is one held by many people, but it has never been the official view of the UK government, and accepting it could have left it and the armed forces open to legal action. Clegg's office had to issue a clarifying statement explaining that he had been speaking in a personal capacity and expressing his own opinion, and that the government would await the result of the Chilcot inquiry.[262]

This was an early example of the box Clegg was in – unable to express his own party's view where it did not reflect government policy, unable to distance himself from the Conservative Party. As one of his advisers, Sean Kemp, reflected to us, when he read out Tory economic lines or attacked Labour, people would read in signals about his openness to a future coalition with the Tories and the impossibility of the Liberal Democrats ever doing a deal with Labour under his leadership, but in reality he had no option. He couldn't reply to a question from Harriet Harman about the iniquities of Tory welfare policy by saying words to the effect of 'I agree with you, the Tories are bad, but we're in coalition and they're the bigger party so it's part of the price we pay to get other things we like.' He had to defend it, and if you're going to defend something you may as well do it forcefully. The problem was that he ended up sounding like – or put himself into a position where he could be portrayed as sounding like – a Tory, which was exactly Labour's characterisation of him in the first place. The hundreds of Tory backbenchers sitting behind him cheering him on only added to the effect.

The problem was made worse by the fact that in addition to the government briefings Clegg was given by civil servants, he was working with political briefings about the Labour Party prepared by the Conservative Research Department. The Liberal Democrats were a small party, with a small staff; meanwhile, the Tories had significant research capacity and were already producing anti-Labour attack briefings, so when they offered them to Clegg it was hard to say no. On the Labour side, we were surprised at first to hear him coming out with such recognisably Tory attacks on us, but that was the material he had to work with. As Harman says, 'You can attack from somebody else's ideological framework and it can work in the moment, but it can then start reinforcing things that people think about you which you don't want people to think about you, like "You're the same as the Tories." So a Tory attack might work to undermine us and the Tories might love it, but it didn't do him any good in the long run.'

In Harman's first outing at PMQs against Clegg in November 2010, she asked him about university tuition fees, which he and his party had promised to abolish before the election and were now in the process of increasing from £3,000 to £9,000. 'We all know what it is like,' she said. 'You are at Freshers' Week. You meet up with a dodgy bloke and you do things that you regret. Is not the truth of it that the deputy Prime Minister has been led astray by the Tories?'[263] This was one of Harman's most successful PMQs in opposition, and one of Clegg's worst: while the policy was defensible on its own terms and Clegg attempted to defend it, there was no getting away from the fact that it was the opposite of what he had promised at the election just a few months earlier.

Clegg used the same civil service PMQs prep team as Cameron, although prepping the Prime Minister's stand-in was a bit of a step down for them: as Sean Kemp put it to us, 'It was a bit like when a professional footballer goes to play for a pub team as a favour.' Like many politicians in our experience, he was desperate to have good jokes to deploy, but not very good at telling them, and when he had one he was keen to use he would crowbar it in much too early instead of waiting for the right set-up line from his opponent. While he carried the fat PMQs file, he hated using it, and was happiest and at his best when he could cast it aside and extemporise. After some early difficulties, he learned to use the hostility and jeers from the Labour side to his advantage: in his best performances you could see him channelling his irritation at his status as a Labour hate figure into a convincing righteous indignation that here he was making tough decisions, trying to act in the national interest, clearing up the mess made by a party that now tried to pose as the sole embodiment of political virtue. The anger was real.

Most of the time, Clegg's role at PMQs during the coalition was not to answer questions but to sit quietly next to David Cameron. The decision to do this had its origins in the Rose Garden press conference after the 2010 general election, when the two leaders stood together to show that they were in it for the long term, but it quickly became obvious, not least to Clegg and his team, that it was a mistake. There was no correct facial expression: if he smiled he was just another Tory; if he pointed and jeered along with George Osborne he was a *massive* Tory; if he frowned or otherwise intimated disapproval of Cameron's words there was a coalition split; if he tried to keep his expression as neutral as possible he just looked sad. As time went on he found more and more excuses not to be there, and it was difficult to blame him.

George Osborne stood in for Cameron three times after the 2015 general election, with the Liberal Democrats out of the picture – an opportunity for someone long thought of as a potential successor, but also a risk. Osborne already had a reputation as an effective parliamentary performer, and his jousts at Treasury Questions with a succession of Labour Chancellors and shadow Chancellors had shown his ability to hammer home key messages, sidestep difficult questions and make good use of scripted jokes. He had long experience, too, from behind the scenes in PMQs prep in both government and opposition, so he knew exactly what was required of him: 'I knew what to do and I wasn't fazed by the process, I didn't have to learn all that. Of course a lot of Leaders of the Opposition or new Prime Ministers, they won't have ever seen, Theresa May would never have prepped for Prime Minister's Questions or seen the room where it's done really or understood the process, so I knew all that, but it's still a huge amount of work and it would take a lot of my time. There was adrenalin, but by then I'd been ten years Chancellor and shadow Chancellor so I was used to a full House of Commons. I'd had lots of exchanges with Ed Balls over the years, so I was kind of used to that bit and I certainly found it much easier once you get into the questions from MPs, I was absolutely used to doing that after things like Autumn Statements.'

But despite, or perhaps because of, having more experience of PMQs than most stand-ins, Osborne understood that this was more difficult than his usual parliamentary appearances: 'One of my theories is that, which was [Gordon] Brown's mistake, being the Chancellor of the Exchequer is not at all like being the Prime Minister, and it's a big step up to be the Prime Minister. And one of the reasons is the Chancellor has few parliamentary appearances, most of which are heavily choreographed, and when you've had a time to put the effort in, you're in charge of the battleground. Broadly speaking, a Chancellor can choose when and where they intervene whereas a Prime Minister can't.' Answering PMQs, says Osborne, is 'technically very complex. It's about the most complex parliamentary thing you have to do by far, much more complex than delivering a Budget, or doing a statement, because you're having to deal with the hostile questions, positive questions, you don't know half the questions.'

George Osborne's PMQs debut in June 2015 was also a debut for Hilary Benn, then Labour's shadow Foreign Secretary. Labour had lost the general election just six weeks earlier and was already in the early stages of a leadership election: nominations for leadership candidates had closed that Monday, and nominations for deputy leader closed at noon on Wednesday, the exact moment that PMQs started. Labour was down; Osborne was at perhaps the height of his powers, one of the architects of the Tories' first overall majority for twenty-three years, the Prime Minister's designated deputy as First Secretary of State, ready to use his first PMQs outing to show his backbenchers and the country what they might have to look forward to next. Indeed, there were suspicions that one of the reasons David Cameron had nominated Osborne as his deputy was precisely to allow him the opportunity to demonstrate his leadership abilities, as the thoughts of the Conservative Party started to turn to the succession. As Osborne says, 'Everyone thought I was a future leadership candidate so I wasn't just a stand-in, I was a player in the current game.'

The wider political context shapes the approach leaders have to take going into PMQs. Labour, beaten, confused, had few attacking options; preparing with Benn, we knew Osborne would want the opportunity to use his prepared attack lines and jokes and demonstrate his mastery of the political scene. So Benn did the only thing that would prevent an easy Osborne victory: he parked the bus. Questions about unaccompanied minors travelling to Syria, about counter-radicalisation strategy and about the refugee crisis choked off Osborne's ability to deliver political attack lines; his one attempted prepared joke – 'we are extremely relieved to see that there is no Benn in the Labour leadership contest but plenty of Bennites'[264] – came across as ill judged when delivered in response to a solemn question. 'I made some nice remark about him but it was inappropriate because he'd raised some terrorism incident. And I knew the moment I said it,' he says. Osborne emerged from the session unscathed because unattacked, but without having enhanced his reputation.

George Osborne's next PMQs outing, in December 2015, was much more conventional. Labour's stand-in for Jeremy Corbyn was Angela Eagle. The decision to appoint her to the job was a last-minute fudge to deal with a sudden self-inflicted political wound, when all of the top jobs in Corbyn's first shadow Cabinet were given to men. A hurried late-night press release had been sent out designating Eagle, already appointed shadow Business Secretary, as shadow First Secretary of State, with responsibilities including standing in for the Leader of the Opposition at PMQs when appropriate.

Eagle was happy to do it: 'I knew that I'd be able to do PMQs. I didn't expect that I would get that much chance but I wasn't remotely worried about being able to do it because of my training at Business Questions; it's different but similar.' Eagle had just spent four years as shadow Leader of the House of Commons doing the weekly Business Questions, which involves giving a short speech of topical political attack, leavened with jokes, in response to the Leader of the House setting out the parliamentary business for the week. Eagle characterises the job as 'a few jabs, dance around, see what you can do, and sometimes obviously you have to be serious, and it's a question of how you go from the one to the other, and you can't do a bit of frippery and then serious, so if it's three, three and a half minutes, you've got to get the rhythm of it right, you've got to get the jokes right, you've got to get the timing right, you've got to get the script right, and it's got to fit together.' She says that she drew on her experience as a chess-player to get herself into the right frame of mind: 'I spent a lot of my time, from eight to twenty, playing tournament chess and walking into situations that were competitive, where my own performance was going to make the difference whether I won or lost. When you do those things, first of all you learn to control your nerves, secondly you learn to concentrate in the way that you need to concentrate, and thirdly you have to be nervous enough but not too nervous, you have to be concentrated enough but not too concentrated, because otherwise you will underperform, and it's getting it just right so that you're actually focused and you can think, and you're not panicking, but you need to have adrenalin, because if you didn't have any adrenalin you'd be useless. So it's that kind of focused calm that is what you need.'

After a few months of Corbyn's low-key PMQs, Eagle was keen to provide some political knockabout and cheer Labour's backbenchers. She did both, teasing Osborne for his leadership ambitions and mocking David Cameron's ongoing efforts at renegotiating Britain's membership of the EU. In a parody of Corbyn's crowdsourcing of PMQs, she produced a letter from 'Donald from Brussels' – a reference to the president of the European Council, Donald Tusk – warning about the destabilising effect of uncertainty about the UK's future in the EU. Osborne was reduced to suggesting that she ask about something else – always a sign of unease with the line of questioning. He told us he felt slightly at a disadvantage against Eagle: 'It was quite asymmetric, I felt, less so with Hilary but with Angela it was like, she only had to hit me once and it was "Oh, Osborne's…" Remember, half the Tory press were out to get me by then.' Eagle is unsympathetic: '*I* knew it was his problem with his own side, *he* must have known it was his problem with his own side. In fact, he should have been much more gracious with me; if he'd been gracious with me it would have been very difficult for me to be quite so mean to him.'

By the end of 2016, politics had moved on. Cameron and Osborne had departed from frontline politics for reasons unconnected with their PMQs performances, Eagle had left the Labour front bench, and the new Leader of the House, David Lidington, standing in for new Prime Minister Theresa May, had to face a different Labour stand-in. Emily Thornberry, substituting for Corbyn, showed that simple forensic questioning, and a willingness to ask the same question again if an answer is not forthcoming, can pay dividends. Lloyd Evans in *The Spectator*, praising Thornberry's 'warm buttery voice, like melting fudge', wrote that her performance 'raises her to the position of heiress-apparent if anything happens to Corbyn'[265] – another example of PMQs as a showcase that can help to make or break a parliamentary reputation.

While Corbyn was generally unwilling to ask about Brexit at PMQs either before or after the EU referendum, his two PMQs stand-ins, Eagle and Thornberry, asked about it repeatedly – after all, it was the dominant political issue of the period. Stand-ins, especially on the opposition side, don't just act as ciphers for their absent leaders ('Nobody from Jeremy's office ever said, "Well done," or anything, I did it in a complete vacuum,' says Eagle); they write their own questions and can test the strengths and weaknesses of an alternative strategy.

One of Nick Clegg's advisers told us that the problem with doing PMQs as a stand-in is that you can never really win – you can only cock up. John Biffen, who stood in twenty-one times for Margaret Thatcher at PMQs between 1983 and 1987 when he was Leader of the House, said that he felt 'like the office boy in the boss's chair'.[266] There's some truth in this. There's an inevitable sense that the B-team is performing when, well, the B-team is performing. If the Prime Minister is on a foreign trip, even the senior political journalists who usually cover PMQs tend to follow her, meaning that they miss the events that take place back home. But PMQs has a special glamour that makes many senior politicians below leadership level seek the right to stand in for their leaders – as Harriet Harman did, assiduously asserting her precedence over Jack Straw as Gordon Brown's PMQs deputy. George Osborne says, 'I'm very pleased I've done it; there's definitely a little thrill when you say, "I had meetings with ministerial colleagues and others earlier today," and all that.' PMQs may not attract the level of attention when the deputies get a run-out that it does when the leaders are present, but it is still a bigger showcase for the substitutes than almost any other parliamentary appearance in their lives. When the Prime Minister jets off to exotic parts of the world, it's a chance for someone else to get their moment in the sun.

II

'THAT IS THAT.
THE END.'

Nobody does PMQs for ever. Some Prime Ministers and Leaders of the Opposition – and their advisers – do their last PMQs without knowing it's their last. When Gordon Brown answered the questions at the last PMQs before the 2010 election he would have hoped to return to answer more, but having lost the election he resigned as Labour leader and never asked a question of Prime Minister David Cameron. Ed Miliband's last ever PMQs, at which he challenged Cameron to rule out raising VAT, and Cameron devastatingly did just that before challenging him to rule out raising national insurance contributions, also came just before an election which he lost: it was not his, or our, finest hour.

A few leaders gradually fade away at PMQs, departing almost unnoticed. Like Brown, John Major took part in a high-octane, noisy shouting match in his last pre-election PMQs as Prime Minister, but unlike Brown he stayed on as Leader of the Opposition for a few months after his defeat. Danny Finkelstein helped him prepare for asking the questions of Tony Blair, 'which we did literally just the two of us, because he was only in his last few weeks. It was an extremely civilised process, he wasn't really interested in making some great political points.'

Some Prime Ministers do get to do their final PMQs knowing, and with everyone else knowing, that it's their last. In some ways that's a mark of success – it only happens if they have won enough elections to be Prime Minister in the first place – but it is the all-political-careers-end-in-failure kind of success. It's almost never fully by choice, and the opposition can rarely take much credit for it. David Cameron resigned as Prime Minister in 2016 after the UK voted to leave the European Union, against his wishes and advice but in a referendum he had chosen to call. Tony Blair succumbed to pressure from within his own party and stepped down in 2007 after ten years in office. Margaret Thatcher was forced out by Conservative MPs in 1990 after failing to get enough votes to defeat a leadership challenge from Michael Heseltine on the first ballot. But all of them were able, after their departures had become certain, to stay on long enough for a valedictory Prime Minister's Questions performance. They went into their final PMQs with their fate already sealed, and with the bittersweet knowledge that they would never have to do it again. Cameron answered his last ever 'engagements question' with a self-aware reference to his imminent new status: 'This morning, I had meetings with ministerial colleagues and others. Other than one meeting this afternoon with Her Majesty the Queen, the diary for the rest of my day is remarkably light.'[267]

Thatcher answered PMQs for the final time on 27 November 1990 – before the votes in the final Conservative Party leadership ballot had been counted and Major announced as her successor later that day. As the longest-serving Prime Minister since the formalisation of PMQs, she had answered a lot of questions between 1979 and 1990: she told the Conservative MP David Wilshire that his was 'the 7,498th oral question to which I have replied in 698 Question Times'.[268] The session was dominated by tributes from her Conservative colleagues, including this one from Dame Jill Knight, the single most sycophantic question we've come across while researching this book: 'May I ask my right honourable friend to reflect with pride that a thousand years from now, when every other member of the House is dead dust, she alone will have a hallowed place in the history books?'[269] It was all too much for Labour's David Winnick, who asked Thatcher if she found it 'the height of hypocrisy and nauseating to be so highly praised by Tory members when, last week, 152 of them stabbed her in the back'. 'I do not find it nauseating,' Thatcher replied; 'I find it very refreshing.'[270]

Outgoing Prime Ministers' final PMQs are a complete dead loss for Leaders of the Opposition – the day isn't about them at all, nobody is interested in what they have to say, and they're hardly going to bring down the Prime Minister. But Neil Kinnock, on his final go against Thatcher, induced an uncharacteristic – if, by this time, irrelevant – slip of the tongue, asking her about what the government officially called the 'community charge' and everyone else called the 'poll tax'. When he asked, 'Why on earth all those now competing for her job are desperately wriggling around trying to find a way out of the poll tax trap?' Thatcher, somewhat carried away, used the popular name for the unpopular tax and had to correct herself: 'On the contrary, I really rather thought that they were keeping the poll— the community charge.'[271] She allowed herself to laugh. It didn't matter any more.

The choreography of Tony Blair's final PMQs on 27 June 2007 was part of a carefully planned handover to Gordon Brown in which one Prime Minister would carry out his final parliamentary duties before driving to Buckingham Palace to resign, and another one would meet the Queen to be appointed, and then arrive in Downing Street. This meant that PMQs itself was largely pointless as an exercise in scrutiny. As Leader of the Opposition David Cameron, unusually but quite reasonably, did not bother to ask six questions, and used his final one to pay tribute to Blair and wish him well for the future.

Among the tributes, two backbench contributions stood out. Liberal Democrat Richard Younger-Ross asked about the relationship between church and state and the disestablishment of the Church of England, provoking the entirely correct answer, 'I am really not bothered about that one.'[272] And Labour's Jeremy Corbyn, who had recently entered his twenty-fifth year as a backbencher, demonstrated the dogged focus on the issues that mattered to him that would eventually propel him to the Labour leadership, asking for a timetable for British troops to be withdrawn from Iraq. He didn't get one.[273]

Blair's last words at PMQs, and his last words in Parliament as Prime Minister, were these:

> Mr Speaker, if I may just finish with two brief remarks – first to the House. I have never pretended to be a great House of Commons man, but I pay the House the greatest compliment I can by saying that, from first to last, I never stopped fearing it.

The tingling apprehension that I felt at three minutes to twelve today I felt as much ten years ago, and every bit as acute. It is in that fear that the respect is contained. The second thing that I would like to say is about politics and to all my colleagues from different political parties. Some may belittle politics but we who are engaged in it know that it is where people stand tall. Although I know that it has many harsh contentions, it is still the arena that sets the heart beating a little faster. If it is, on occasions, the place of low skulduggery, it is more often the place for the pursuit of noble causes. I wish everyone, friend or foe, well. That is that. The end.[274]

He departed to applause which was both a sincere tribute to his political achievements and talent and to his ten years as Prime Minister and, at least on the Conservative side, part of the modernisers' strategy of praising him in order to heighten the contrast with his successor, Gordon Brown.

That was the most memorable moment of the session, but it was not the most significant. The question and answer that mattered most came when Conservative backbencher Sir Nicholas Winterton complained that 'a majority of the people of the United Kingdom feel betrayed by the fact that they are being drawn down further into the suffocating quicksand and expensive bureaucracy of the European Union', and called for a referendum on the new EU treaty. Blair observed, 'After the guttural roar from his own benches that greeted his statement, I really believe that if I were the leader of the Conservative Party I would be worried about that.'[275] He had a point. Nine years later, that leader of the Conservative Party, David

Cameron, made his own final PMQs appearance after losing a referendum on the EU.

It came sooner than most would have expected, just fourteen months after delivering the Conservative Party's first overall majority since 1992 at the 2015 general election. Even when he announced his intention to resign as Prime Minister immediately after the referendum, Cameron anticipated a three-month leadership election process. But Theresa May found herself the last candidate standing just three weeks later, when Andrea Leadsom pulled out of the contest. On 13 July 2016, Cameron took PMQs for the last time. As usual, he was comfortable: reading out lists of his achievements in office, attacking Jeremy Corbyn and even producing a photo of himself holding Larry the Downing Street cat, to put to rest 'the rumour that I do not love Larry; I do, and I have photographic evidence to prove it'.[276] As with so many of Cameron's PMQs answers, it sounded convincing enough in the moment and then, when you started to think about it, it turned out to prove nothing of the sort. One member of Ed Miliband's old PMQs prep team made a small contribution to Cameron's last appearance, sending over Jeff Smith's transparently Milibandesque question, 'The Prime Minister came to office promising to keep the UK's triple-A rating, to end top-down NHS reorganisations and to stop his party banging on about Europe. How would he say that has gone?'[277] True to form and as expected, Cameron gave a robust defence of his record.

Fittingly, Cameron's last ever PMQs answer dodged the question, from veteran Tory Kenneth Clarke: 'Although, no doubt, he will have plans for a slightly more enjoyable and relaxed Wednesday morning and lunchtime in the future, may I ask that he will nevertheless still be an active participant in this House as it faces a large number of problems over the next few years?' Cameron made no commitment either way – and resigned as an MP two months later. Instead, Cameron used his final answer to praise Parliament, as Blair had done nine years earlier, and signed off with 'Nothing is really impossible if you put your mind to it. After all, as I once said, I was the future once.'[278] It might seem odd for a Prime Minister who was leaving office as a result of losing a career- and nation-defining referendum to say, 'Nothing is really impossible if you put your mind to it,' but, like Blair, he left the Chamber to applause.

For all the satisfaction they can derive from an effective perform-ance, few leaders enjoy PMQs. The stakes are too high, the preparation too time-consuming, the risk of humiliation too great. Cameron told us, 'At five minutes to twelve you think, "God, I wish I wasn't doing this," and that's on both sides, whether you're Leader of the Opposition or Prime Minister.' Years after stepping down as Prime Minister, Tony Blair wrote, 'Even today, wherever I am in the world, I feel a cold chill at 11.57 a.m. on Wednesdays, a sort of prickle on the back of my neck, the thump of the heart.'[279] It's worth keeping that, the recurring fear of PMQs, in mind when thinking about Blair's last words at his last PMQs, 'That is that. The end.'

Harriet Harman, uniquely, had two final PMQs as Leader of the Opposition: once in September 2010 before Ed Miliband's election as Labour leader, and once in September 2015 before Jeremy Corbyn's ('It's quite surprising to discover that I am not old enough or posh enough to be the front-runner of this current leadership election,' she joked afterwards).[280] She says: 'I'm sure there isn't anybody who's done Prime Minister's Questions who isn't really pleased when they stop doing it. I've never heard anybody saying, "I so miss Prime Minister's Questions, I wish I was still Leader of the Opposition or Prime Minister because I miss Prime Minister's Questions." I suspect nobody says, "I just used to love Prime Minister's Questions so much." You love it when it's finished. For ever.'

12

PUNCH AND JUDY
POLITICS

Every Prime Minister or Leader of the Opposition who has ever asked or answered questions at PMQs remembers the fear. David Cameron told us, 'It doesn't matter how many times you've done it, you get nervous, because it's such a tight theatre. You were always nervous. Because the effective attack against you, you feel instantly; the effective attack you make that works, it's very instant.' John Whittingdale says that for Margaret Thatcher it was 'the most terrifying thing of the week, and she was always nervous, always nervous'. In his memoirs, Tony Blair describes PMQs as 'the most nerve-racking, discombobulating, nail-biting, bowel-moving, terror-inspiring, courage-draining experience in my prime ministerial life, without question. You know that scene in *Marathon Man*, where the evil Nazi doctor played by Laurence Olivier drills through Dustin Hoffman's teeth? At around 11.45 on

Wednesday mornings, I would have swapped thirty minutes of PMQs
for thirty minutes of that.'[281] William Hague says that before PMQs he
would feel 'nervous in a productive-excitement kind of way. There
are two types of nervousness, aren't there? There's nervous terror
that stops your brain working, then there's a productive nervousness
which is you're on peak fighting form, and preferably it's that second
one. But that's still nervous, you still feel it as nervousness, your
heart's going and you're feeling pretty much under pressure.' For Ed
Miliband it was the moments just before PMQs that were the worst:
'I found the bit beforehand, just before, more nerve-racking than the
bit when you're actually in there. Walking over, being in the room
behind the Speaker's chair.' Even the Speaker is nervous beforehand.
'I think if the adrenalin isn't flowing there's something wrong, you're
probably making a complete hash of it,' says John Bercow. 'Precisely
because it is heavily viewed, I do feel this tingle of anticipation, a
very slight nervousness.'

Yet for an event that inspires so much fear, takes so much preparation and is supposed to be a highlight of the parliamentary week,
Prime Minister's Questions has fewer highlights than you might
hope. Ed Miliband pointed out to us, rightly, that many of the
most famous, memorable and defining political and parliamentary
moments of the last few decades did not happen at PMQs at all.
PMQs is 'a mood-definer', he says. 'Even though it's these moments
of joust, it's the background music, partly because there's so many of
them.' That isn't to say that there haven't been some great PMQs
moments over the years, many of which have already been discussed
in this book. A rough list of the top twenty PMQs moments referred
to in this book – this is a personal list, which like this book is rather

skewed towards the last couple of decades when we have been paying the most attention; and of course we know that everyone's list
will be different – might look something like this, in chronological
order.

1) Frit? Margaret Thatcher turns on her opponents

Margaret Thatcher, challenged by Denis Healey to call an election in 1983, went after him, using a Lincolnshire dialect word:
'Afraid? Frightened? Frit? Could not take it? Cannot stand it?' The
word passed into general use, at least among political obsessives
(Chapter 7).

2) Advisers advise and ministers decide: the undisclosed resignation

When Neil Kinnock asked Margaret Thatcher in 1989 about the
conflict at the top of her government between Chancellor Nigel
Lawson and economic adviser Sir Alan Walters, Thatcher gave a
robust defence of her economic policy. Nobody could have guessed
that Thatcher had taken Lawson's resignation letter an hour
beforehand, slipped it into her handbag and set off for PMQs as if
nothing had happened (Chapter 5).

3) As seen on TV: a new audience

The first televised PMQs in 1989 was almost entirely unmemorable,
and the questions and answers had little long-term political
significance. In that sense, it was a more typical PMQs than we
might like to think. But this was a major event: televising the event
transformed the way it was used by both sides. Without television,
PMQs would matter a lot less (Chapter 1).

4) Weak, weak, weak: Tony Blair's brutal attack on John Major

Arguably the high point, at least at PMQs, of Labour's assault on the Major government in the run-up to the 1997 election. Tony Blair wrapped up an attack on John Major's failure to hold his party together over Europe with three devastating words, summing up the contrast he wanted to make between the leadership of the two main parties (Chapter 6).

5) The unread book: William Hague's deconstruction of the Budget

William Hague took advantage of the 24-hour period between the Tuesday Budget and the Wednesday PMQs in 1998 to go through the numbers in the small print and challenge Tony Blair on the tax burden on businesses. 'That is in the Red Book – or, apparently, in the Prime Minister's case, the unread book,' he teased. The Budget was soon moved to Wednesdays, just after PMQs (Chapter 2).

6) Turning the tables: Tony Blair ambushes William Hague on Lords reform

If William Hague had known that the Conservative leader in the House of Lords, Lord Cranborne, had already done a deal with the Labour government on Lords reform in 1998, he would never have asked Tony Blair about it at PMQs. But he didn't know. Blair crushed him (Chapter 2).

7) Tony Blair's political philosophy: the killer backbench question

Labour backbencher Tony McWalter completely stumped Tony Blair in 2002 by innocently asking what his political philosophy was: the

Prime Minister floundered, and failed to come up with a convincing response. Asking about something that's not in the briefing book, and not even about policy, can be deadly – even if you're not trying to be (Chapter 8).

8) How many? The heckle that put a nail in Iain Duncan Smith's coffin

Labour's Kevin Brennan wrecked Iain Duncan Smith's long-running 'ask Tony Blair for an obscure number' strategy in 2002 by asking the beginning of the question for him in the pause before he spoke. If you're too predictable at PMQs, people will take advantage (Chapter 2).

9) Purple powder protest: PMQs suspended

In 2004 Tony Blair was in the middle of answering a question from Conservative leader Michael Howard when he was hit on the back by a condom filled with purple flour, part of a protest by so-called fathers' rights protest group Fathers4Justice, which probably made sense to them at the time. The sitting was suspended (Chapter 9).

10) He was the future once: David Cameron's confident debut

In his first PMQs as Conservative leader in 2005, David Cameron managed to put down some important markers – attack the yelling of Labour's Chief Whip, signal support for some Blairite public service reforms and demonstrate his modernisation of the Conservative Party, cast himself as the 'heir to Blair' and implicitly contrast both himself and Blair favourably with Gordon Brown. As strategic, impactful uses of PMQs go, it has few equals (Chapter 6).

11) That is that, the end: Tony Blair's farewell

Tony Blair's final PMQs in 2007 was a stage-managed but emotional affair in which he paid tribute to the House of Commons – 'The tingling apprehension that I felt at three minutes to twelve today I felt as much ten years ago, and every bit as acute' – and then left to applause from both sides (Chapter 11).

12) Stalin to Mr Bean: Vince Cable's perfect phrase

Stand-in Liberal Democrat leader Vince Cable summed up Gordon Brown's declining fortunes after 2007's 'election that never was' in one short phrase: 'The House has noticed the Prime Minister's remarkable transformation in the past few weeks from Stalin to Mr Bean.' Cable showed that the leader of the third party can have an impact at PMQs and make a reputation there, and that a good line can be at least as effective and wounding as a forensic deconstruction of policy (Chapter 8).

13) The man in the baseball cap: Harriet Harman uses humour to beat William Hague

The pressure was on Harriet Harman in 2008, the first time she stood in for Gordon Brown against William Hague: he was funnier than her and had more PMQs experience, and everyone expected her to lose, especially after she was photographed wearing a stab vest in her constituency. She and her team predicted his joke and prepared their own gag – 'If I were looking for advice on what to wear or what not to wear, the very last person I would look to is the man in the baseball cap.' Harman brought the house down, and won the day by exceeding expectations (Chapter 10).

14) Saving the world: Gordon Brown's slip of the tongue

It was obvious what he meant, he corrected himself almost imme-diately and he arguably had a point anyway, but Gordon Brown's accidental claim to have 'saved the world' rather than 'saved the banks' through recapitalisation in 2008 was easy for the Conservatives to portray as hubristic self-delusion (Chapter 7).

15) Wooooooo! The haunting of David Cameron

A Labour MP contributed ghostly sound effects when David Cameron was warned in 2010 that if he screwed up the NHS, the recently deceased former president of the Patients Association, Claire Rayner, would come back and haunt him. It may not be the most significant of PMQs moments, but we like it (Chapter 7).

16) Calm down, dear: Flashman and the perils of overconfidence

It may just have been a line from an insurance advert, and it may even have been aimed at Ed Balls, but David Cameron's snapped 'Calm down, dear' in the face of heckling from Angela Eagle in 2011 summed up everything Labour wanted people to think about his character – arrogant, superior, hot-tempered – and added a dose of apparent sexism too (Chapter 7).

17) Is there anything he could organise in a brewery? The deadly opening gag

One of our proudest moments: Ed Miliband wrong-footed David Cameron in 2013 by opening with a joke which had no possible serious answer – 'In the light of his U-turn on alcohol pricing, is there anything the Prime Minister could organise in a brewery?'

– and which gave him no time to come up with a better joke back. Cameron came back with a much worse joke instead, and the day was won (Chapter 2).

18) Never ask a question you don't know the answer to: Ed Miliband's last PMQs

Not one of our proudest moments: in the last PMQs before the 2015 election, Ed Miliband asked David Cameron to rule out increasing VAT. Cameron, disastrously for Labour, obliged, and comprehensively won the exchange and, a few weeks later, the election (Chapter 4).

19) My questions will be your questions: Jeremy Corbyn's new kind of politics

Following a leadership campaign which promised to take back control from a closed elite circle, Jeremy Corbyn asked his supporters to send in their own suggested questions for his first PMQs as Labour leader in 2015. They may not have been particularly challenging to David Cameron, but they embodied the change Corbyn wanted to make to politics, as well as functioning as a useful defensive shield (Chapter 2).

20) Remind him of anybody? Theresa May's false dawn

As a brand new Prime Minister in July 2016 Theresa May closed her first ever PMQs with a memorable line, directed at Jeremy Corbyn: a Thatcheresque 'Remind him of anybody?' The resemblance was deliberate, unmistakable and ominous – but May's loss of her majority in an unforced general election less than a year later was rather less reminiscent of Britain's first female Prime Minister (Chapter 6).

Lists like these are fun to compile, and the moments in them are all memorable and all, in their own way, politically important. Arguing about which ones should be taken off, and which ones should replace them, is part of what political observers and obsessives – we plead guilty to both charges – like doing. And of course, the greatest PMQs moment of all time might happen this week, or next week, although at the time of writing we wouldn't bet on it. But these moments are the exceptions, not the rule. PMQs often seems to be more hype than substance, an event built up by broadcasters, accompanied by plenty of noise from MPs but adding little to our understanding of the week's political stories. It's no surprise that many people say they dislike it, and that many leaders, especially new leaders, say they want to change it.

When David Cameron, as the newly elected leader of the Conservative Party in 2005, said that he wanted to see an end to 'Punch and Judy politics' – the phrase that gives this book its title – he wasn't, mostly, talking about Prime Minister's Questions. He was drawing a contrast between an approach to politics which is constantly, instinctively adversarial and one – which he hoped his leadership would exemplify – where opposition parties work constructively with governments when they do the right thing. 'We need to change, and we will change, the way we behave,' he said. 'I'm fed up with the Punch and Judy politics of Westminster, the name-calling, backbiting, point-scoring, finger-pointing. I want and I will lead a Conservative Party that when the government does the right thing, we will work with them, and when they do the wrong thing we will call them to account and criticise them.'[282]

Cameron had used the phrase over a year before he became Conservative leader in a speech at a fringe event at the Conservative

Party conference in 2004, warning that 'we don't win by a fruitless search for differences between us and our opponents where none really exist. It's opportunist Punch and Judy politics. It's unattractive and it doesn't work.'[283] He used it in the same sense throughout his campaign for the Conservative leadership. (By the way, remember our reference to the David Cameron quotes catalogue in Chapter 3? Here it is in action.) 'Punch and Judy politics' was a phrase that described a crucial element of the Cameron modernisation project: a new accommodation towards certain elements of New Labour to which many Conservatives were not in fact reconciled, in order both to demonstrate to the country that his party had changed and to create embarrassment for Tony Blair. It dramatised to the wider Labour Party the fiction that Blair was just a Tory in disguise by identifying parts of his programme which many Labour MPs disliked but which Tories could vote for.

The problem with lumping all of this together under the 'Punch and Judy politics' heading was that PMQs was, and is, the political event at which the 'name-calling, backbiting, point-scoring, finger-pointing' is most on public display, and not only did Cameron never really seek to change it – it turned out he was bloody good at it. Ed Miliband, who came up against Cameron more than any other Labour leader, acknowledges his opponent's skill, albeit in a slightly backhanded way: 'I think Cameron was good at it. Cameron is fleet of foot and he didn't care about the conventions. He didn't care if he spent five questions asking me a question. He didn't care about answering the questions, he didn't really attempt to answer the questions. I mean he basically decided survival is what matters and by any means necessary.'

Cameron's PMQs proficiency meant that the 'Punch and Judy politics' line was a constant source of low-level embarrassment to him over the next decade. Interviewer after interviewer pointed to his willingness to play the game at PMQs as evidence that he had failed to follow through on his own 'end to Punch and Judy politics' commitment. Like PMQs itself, the phrase has a deeper meaning than appears on the surface – and the surface appearance can be difficult to defend. As Cameron ruefully told Dominic Lawson in November 2008, 'The idea that there's a non-confrontational, more chummy way of doing PMQs, it's just not the case. I thought it might be possible. I was wrong. I thought maybe it could be different, and actually it can't be. The fact is, Prime Minister's Questions is an adversarial occasion. It's about me asking quite tough questions on behalf of the public. It's the questions they want answered. And you can't pull your punches.'[284] He said to us, 'My criticism of the former, previous Tory leaders was that we were doing just too much opposition for opposition's sake. What I said about PMQs was an extension of that, and was the bit that was undeliverable, but the thought behind it was deliverable. And that's the sort of terrible self-justification you can put in your book.' Well, there it is.

Nevertheless, he says, 'If you look at what I did with Blair, I did vary the approach a lot. I did soft subjects, hard subjects, aggressive politics, consensual, and I think a bit of that is good. Always the colleagues behind you say, 'Oh *bor-ing*, why do we have to have six questions on Afghanistan?' but actually you want the warp and weft and the variety. But I think you can't forever take out the Punch and Judy nature because it is a piece of theatre.' As the veteran political journalist Peter Riddell wrote, 'Too often attempts at self-conscious bipartisanship can result in a suspension of proper scrutiny and accountability. Occasions when the House of Commons unites and are said to be at its best can be the reverse, exercises in pious plati-tudes, necessary perhaps to handle immediate grief, but, rightly, unsustainable.'[285]

Ed Miliband did try consciously to change the tone of PMQs at least once. In February 2011, just a few months into his leadership, he asked six consensual questions about the Arab Spring in Egypt and the situation in Afghanistan. He did so not because he had had a bad week or was worried about attacks Cameron might make on him if he was more party political, and not because his chosen topics were dominating the news so much that avoiding them would have looked negligent, but to make a point about how PMQs could be done differently in a less Punch and Judy style. Perhaps he was also trying to set a precedent he could point to on future occasions when bipartisanship was being used as a tactic to avoid obvious attacks. The closing exchanges between the two leaders, as dissatisfied mur-murings from the back benches on both sides demonstrated their impatience, were almost unbearably self-congratulatory, with Ed joking, 'I sense that people are not used to this kind of Prime Minis-ter's Questions,' and Cameron responding, 'From all the noises off, it is clear that people would prefer a bunfight, but sometimes it is sensible to have a serious conversation about the issues that we face.'[286] With no political edge, the session was excruciatingly dull; we didn't try it again.

Tony Blair is another leader who started out wanting to try a more consensual approach at PMQs and soon realised it was a non-starter. 'Forget all that,' he told us. 'Everyone always thinks they should do this, and it's completely futile for this very simple reason: you put 600 of the most reasonable people in the world into a confined space and ask them to debate extremely controversial topics; I promise you, within twenty minutes they'll be shouting and bawling at each other, it's just the way it is. And so, honestly, everyone always thinks that it would be good to do that, and I came to the conclusion it was total fantasy, it was never going to happen. I began as Leader of the Opposition in this very reasonable way. And then I realised after about three or four PMQs, and I remember Alastair [Campbell] and I having a chat about it, that my own side of course, they were wanting me to go and *belt* the guy, and I was sitting there and sort of stroking him round the cheeks. And of course, for the Prime Minister it's absolutely perfect. You know, no one's being very threatening to you. So we had to shift gear. That's where I learned it's just never going to work because quite apart from the general atmosphere, your own side end up thinking, "What the hell did we employ this guy for?" It's like putting a prize fighter in the ring and he's kind of dancing around waving at the crowds, and they're going, "Get in there and hit him!"'

Whether you like PMQs or not, as Tony Blair said to us, 'If you're going to have to do it, you might as well do it well, not badly.' One Conservative adviser told us: 'If Jeremy Corbyn was more theatrical he'd have given Theresa May a lot of trouble, because that's not her strength. And funnily enough he plays to her strength, so these encounters are low-wattage, and therefore as entertainment they're less interesting, but actually they are proper exchanges on issues of substance.'

If you've chosen to take part in a contest, you have to try to win it. As Harriet Harman told us, if you try to change it before you've shown you're good at it, 'it looks like you're trying to do it because you couldn't succeed. And all the build-up to me doing PMQs when I was standing in for Gordon [Brown], which is the first time I did it, was all about how I was going to be hopeless, so it's quite difficult in those circumstances to seek to change the terms of it. You can only really change the terms of something from a position of strength. And the difficulty is that a lot of Prime Ministers start out with "No more Punch and Judy" but you've got to have both sides wanting at the same time to change it. If you're in opposition you want to be battering the Prime Minister, so you don't want when you're in opposition to change the terms of it, because that would be giving the Prime Minister a free ride. And when you're the Prime Minister you don't want to change the terms of it because you want to be laying about yourself with all the government's achievements and generally battering the opposition, so its controversial, its combative status is locked in.' This is of course the same logic as that used by opponents of unilateral nuclear disarmament, so perhaps it's not surprising that the unilateralist Jeremy Corbyn is the recent party leader who has had the most success in breaking free from it.

Corbyn's style of questioning really has helped to change the tone of PMQs, although not necessarily for the better. The use of crowd-sourced questions from real members of the public, as discussed in Chapter 2, helps to disarm certain kinds of political attack. But more significant in making PMQs less combative is that his questions have consistently been far longer and far more scripted than any previous leader's, and performed in a way that makes this fact obvious. There is less improvisation and few rejoinders, scripted or otherwise, to the Prime Minister's responses – which means that Corbyn has only rarely taken advantage of obvious openings that David Cameron's or Theresa May's answers leave for him.

Corbyn is not the first Leader of the Opposition to be tempted to speak at greater length than necessary: when preparing Iain Duncan Smith for PMQs Cameron 'almost always urged economy of expression' on him, for he 'liked to go "off piste", as one of his former team puts it'.[287] But where previous Leaders of the Opposition have either been naturally light on their feet or worked very hard to appear so, Corbyn has been content to plod on relentlessly – an approach that, to be fair, has served him well since 1983. The scripts themselves tend to be written with little regard for how easy they are to read out loud, or to listen to. As one Labour MP said to us, 'He has some rejoinders written down but they're always quite tedious. And they're too po-faced. I think if you haven't done it or you haven't been in the Chamber it's quite difficult to write a script for somebody, and I don't think Jeremy writes his own. It doesn't come over like he does.' Corbyn's PMQs have never been consensual or bipartisan, but they have often been lower-key. And almost everyone we spoke to in the course of writing this book agreed that he, with the help of Theresa May, has succeeded in making PMQs less exciting, and therefore less important, than it had been for many years. Most of them regretted this; but what political professionals see in PMQs, and what the public see in it, can be very different things.

It is easy to make the case against PMQs. It's rowdy, childish and badly behaved. Too many of the questions from the government side are pointless and sycophantic, and the difficult questions are too often dodged. MPs on all sides seem more interested in making terrible jokes, or shouting each other down, than in holding the government properly to account or explaining the government's policies – and especially its failures. It's hard to understand and packed with archaic procedure, and those who say they like it are already part of a political establishment which knows how to navigate the rules, gets the in-jokes and can afford to exclude people who don't work in politics but who still care deeply about the state of the country, worry about how much they are paid and how heavily they are taxed, run businesses, use or work in public services, and simply haven't got time for all this nonsense. Most of all, as Parliament's showpiece event, it's a terrible advertisement for Parliament, for politicians and for politics in general. Aren't they supposed to be running the country?

A report by the Hansard Society in 2014, based on opinion polling and focus groups with members of the public from a range of backgrounds, found that PMQs was 'a significant contributory factor' in a wider dissatisfaction with the culture and conduct of politics.[288] One participant 'was put off by the fact that the point-scoring was "often cringe-worthy"'.[289] Given that the example of PMQs shown to the focus group, from 11 September 2013, was one in which David Cameron finished his final answer to Ed Miliband with one of his worst ever lines – 'I will tell the right honourable gentleman what is a disgrace, and that is going down to Bournemouth and caving in to the trade unions. We were promised this great big, tough fight and great big, tough speech. He told us it was going to be *Raging Bull*; he gave us *Chicken Run*'[290] – this assessment isn't unreasonable, even if the gag isn't really representative.

Vince Cable rightly pointed out to us that PMQs is 'out of character with most of parliamentary life, which is pretty dull, slow-moving, undramatic and at its best business-like but rarely confrontational, rarely theatrical in the way that PMQs is. And I think that part of the problem is that the public assume that's the way Parliament works but it's just half an hour of bunfight in the middle of what is usually much more, I won't say gentle, but much less lively.' David Cameron told Sky News in 2012 that 'MPs work very hard, they are all day doing letters and meetings and the feeling is that they come to the House of Commons at twelve on a Wednesday for a bit of ... the Circus Maximus.'[291]

But for a general public who for perfectly good reasons aren't paying much attention to Parliament, and for whom heavily edited highlights of PMQs on the news are the main thing they see of it, complaining that what they see is unrepresentative would be to miss the point. While the charge that politicians are all the same is, once you look at the policy differences between different parties, clearly unsustainable, it's difficult to deny that when they are all in the same room and behaving in indistinguishable ways they just *do* all *look* the same. And when the ways they are seen behaving involve shouting and jeering at each other, and attempting to score points on issues other than policy, it's easy to see why many people find it off-putting. The Hansard Society's focus group participants said things like 'If I went off like that in my job I would be sacked,' and 'My grandchildren have more manners than our politicians.'[292] If you only see your grandchildren when they are interacting with their grandparents, and your politicians when they are at PMQs, you will almost certainly get a misleading impression of the manners of both. But it is certainly unfortunate for politicians that the time when they are most visible to the public – unlike the time grandchildren are most visible to their grandparents – is the time when they are on their worst behaviour.

The Hansard Society's report notes that 'a number of participants thought about accountability in Parliament through the lens of their own personal experience of accountability in the workplace'.[293] It quotes Lynne Featherstone, then a Liberal Democrat MP, asking, 'Can you imagine running a workplace on that basis? Judge a manager by how loudly his or her staff shout and heckle other managers at the weekly staff meeting? Bizarre. Yet this is meant to pass for normal adult behaviour in the Palace of Westminster.'[294]

Featherstone's analogy with a weekly staff meeting is not a particularly helpful or accurate one, not least because Parliament is not the kind of workplace in which everyone is on the same side, or even – as with some other workplaces – pretending to be. Opposing the government is part of the job of opposition politicians; defeating the opposition is part of the government's job; complaining that this leads to an adversarial atmosphere is to miss the point of why everyone in Parliament has turned up to work in the first place. Nevertheless, this of course makes it an unusual workplace, and there's no doubt that the rowdy atmosphere at PMQs can look alienating.

Angela Eagle – a self-confessed heckler – is happy to defend MPs who are vocal in the House of Commons Chamber, pointing out that given the importance of the issues being discussed to those taking part, silence would be more unnatural: 'I'm sorry, at some stage in their lives everybody does that, we all feel our politics very strongly, we're all partisans, that's why we came into politics, and of *course* we're going to say, "Oh well, that's a load of rubbish."' She gave us an example of a recent parliamentary event at which she openly admitted she shouted at her Conservative opponents: 'I was at it the other day in the universal credit thing, because to think that people who've got nothing can wait for six weeks and can somehow manage in that time is a *joke*, and anyone who thinks that way, saying, "Oh that'll be fine and this isn't a problem and you're scaremongering" – come and see my constituents, of course I'm very annoyed about it. And so yes, I did shout "Rubbish" on quite a few occasions during that particular debate.' It isn't as if political debates to which members of the public are invited, or TV political discussion shows with a studio audience such as *Question Time*, are any more respectful than Parliament: heckles, jeers, booing and applause (applause is banned, of course, in the House of Commons) are the order of the day.

People might not like the noise, but although it might get out of hand sometimes, it's better to have a parliament of disagreement and argument than one of silent consensus. As William Hague says, 'There are quiet parliaments in the world but the quietest are in Pyongyang and Beijing.' Scrutiny is important; Hague told us, 'I often think how much US government would benefit if the President of the United States had to answer complex questions from any member of Congress on a regular basis, and Americans think that too.' Especially right now. John Bercow says: 'I feel that the scrutiny process is important. Whether Prime Minister's Questions is the best form of scrutiny is another matter, but it is in my view a form of scrutiny. It's not necessarily the best and it's certainly not the only club in the golf bag, but I think it is quite an important opportunity for people to speak truth to power and to hold prime ministerial feet to the fire.'

In the Hansard Society's focus group, several participants disliked the 'theatrical' aspect of PMQs.

Some queried whether the Prime Minister knows the questions in advance, whether the whole of PMQs is scripted beforehand,

and each of the key players merely acts out their assigned role.
'I wonder' said one of the non-voters, 'if they put on a big show
for the cameras, then go off down the pub together and have a
good laugh at us.'[295]

It was this kind of scepticism of the artifice of PMQs and of Parliament more generally which Jeremy Corbyn echoed when, in his first
PMQs as Leader of the Opposition, he said that 'many told me that
they thought Prime Minister's Question Time was too theatrical, that
Parliament was out of touch and too theatrical, and that they wanted
things done differently'.[296] Of course, there is as much scripting
beforehand, and as much artifice, in Corbyn's PMQs performances
as in anyone else's. But, especially in his early sessions, there was a
reluctance to engage in the joust of PMQs which reflected a wider
public impatience with the whole enterprise.

PMQs takes place in public and therefore just does involve performance, like anything that happens in front of an audience. There's
a theatrical element to political speeches and rallies, too; what there
isn't, unless something goes wrong, is a back-and-forth argument
between two opposing sides: speeches and rallies to friendly audiences
are less risky, more sanitised, than making an argument in front of
people who are convinced you are wrong and can answer back. As a
politician, anything you do in front of an audience is worth getting
right, and anything you do in front of an audience where someone is
going to argue against you, perhaps convincingly, is worth thinking
through. Dennis Skinner says, 'For a lot of people it's their political
half-hour. That's their politics for the week. It shouldn't be, but it
is. You've got to bear in mind there's a lot of people watching it,

more than any other parliamentary programme.' Most people, of course, aren't watching it – a fact that's true of almost every television programme ever broadcast. But that doesn't mean they don't get a sense of whether politicians are good at it or not, and of different politicians' leadership qualities. Alastair Campbell told us: 'I do think it matters. I do think if you do PMQs well, the public sort of get to know about it, even if they don't see it. I used to meet people, like at a football match, who would say, "Ah, I like that Tony Blair, he knows how to do that Prime Minister's Questions, oh I wouldn't like to do that." It sort of gets out there.'

There are other ways of holding the Prime Minister to account which are lower-profile and lower-octane. For a start, the Prime Minister is sometimes interviewed in the media; but this does not happen on a weekly basis, and she is in a position to refuse to appear, or to pick her outlets, or to set her own ground rules. John Whittingdale pointed out to us that in Margaret Thatcher's day, she would regularly – though certainly not weekly – submit herself to television interviews which could last up to an hour, something unheard of today. But, he says, 'The reason she was so good at the hour's interview with Brian Walden or David Frost was PM's Questions, because whatever he asked she'd probably answered at some point, she was constantly match fit.' The Prime Minister appears about three times a year in front of the House of Commons Liaison Committee, which consists of the chairs of all of the select committees. They can provide tough and sometimes illuminating questioning but, as Harriet Harman says, 'it's not attended by the mob of all the MPs. It's the attendance of the mob that makes PMQs particularly perilous for a Prime Minister, because the Liaison Committee, with all the select committee chairs, becomes a bit of a chat amongst chums. You've got to have the hordes of MPs there, or else it can get very cosy.'

And crucially, neither media interviews with the Prime Minister nor the Liaison Committee provide any sort of platform for the Leader of the Opposition, either to select and ask the questions or to be put under scrutiny for his performance (of course Leaders of the Opposition are interviewed in the media too, but this is a completely different ordeal from putting the questions at PMQs). Neither provides the opportunity for direct comparison between the two people putting themselves forward as national leaders, and neither allows them to take each other on directly. In an adversarial political system, an adversarial format is useful.

There are two obvious examples of politicians whose overall success or failure can be cited as proof that PMQs doesn't matter very much. One is William Hague, who even his greatest detractors would acknowledge was a superb PMQs performer, but who was crushed by Tony Blair's Labour Party in the 2001 election. The other is Jeremy Corbyn, who even his greatest admirers would acknowledge is not particularly adept at PMQs, but who defied almost everyone's predictions to make gains against Theresa May's Conservative Party in the 2017 election.

While Hague and Corbyn are both instructive cases, they are not conclusive. For a start, Hague was up against Tony Blair, another strong PMQs performer who was at the height of his popularity and power at the time – Hague's PMQs success was never going to be enough to win him the 2001 election, but he did use his debating skills to give himself and his party a bit of dignity. 'I do think these were classic encounters. The best questioner of the modern era was William

Hague, and the best answerer was Blair,' says Danny Finkelstein. 'They were sort of the Arsenal *v* Manchester United of encounters.' And Corbyn was up against Theresa May, for whom PMQs was also not her forte. In both cases, their over- and underperformance was to a significant extent cancelled out by their opponent.

For another thing, the House of Commons Chamber was probably Hague's strongest environment as a politician, and probably Corbyn's weakest – so if we look only at PMQs we are likely to overestimate Hague and underestimate Corbyn, who in leadership elections and general elections, if not in referendums, has shown himself to be at his most effective as a campaigner out in the country. And Hague told us that PMQs competence is more important for the Prime Minister than for the Leader of the Opposition anyway: 'A Prime Minister who was truly terrible at it, I think it would be quite a weakness in that Prime Minister, more than a weakness or a strength for a Leader of the Opposition. So it matters a bit more than my case or the Corbyn case might show.'

A Labour MP points out that whether Leaders of the Opposition like Parliament or not, if they become Prime Minister they will be accountable to it – so they need to make sure they get good at performing there: 'Demonstrating that the other side are useless in Parliament is quite important, and you only do that by being good in Parliament yourself, in my book. And if you're not, or if you neglect being good in Parliament, then you'll be shit as a minister, because in the end what will happen is that you *will* need to be good in Parliament because there's some crisis, and you won't be able to do it.'

The central question for this book is: does PMQs matter? It does: for a start, simply because it's there. Nothing that so dominates the lives and thoughts of the leaders of the government and opposition can be treated as unimportant, even if both resent it. ('How would you change PMQs?' we asked Ed Miliband. 'Abolish it!' he immediately replied, laughing, before swiftly backtracking.) Tony Blair told us, 'I never enjoyed doing it, because I never thought it was particularly important. Sorry, it was *really* important without being *truly* important, if you can see what I mean.' Simply because it was there, he had to be good at it – 'the thing about Prime Minister's Questions is that it is intimately linked to your authority as leader of your own side, so if you do badly, it's *bad*, and if you do a string of really bad PMQs you know you're in trouble' – even though he would rather have been anywhere else in the world at noon on a Wednesday.

The role of PMQs in defining both leaders' authority makes it vital that they perform well at it. All leaders have good weeks and bad weeks. Ed Miliband told us some advice he had been given by Blair: the trouble with PMQs is that if you have three bad ones your troops start to get a bit restive. Our own experience of working with him over the four and a half years of his leadership was that although he certainly did have bad weeks, he generally managed to produce a good performance when he really needed one, which may be one reason why he got from 2010 to 2015 without facing a leadership challenge. MPs on both sides are watching closely, and their sense of whether a leader is doing well or badly is absolutely sincere and instinctive. As Harriet Harman says, 'Any weaknesses you've got will be absolutely there for everybody to see. And that's another thing that TV and radio doesn't pick up. It doesn't see the faces of your ranks, of your side, party members watching it on TV. And those are the people who need to be going out and working hard for the party, supporting you in your work as leader, and they don't want to feel a kick in the stomach in the middle of the week. They want to go out feeling pumped up and ready to work twice as hard, reconvinced of the authority of the project.'

Doing badly at PMQs, as John Whittingdale told us, 'undermines a leader faster than anything. And I love him to bits but it probably wasn't Iain Duncan Smith's strength, and so every week he would be seen taking on Blair, who actually *was* good, and clearly not really landing a blow, and that will have probably contributed to the letters going in saying he's not up to the job.' Danny Finkelstein says that PMQs matters 'in terms of your relationship with your parliamentary party, which is crucial because you are the head of the parliamentary party, and it's important that they should regard you as their leader and the person putting the arguments forward in the best way'. He recalls one moment at PMQs in which William Hague, thinking on his feet at a moment of peril, produced an unscripted comeback to Tony Blair that was 'completely brilliant. And at that moment I thought to myself, "My God, thank God you're the leader, not me!" And everyone's got to feel that: "Thank God you're the leader, not me." That's a very important part of being able to lead a party full of people who think they're political professionals themselves, they've got to think, "Thank God you're doing it, not me." Rather than, sometimes with Iain Duncan Smith I was thinking, "Look, just hand me the papers, I'll do it."'

At its best, PMQs acts as a kind of quality control for our political leaders. David Cameron wrote in 2002 that 'a Prime Minister or Leader of the Opposition who was slow-witted, corrupt or simply not up to the job would not survive',[297] and Tony Blair wrote in his memoirs that 'an idiot couldn't survive one session. To survive and hold your head up over a period of time – let's say a year of being opposition leader – you have to be clever, significantly past a basic intellectual threshold, otherwise you will be eaten alive.'[298] Alastair Campbell states its importance even more simply: 'I do think one of the reasons that Tony lasted three terms was because he was good at PMQs.' Leaders who are good at PMQs do sometimes lose elections, but – at least since Parliament has been televised – no leader who is bad at PMQs has ever won one. (Margaret Thatcher in 1979 was probably the last poor PMQs performer to win an election; by her second election victory in 1983 she was much improved. In 2017, two leaders who were not particularly good at PMQs both failed to win a general election outright.)

Many of the people we spoke to for this book, in the second half of 2017, thought that PMQs was lower-key, and less important as a means of scrutinising the government, than it had been for some time, given the fact that neither Jeremy Corbyn nor Theresa May are natural star performers at the dispatch box, and that Corbyn's approach has taken some of the heat out of the exchanges. As a senior Conservative reflected to us, 'One argument would be, Corbyn is taking politics away from Parliament, and maybe Parliament doesn't matter any more. But on the other hand I think May would be completely finished if there was a decent Leader of the Opposition, she'd be screwed every week. She's not very good, she's pretty wooden and you'd have someone absolutely mercilessly pulling her apart on what Boris Johnson said or whatever, but Corbyn doesn't do that. And Corbyn might argue that that's all the politics of the past, and maybe we've moved into a new era of British politics, but I don't know. And actually with no majority in Parliament, exposing the weaknesses of the government on a daily basis, and thinking of topics that really identify where the government's weak, is very important.'

PMQs doesn't just test the leaders. It tests the entire operations that sit beneath both of them. The role of PMQs in holding the government to account is real, but it exists more in the vast preparation exercises that go on on both sides, in the process of identifying and dealing with weaknesses in order to head off the risk of embarrassment in the House of Commons Chamber, than in the questions and answers themselves. As William Hague says, 'A lot of the benefit of it is the hidden effect it has on governments: think of all the extra things governments would get away with if Question Time didn't exist.' Alastair Campbell told us, 'We would quite often go away afterwards and say, "Oh, that thing they said about such and such, that's a problem."'

Most obviously for the government but for the opposition too, PMQs is the political event that most drives self-analysis and bomb-proofing. Campbell says: 'I'd say most of our focus was on absolutely drilling down on detail and working out a line. And working out where we were vulnerable. I don't know if that's how we thought about it at the time, but it feels looking back that we were just constantly trying to make sense of all this big stuff and get it down into very tough questions, single lines, arguments that really were robust.' It forces the government to ask internally about, and find satisfactory answers to, everything that could conceivably be asked by an MP – a process that's worthwhile even if no MP actually asks the most difficult question. It forces the opposition to spot what the most difficult questions for the government are, and to identify its own political priorities and weaknesses. The fact that the Prime Minister will respond to the Leader of the Opposition means that the opposition has to ensure that its attacks on the government are grounded in reality, not just in wishful thinking and sloganising, and that its own alternative policy programme can stand up to scrutiny. It drives opposition policy-making too: if we're criticising this government failure, how far are we prepared to go in rectifying it, what can we commit to spending, do we have a credible alternative set of measures to put in place, or are we just cross?

An opposition that hasn't done this work and doesn't have a credible alternative will be easy to unpick at PMQs. As Neil Kinnock says, 'Obviously there is plenty of justification in complaining and protesting, on a galaxy of issues, but that's never enough. I don't mean in one Prime Minister's Questions session, it could be enough in one, but cumulatively it's not enough. In addition to complaint and protest you have to be able to declare a realistic alternative, and to do that, first of all the alternative must have substance and secondly the person offering the alternative has got to have credibility.'

As well as its role in developing policy, PMQs helps both sides develop a political narrative. David Cameron says: 'You soon find out your strongest defence lines, and they're partly dependent on what switches on the people behind you, and partly what your opponents see as potential weaknesses, so economic inheritance, perceived political weakness, whatever it was, you'd just keep hammering the same things.' It works the other way too, he told us: 'Attack lines work in the Commons sometimes better than they work in the country, but if you want to know whether a position you have is vulnerable the Commons is a good place to test it out.' Alastair Campbell says:

'I think over time we developed a sense of how important it could be. We definitely used it as a kind of strategic anvil. Partly it's the fact that we were all obsessed with our opponents all the time, they were in our heads all the time, we thought about them all the time. But I think we used PMQs quite well with all of them to work out their weaknesses, and also to destabilise them, diminish some of their strengths.'

We started writing this book knowing that PMQs is loathed as well as loved: loathed not just by many of the leaders who have to do it every single week, and by the advisers for whom the weekly PMQs grind is more chore than pleasure, but by many members of the public, and by professional politicians and observers of politics, who think it projects an image of politics, and of Westminster in particular, that is alienating, self-absorbed and inaccessible. They have a point. But we both know that when we were doing it, there was no political event we would rather have been working on. The high of knowing you've written a gag, or crafted a line of questioning, or uncovered an inconvenient fact, that's played a part in getting the better of the Prime Minister at PMQs is better than almost any other feeling in politics, apart from winning a general election; and it's a long time since anyone in the Labour Party has experienced that.

Prime Minister's Questions is still an important moment in the political week; when used well, and perhaps when used especially badly, it can be the most important moment. It's an opportunity to hold the most powerful person in the country to account, and a place where any backbencher, however little influence they may have with their party's leadership, can raise any issue they like and be guaranteed some prime ministerial attention. It's a place where the Prime Minister can demonstrate her command of the agenda, or her lack of it, and a means for her to exert control over the sprawl of government. It's a platform for the Leader of the Opposition to prosecute an argument and show the world why he should be in charge. It's a forum in which MPs can see what their leaders are made of, and leave with confidence or apprehension about their party's immediate political future. We can't defend every element of the noise and rowdiness of the packed House of Commons Chamber; but a sanitised, silent, polite PMQs would make life easier for the Prime Minister of the day. That is the opposite of what PMQs is meant to do. It is meant to put the Prime Minister – and the Leader of the Opposition – under pressure. The job of leading one's party and one's country, of achieving the office and of staying in it, should be hard.

The case for PMQs is not that with a few deft questions a Leader of the Opposition, or even a backbench MP, can expose the hollowness of a government's entire programme and bring down a Prime Minister. That would be to expect too much of it, and to misunderstand its role. PMQs is a weekly routine check-up, not major surgery. It helps governments to discover weaknesses and problems, and to take action to rectify them. It helps both sides to test arguments that they will later make elsewhere. It reveals to all of us what the parties' key themes and arguments are, where they think the other side is weak and, implicitly, where they think they have their own weaknesses: which areas they want to talk about and which they want to avoid. It tests the skills, judgement, resilience and, yes, wits of our political leaders, revealing aspects of their character which tell us much about what they consider important and unimportant, how they handle pressure, how they react when cornered and whether we should want them anywhere near power. It tells us whether they can make a persuasive argument in a compelling way in the face of instant criticism. In a world in which much of politics consists of two sides making their case independently of each other to separate audiences, it forces a direct clash of arguments, and of the skills of the two people entrusted by their parties with making those arguments, in the same place at the same time.

PMQs doesn't change the course of history. But it nudges it gently, and helps to identify the most promising places to push it. It absolutely still matters. For all its flaws, for all the noise and pantomime, it is a reflection of the best and worst of British politics, and a unique test of some of the skills which it is reasonable to expect of our political leaders. It is, in the end, a good thing that every Wednesday at noon the Prime Minister has to answer questions from all sides, including from people who want her job, and a good thing that the people who want her job have to show why they're worthy of it. Anything our political leaders fear so much is worth keeping.

NOTES

Introduction

1   Margaret Thatcher, *The Downing Street Years* (HarperCollins, 1993), p. 41.
2   George H. W. Bush, C-SPAN, 20 December 1991, available at https://youtube/tR7EUbnvNqY (accessed 28 February 2018).

Chapter 1: Evolution

3   G. W. Jones, 'The Prime Minister and Parliamentary Questions', *Parliamentary Affairs*, March 1973, p. 260.
4   Roy Jenkins, *Churchill: A Biography* (London: Macmillan, 2001), p. 336.
5   Jones, 'The Prime Minister and Parliamentary Questions', p. 262.
6   Jones, 'The Prime Minister and Parliamentary Questions', p. 261.
7   Peter Catterall (ed.), *The Macmillan Diaries: Prime Minister and After, 1957–66* (London: Macmillan, 2011), pp. 340–1.
8   Hansard, HC Deb, 18 June 1961, vol. 644, col. 1053.
9   Hansard, HC Deb, 24 October 1961, vol. 646, col. 740.
10 Hansard, HC Deb, 24 October 1961, vol. 646, col. 741.
11 Tam Dalyell, 'On the Decline of Intelligent Government', in Ivo Mosley (ed.), *Dumbing Down: Culture, Politics and the Mass Media* (Exeter: Imprint Academic, 2000), p. 12.
12 Hansard, HC Deb, 29 April 1975, vol. 891, col. 90W.
13 'MP's marathon speech sinks bill', BBC News, 2 December 2005, http://news.bbc.co.uk/1/hi/uk_politics/4492688.stm (accessed 28 February 2018).
14 Hansard, HC Deb, 13 February 1968, vol. 758, cols 1136–41.
15 Hansard, HC Deb, 29 June 1971, vol. 820, col. 200.

16   Matthew Parris, *I Couldn't Possibly Comment... Sketches and Follies from the Commons Again* (London: Robson, 1997), p. 242.

17   Hansard, HC Deb, 21 May 1997, vol. 294, col. 702.

18   Catterall (ed.), *The Macmillan Diaries*, p. 312.

19   Hansard, HC Deb, 5 July 1960, vol. 626, cols 227–30.

20   Jones, 'The Prime Minister and Parliamentary Questions', p. 265.

21   Hansard, HC Deb, 12 July 1979, vol. 970, col. 663.

22   Hansard, HC Deb, 12 July 1979, vol. 970, col. 664.

23   Hansard, HC Deb, 24 March 1964, vol. 692, col. 242.

24   Jones, 'The Prime Minister and Parliamentary Questions', p. 271.

25   John Campbell, *Margaret Thatcher, vol. 2: The Iron Lady* (London: Jonathan Cape, 2003), p. 453.

26   Peter Hennessy, *The Prime Minister: The Office and Its Holders since 1945* (London: Allen Lane, 2000), p. 81.

27   Dalyell, 'On the Decline of Intelligent Government', p. 12.

28   Margaret Thatcher, *The Downing Street Years* (London: HarperCollins, 1993), p. 41.

29   Hansard, HC Deb, 1 July 2015, vol. 597, col. 1477.

30   Theo Bertram, 'The Power and Purpose of PMQs', *Medium*, 3 March 2017, https://medium.com/@theobertram/the-power-and-purpose-of-pmqs-861c95d4e0f5 (accessed 28 February 2018).

31   Hansard, HC Deb, 22 February 1962, vol. 654, col. 629.

32   Charles Moore, *Margaret Thatcher: The Authorized Biography, vol. 1: Not for Turning* (London: Penguin, 2013), p. 385.

33   Hansard, HC Deb, 20 November 1985, vol. 87, col. 301.

34   John Campbell, *Margaret Thatcher, vol. 2: The Iron Lady* (London: Jonathan Cape, 2003), p. 458.

35   Hansard, HC Deb, 20 November 1985, vol. 87, col. 305.

36   Nick Robinson, *Live from Downing Street: The Inside Story of Politics, Power and the Media* (London: Bantam Press, 2012), p. 242.

37   Christopher Hope and Lydia Willgress, 'Margaret Thatcher's television training before cameras first broadcast from House of Commons revealed', *Daily Telegraph*, 1 January 2017, http://www.telegraph.co.uk/news/2017/01/01/margaret-thatchers-television-training-cameras-first-broadcast (accessed 28 February 2018).

38   Robinson, *Live from Downing Street*, p. 243.

39   Hansard, HC Deb, 24 February 2016, vol. 606, col. 291.

40   Jeremy Corbyn, Twitter, 24 February 2016, https://twitter.com/jeremycorbyn/status/702472149001478145 (accessed 28 February 2018).

41   Tom Newton Dunn, 'SUITS YOU, JEZ! Jeremy Corbyn's aides have forced him to wear blue suits so voters see him as PM material', *The Sun*, 30 May 2017, https://www.thesun.co.uk/news/3684529/jeremy-corbyns-aides-have-forced-him-to-wear-blue-suits-so-voters-see-him-as-pm-material (accessed 28 February 2018).

42   Gyles Brandreth, *Breaking the Code: Westminster Diaries, 1990–2007* (London: Biteback, 2014), p. 437.

43   Brandreth, *Breaking the Code*, p. 438.

44   Dalyell, 'On the Decline of Intelligent Government', p. 11.

45   Hansard, HC Deb, 12 May 1964, vol. 695, col. 218.

46   Hansard, HC Deb, 12 May 1964, vol. 695, col. 220.

47   Hansard, HC Deb, 12 May 1964, vol. 695, col. 224.

48   Norman Shrapnel, *The Performers: Politics as Theatre* (London: Constable, 1978), p. 65.

49   Alwyn W. Turner, *Crisis? What Crisis? Britain in the 1970s* (London: Aurum Press, 2008), p. 18.

50   Shrapnel, *The Performers*, p. 65.

51   John Bercow, speech to the Centre for Parliamentary Studies, 6 June 2010, http://www.johnbercow.co.uk/content/speech-centre-parliamentary-studies (accessed 28 February 2018).

52   Bercow, speech to the Centre for Parliamentary Studies.

53   Bercow, speech to the Centre for Parliamentary Studies.

54   Andy McSmith, *John Smith: Playing the Long Game* (London: Verso, 1993), p. 233.

55   Hansard, HC Deb, 9 June 1993, vol. 226, col. 292.

56   Hansard, HC Deb, 26 October 1993, vol. 230, col. 687.

57   Hansard, HC Deb, 12 May 1994, vol. 243, col. 429.

58   Hansard, HC Deb, 6 December 1994, vol. 251, col. 139.

59   Bercow, speech to the Centre for Parliamentary Studies.

60   Labour Party manifesto 1997, available at http://www.politicsresources.net/area/uk/man/lab97.htm (accessed 1 March 2018).

61   Tony Blair, *A Journey* (London: Hutchinson, 2010), p. 108.

62   Hansard, HC Deb, 21 May 1997, vol. 294, col. 703.

63   'Blair's a bore in USA: American viewers critical of Tony Blair's question time', *The People*, 15 June 1997.

64   Blair, *A Journey*, p. 108.

65   Sarah Womack, 'I was no elected dictator, says Lady Thatcher', *Daily Telegraph*, 2 June 2001, http://www.telegraph.co.uk/news/uknews/1311216/I-was-no-elected-dictator-says-Lady-Thatcher.html (accessed 1 March 2018).

66   Michael Prescott, 'Blair will cut question time', *Sunday Times*, 27 April 1997.

67   Betty Boothroyd, interview with Dominic Sandbrook, 'Mind Your PMQs', *Archive on 4*, BBC Radio 4, 22 October 2011, http://www.bbc.co.uk/programmes/b0167rdw (accessed 1 March 2018).

68   Hansard, HC Deb, 4 June 1997, vol. 295, col. 350.

Chapter 2: The Questions

69   Hansard, HC Deb, 29 April 2009, vol. 491, cols 858–60.

70   Hansard, HC Deb, 7 March 2007, vol. 457, col. 1513.

71   Alistair Horne, *Macmillan, 1957–1986: Volume II of the Official Biography* (London: Macmillan, 1989), p. 156.

72   Hansard, HC Deb, 28 October 1998, vol. 318, cols 329–30.

73   Hansard, HC Deb, 18 March 1998, vol. 308, col. 1282.

74   Hansard, HC Deb, 1 July 2009, vol. 495, col. 294.

75   Hansard, HC Deb, 7 June 1990, vol. 173, cols 783–4.

76   Hansard, HC Deb, 9 October 2013, vol. 568, col. 151.

77   Charles Moore, *Margaret Thatcher: The Authorized Biography, Volume Two: Everything She Wants* (London: Allen Lane, 2015), p. 165.

78   Hansard, HC Deb, 11 January 2012, vol. 538, cols 172–3.

79   Hansard, HC Deb, 8 February 2017, vol. 621, cols 420–2.

80   Hansard, HC Deb, 15 October 2014, vol. 586, col. 292.

81   Hansard, HC Deb, 25 November 2009, vol. 501, col. 525.

82   Hansard, HC Deb, 30 November 2009, vol. 501, col. 836.

83   Iain Martin, 'Michael Gove in the Cameron Dog House', *Wall Street Journal*, 30 November 2009, https://blogs.wsj.com/iainmartin/2009/11/30/michael-gove-in-the-cameron-dog-house (accessed 1 March 2018).

84   Hansard, HC Deb, 13 March 2013, vol. 560, col. 297.

85   Hansard, HC Deb, 13 March 2013, vol. 560, col. 298.

86   Hansard, HC Deb, 5 July 2000, vol. 353, col. 323.

87   Hansard, HC Deb, 27 Feb 2002, vol. 380, col. 703.

88   Hansard, HC Deb, 26 February 2003, vol. 400, col. 253.

89   Hansard, HC Deb, 22 October 2003, vol. 411, col. 637.

90   Hansard, HC Deb, 19 June 2002, vol. 387, col. 268.

91   Hansard, HC Deb, 3 July 2002, vol. 388, col. 220.

92   Hansard, HC Deb, 8 January 2003, vol. 397, col. 166.

93   Hansard, HC Deb, 5 December 1996, vol. 286, col. 1199.

94   Hansard, HC Deb, 5 December 1996, vol. 286, col. 1200.

95   Hansard, HC Deb, 5 December 1996, vol. 286, col. 1200.

96   Alastair Campbell, *The Blair Years: Extracts from the Alastair Campbell Diaries* (London: Hutchinson, 2007), p. 140.

97   Ed Miliband, *The Andrew Marr Show*, BBC One, 27 July 2014, http://news.bbc.co.uk/1/shared/bsp/hi/pdfs/100101.pdf (accessed 1 March 2018).

98   Jeremy Corbyn, email to Labour Party members, 12 September 2015.

99   Hansard, HC Deb, 16 September 2015, vol. 599, col. 1037.

100 Hansard, HC Deb, 16 September 2015, vol. 599, col. 1037.

101 Hansard, HC Deb, 28 June 2017, vol. 626, cols 585–98.

102 Hansard, HC Deb, 21 October 2015, vol. 600, col. 950.

Chapter 3: Norman Shaw South

103 Alastair Campbell, *The Blair Years: Extracts from the Alastair Campbell Diaries* (London: Hutchinson, 2007), p. 69.

104 Tony Blair, *A Journey* (London: Hutchinson, 2010), p. 111.

105 Ben Wright, *Order, Order! The Rise and Fall of Political Drinking* (London: Duckworth Overlook, 2016), p. 159.

106 Francis Elliott and James Hanning, *Cameron: Practically a Conservative* (London: Fourth Estate, 2012), p. 224.

107 Peter Snowdon, *Back from the Brink: The Inside Story of the Tory Resurrection*, (London: HarperPress, 2010), p. 104.

108 Rachel Sylvester, 'Power exposes the Tories' internal tensions', *The Times*, 17 April 2012, https://www.thetimes.co.uk/article/power-exposes-the-tories-internal-tensions-8zmwogpdqtpm (accessed 14 March 2018).

109 Hansard, HC Deb, 18 April 2012, vol. 543, col. 314.

110 Alistair Horne, *Macmillan, 1957–1986: Volume II of the Official Biography* (London: Macmillan, 1989), p. 153.

111 Hansard, HC Deb, 9 April 2014, vol. 579, col. 258.

112 Hansard, HC Deb, 15 March 2017, vol. 623, col. 387.

113 Hansard, HC Deb, 15 March 2017, vol. 623, col. 386.

114 Hansard, HC Deb, 13 October 2010, vol. 516, col. 323.

115 Patrick Wintour and Allegra Stratton, 'Ed Miliband sets out "profound" changes to Labour party', *The Guardian*, 22 November 2010, https://www.theguardian.com/politics/2010/nov/21/ed-miliband-profound-changes-labour (accessed 2 March 2018).

116 Hansard, HC Deb, 24 November 2010, vol. 519, col. 259.

117 Hansard, HC Deb, 11 September 2013, vol. 567, col. 971.

118 John Healey, speech to the King's Fund, 20 January 2011, available at http://www.healthpolicyinsight.com/?q=node/922 (accessed 2 March 2018).

119 Hansard, HC Deb, 9 February 2011, vol. 523, col. 299.

120 Hansard, HC Deb, 7 February 2001, vol. 362, col. 918.

121 Hansard, HC Deb, 15 March 2006, vol. 443, col. 1449.

122 Sam Jones, 'Clegg tots up sex encounters in *GQ* interview', *The Guardian*, 1 April 2008, https://www.theguardian.com/politics/2008/apr/01/nickclegg.pressandpublishing (accessed 2 March 2018).

123 Hansard, HC Deb, 10 December 2008, vol. 485, col. 530.

124 Hansard, HC Deb, 10 December 2014, vol. 589, cols 864–5.

Chapter 4: The Answers

125 Hansard, HC Deb, 13 September 2017, vol. 628, col. 833.

126 *More or Less*, BBC Radio 4, 17 September 2017.

127   Giles Kenningham, 'The art of PMQs (it helps if the opposition text you ideas)', *The Times*, 7 February 2018, https://www.thetimes.co.uk/article/the-art-of-pmqs-it-helps-if-the-opposition-text-you-ideas-kh8wgmnqr (accessed 16 March 2018).

128   Hansard, HC Deb, 12 February 2014, vol. 575, col. 842.

129   Hansard, HC Deb, 16 February 2011, vol. 521, col. 952.

130   Hansard, HC Deb, 25 January 2017, vol. 620, cols 285–6.

131   Hansard, HC Deb, 11 October 2017, vol. 629, col. 323.

132   Hansard, HC Deb, 15 November 2017, vol. 631, col. 357.

133   Hansard, HC Deb, 25 March 2015, vol. 594, col. 1423.

134   Hansard, HC Deb, 14 December 2011, vol. 537, col. 785.

135   Hansard, HC Deb, 30 April 2014, vol. 579, col. 820.

136   Hansard, HC Deb, 4 November 2009, vol. 498, col. 849.

137   Hansard, HC Deb, 6 December 2017, vol. 632, col. 1027.

138   Tony Blair, *A Journey* (London: Hutchinson, 2010), p. 489.

139   Hansard, HC Deb, 6 September 2017, vol. 628, col. 150.

140   Hansard, HC Deb, 1 February 2017, vol. 620, col. 1017.

141   Hansard, HC Deb, 19 October 2016, vol. 615, col 799.

Chapter 5: No. 10 Downing Street

142   Alistair Horne, *Macmillan, 1957–1986: Volume II of the Official Biography* (London: Macmillan, 1989), p. 154.

143   G. W. Jones, 'The Prime Minister and Parliamentary Questions', *Parliamentary Affairs*, March 1973, p. 270.

144   Hansard, HC Deb, 19 November 1997, vol. 301, col. 323.

145   Hansard, HC Deb, 23 October 1984, vol. 65, col. 552.

146   Jones, 'The Prime Minister and Parliamentary Questions', p. 269.

147   John Campbell, *Margaret Thatcher, vol. 2: The Iron Lady* (London: Jonathan Cape, 2003), p. 479.

148   Hansard, HC Deb, 29 February 2012, vol. 541, cols 283–4.

149   Hansard, HC Deb, 4 July 2007, vol. 462, cols 951–2.

150   Hansard, HC Deb, 26 October 1989, vol. 178, cols 1044–5.

151   Nigel Lawson, *The View From No. 11: Memoirs of a Tory Radical* (London: Bantam Press, 1992), p. 963.

Chapter 6: The Joust

152   Hansard, HC Deb, 8 December 2010, vol. 520, col. 300.

153   Hansard, HC Deb, 26 June 2013, vol. 565, cols 292–3.

154   Hansard, HC Deb, 18 March 2009, vol. 489, cols 901–2.

155   Hansard, HC Deb, 11 May 2011, vol. 527, col. 1155.

156 Hansard, HC Deb, 25 October 2017, vol. 630, cols 294–5.

157 Hansard, HC Deb, 23 April 2008, vol. 474, col. 1305.

158 Hansard, HC Deb, 20 November 2013, vol. 570, col. 1222.

159 Hansard, HC Deb, 30 January 1997, vol. 289, cols 502–4.

160 Alastair Campbell, *The Blair Years: Extracts from the Alastair Campbell Diaries* (London: Hutchinson, 2007), p. 55.

161 Gyles Brandreth, *Breaking the Code: Westminster Diaries, 1990–2007* (London: Biteback, 2014), p. 290.

162 Hansard, HC Deb, 25 April 1995, vol. 258, cols 655–6.

163 Hansard, HC Deb, 20 July 2016, vol. 613, col. 819.

164 Hansard, HC Deb, 7 December 2005, vol. 440, col. 861.

165 Hansard, HC Deb, 7 December 2005, vol. 440, col. 861.

166 See for example Hansard, HC Deb, 26 January 1995, vol. 253, col. 468.

167 Hansard, HC Deb, 7 December 2005, vol. 440, col. 861.

168 Hansard, HC Deb, 13 June 2012, vol. 546, col. 317.

169 Hansard, HC Deb, 3 December 2003, vol. 415, col. 498.

170 Hansard, HC Deb, 3 December 1997, vol. 302, col. 347.

171 Hansard, HC Deb, 7 June 1989, vol. 154, col. 249.

172 Hansard, HC Deb, 17 November 1999, vol. 339, col. 16.

173 Hansard, HC Deb, 4 February 2015, vol. 592, col. 265.

174 Hansard, HC Deb, 10 June 1993, vol. 227, col. 168.

175 Norman Shrapnel, *The Performers: Politics as Theatre* (London: Constable, 1978), p. 190.

176 Hansard, HC Deb, 27 February 2013, vol. 559, col. 305.

177 Hansard, HC Deb, 27 November 2013, vol. 571, col. 251.

178 Hansard, HC Deb, 2 April 2014, vol. 578, col. 877.

179 Hansard, HC Deb, 7 September 2016, vol. 614, col. 325.

180 Hansard, HC Deb, 18 January 2017, vol. 619, col. 928.

Chapter 7: The Chamber

181 'PMQs noise levels tested by Alun Cairns and Tessa Munt', BBC News, 17 July 2013, http://www.bbc.co.uk/news/av/uk-politics-23346854/pmqs-noise-levels-tested-by-alun-cairns-and-tessa-munt (accessed 6 March 2018).

182 'MP mimics Ed Miliband's questions in Commons', *The Telegraph*, 25 November 2011, http://www.telegraph.co.uk/news/newsvideo/uk-politics-video/8915110/MP-mimics-Ed-Milibands-questions-in-Commons.html (accessed 6 March 2018).

183 'Ed Miliband PMQs briefing notes left in Commons toilets', BBC News, 3 July 2013, http://www.bbc.co.uk/news/uk-politics-23166053 (accessed 6 March 2018).

184 Hansard, HC Deb, 9 February 2000, vol. 344, col. 243.

185 Hansard, HC Deb, 9 February 2000, vol. 344, col. 246.

186 Gyles Brandreth, *Breaking the Code: Westminster Diaries, 1990–2007* (London: Biteback, 2014), p. 227.

187 Alistair Horne, *Macmillan, 1957–1986: Volume II of the Official Biography* (London: Macmillan, 1989), pp. 153–4.

188 Hansard, HC Deb, 9 December 2015, vol. 603, col. 985.

189 Hansard, HC Deb, 20 March 1997, vol. 292, col. 1072.

190 Hansard, HC Deb, 13 January 2010, vol. 503, cols 684–5.

191 Hansard, HC Deb, 4 March 2015, vol. 593, col. 938.

192 Hansard, HC Deb, 13 October 2010, vol. 516, col. 327.

193 Hansard, HC Deb, 10 December 2008, vol. 485, col. 527.

194 Hansard, HC Deb, 14 October 2015, vol. 600, col. 433.

195 Hansard, HC Deb, 22 February 2016, vol. 606, col. 26.

196 Andrew S. Crines, Timothy Heppell and Peter Dorey, *The Political Rhetoric and Oratory of Margaret Thatcher* (London: Palgrave Macmillan, 2016), p. 25.

197 Hansard, HC Deb, 22 May 1979, vol. 967, col. 867.

198 Margaret Thatcher in *Daily Mail*, 4 May 1989, quoted in Patrick Dunleavy, G. W. Jones and Brendan O'Leary, 'Prime Ministers and the Commons: Patterns of Behaviour, 1868 to 1987', *Public Administration*, vol. 68 (1990), p. 135.

199 Norman Shrapnel, *The Performers: Politics as Theatre* (London: Constable, 1978), p. 126.

200 Lesley Abdela, *Women with X Appeal: Women Politicians in Britain Today* (London: Optima, 1989), p. 23.

201 Jackie Ashley, 'Bullied, patronised and abused – women MPs reveal the truth about life inside Westminster', *The Guardian*, 7 December 2004, https://www.theguardian.com/politics/2004/dec/07/uk.gender (accessed 7 March 2018).

202 Abdela, *Women with X Appeal*, pp. 27–8.

203 Sophy Ridge, *The Women Who Shaped Politics: Empowering Stories of Women Who Have Shifted the Political Landscape* (London: Coronet, 2017), p. 225.

204 '"School pioneer" Toby Young tweets about MP's breasts during PMQs', Political Scrapbook, 7 March 2012, https://politicalscrapbook.net/2012/03/school-pioneer-toby-young-tweets-about-mps-breasts-during-pmqs/ (accessed 15 March 2018).

205 Hansard, HC Deb, 5 February 2014, vol. 575, col. 265.

206 Hansard, HC Deb, 27 April 2011, vol. 527, col. 170.

207 Hansard, HC Deb, 7 September 2011, vol. 532, col. 354.

208 Ed Balls, *Speaking Out: Lessons in Life and Politics*, (London: Arrow, 2017), p. 345.

209 Balls, *Speaking Out*, p. 346.

210 Hansard, HC Deb, 23 May 2012, vol. 545, col. 1131.

211 Oliver Wright, 'Cut out the Flashman act, aides tell David Cameron', *The Independent*, 10 May 2011, http://www.independent.co.uk/news/uk/politics/cut-out-the-flashman-act-aides-tell-david-cameron-2282105.html (accessed 7 March 2018).

212 Hansard, HC Deb, 11 June 2011, vol. 527, col. 1156.

213 Andy McSmith, *John Smith: Playing the Long Game* (London: Verso, 1993), p. 249.

214 Hansard, HC Deb, 17 June 1993, vol. 226, col. 989.

215 Hansard, HC Deb, 3 November 1999, vol. 337, col. 286.

216 Hansard, HC Deb, 10 October 2007, vol. 464, col. 287.

217 Hansard, HC Deb, 19 April 1983, vol. 41, col. 159.

Chapter 8: Backbenchers and Smaller Parties

218 Paul Flynn, *How to Be an MP* (London: Biteback, 2012), p. 45.

219 Hansard, HC Deb, 24 April 2002, vol. 384, col. 328.

220 David Cameron, 'Taking on No. 10', *The Guardian*, 2 May 2002, https://www.theguardian.com/politics/2002/may/02/davidcameron.politicalcolumnists (accessed 7 March 2018).

221 Hansard, HC Deb, 9 March 2016, vol. 607, col. 271.

222 Hansard, HC Deb, 19 December 2012, vol. 555, col. 849.

223 Hansard, HC Deb, 30 January 2013, vol. 557, col. 904.

224 Hansard, HC Deb, 27 February 2002, vol. 380, col. 698.

225 Flynn, *How to Be an MP*, pp. 46–7.

226 Hansard, HC Deb, 13 April 1989, vol. 150, col. 1056.

227 Cameron, 'Taking on No. 10'.

228 Hansard, HC Deb, 19 December 2012, vol. 555, col. 841.

229 Hansard, HC Deb, 27 February 2013, vol. 559, col. 302.

230 Hansard, HC Deb, 27 February 2013, vol. 559, col. 302.

231 Emily Ashton, 'How Prime Minister's Questions is staged by Tory MPs', *Buzzfeed*, 29 January 2015, https://www.buzzfeed.com/emilyashton/how-prime-ministers-questions-is-staged-by-tory-mps (accessed 7 March 2018).

232 G. W. Jones, 'The Prime Minister and Parliamentary Questions', *Parliamentary Affairs*, March 1973, p. 263.

233 Stephen R. Bates, Peter Kerr, Christopher Byrne and Liam Stanley, 'Questions to the Prime Minister: A Comparative Study of PMQs from Thatcher to Cameron', *Parliamentary Affairs*, April 2014, p. 268.

234 Gyles Brandreth, *Breaking the Code: Westminster Diaries, 1990–2007* (London: Biteback, 2015), p. 219.

235 Hansard, HC Deb, 18 March 1998, vol. 308, col. 1288.

236 Ashton, 'How Prime Minister's Questions is staged by Tory MPs'.

237 Ashton, 'How Prime Minister's Questions is staged by Tory MPs'.

238 Hansard, HC Deb, 10 June 2009, vol. 493, col. 785.

239 Menzies Campbell, *My Autobiography* (London: Hodder & Stoughton, 2008), p. 258.

240 Quoted in Flynn, *How to Be an MP*, p. 48.

241 Hansard, HC Deb, 11 January 2006, vol. 441, col. 279.

242 Campbell, *My Autobiography*, p. 246.

243 Hansard, HC Deb, 10 May 2006, vol. 446, col. 308.

244 Campbell, *My Autobiography*, p. 258.

245 Hansard, HC Deb, 28 November 2007, vol. 468, col. 275.

246 Theo Bertram, interviewed in 'How to Fix… PMQs', *Prospect* podcast, 3 October 2017, https://www.prospectmagazine.co.uk/howtofix (accessed 7 March 2018).

Chapter 9: The Spinners and the Lobby

247 Patrick Kidd, 'The Times Diary: an oldie but a goodie', *The Times*, 4 February 2016, https://www.thetimes.co.uk/article/the-times-diary-an-oldie-but-a-goodie-9t27vqs90 (accessed 8 March 2018).

248 Chris Moncrieff, '50 years of PMQs', *The Independent*, 16 July 2011, http://www.independent.co.uk/news/uk/politics/50-years-of-pmqs-2314966.html (accessed 8 March 2018).

249 Hansard, HC Deb, 17 October 2012, vol. 551, col. 316.

250 Quoted in 'People: Penelope Keith, Bruce Forsyth and David Cameron', *The Times*, 19 February 2008, https://www.thetimes.co.uk/article/people-penelope-keith-bruce-forsyth-and-david-cameron-9mzqnzttk5v (accessed 8 March 2018).

251 *Q*, October 2016.

Chapter 10: Stand-Ins and Deputies

252 'Attendance of the Prime Minister at Prime Minister's Questions (PMQs) since 1979', House of Commons Library briefing paper, 18 May 2016, http://researchbriefings.parliament.uk/ResearchBriefing/Summary/SN04401 (accessed 8 March 2018).

253 Hansard, HC Deb, 15 February 2006, vol. 442, col. 1413.

254 Michael Crick, *Militant* (London: Biteback, 2016), pp. vii–viii.

255 Hansard, HC Deb, 15 October 2014, vol. 586, col. 290.

256 Tony Blair, *A Journey* (London: Hutchinson, 2010), p. 330.

257 Simon Hoggart, 'Winning the heart disease with Bruiser Prescott', *The Guardian*, 25 March 2004, https://www.theguardian.com/politics/2004/mar/25/houseofcommons.politicalcolumnists (accessed 8 March 2018).

258 Simon Hoggart, 'Prescott plunges into shark infested waters', *The Guardian*, 1 November 2001, https://www.theguardian.com/politics/2001/nov/01/houseofcommons.politicalcolumnists (accessed 8 March 2018).

259 Hansard, HC Deb, 2 April 2008, vol. 474, col. 761.

260 Hansard, HC Deb, 2 April 2008, vol. 474, col. 761.

261 Hansard, HC Deb, 21 July 2010, vol. 514, col. 346.

262 Andrew Porter, 'Coalition confusion as Nick Clegg tells Commons that the Iraq war was illegal', *Daily Telegraph*, 21 July 2010, http://www.telegraph.co.uk/news/politics/nick-clegg/7903576/Coalition-confusion-as-Nick-Clegg-tells-Commons-that-the-Iraq-war-was-illegal.html (accessed 8 March 2018).

263 Hansard, HC Deb, 10 November 2010, vol. 518, col. 280.

264 Hansard, HC Deb, 17 June 2015, vol. 597, col. 310.

265 Lloyd Evans, 'Emily Thornberry's PMQs performance should worry Jeremy Corbyn', *The Spectator*, 7 December 2016, https://blogs.spectator.co.uk/2016/12/emily-thornberrys-pmqs-performance-worry-jeremy-corbyn/ (accessed 9 March 2018).

266 Chris Moncrieff, '50 years of PMQs', *The Independent*, 16 July 2011, http://www.independent.co.uk/news/uk/politics/50-years-of-pmqs-2314966.html (accessed 8 March 2018).

Chapter 11: 'That is that. The end.'

267 Hansard, HC Deb, 13 July 2016, vol. 613, col. 284.

268 Hansard, HC Deb, 27 November 1990, vol. 181, col. 740.

269 Hansard, HC Deb, 27 November 1990, vol. 181, col. 739.

270 Hansard, HC Deb, 27 November 1990, vol. 181, col. 740.

271 Hansard, HC Deb, 27 November 1990, vol. 181, col. 738.

272 Hansard, HC Deb, 27 June 2007, vol. 462, col. 330.

273 Hansard, HC Deb, 27 June 2007, vol. 462, col. 330.

274 Hansard, HC Deb, 27 June 2007, vol. 462, cols 333–4.

275 Hansard, HC Deb, 27 June 2007, vol. 462, cols 330–1.

276 Hansard, HC Deb, 13 July 2016, vol. 613, col. 289.

277 Hansard, HC Deb, 13 July 2016, vol. 613, col. 291.

278 Hansard, HC Deb, 13 July 2016, vol. 613, col. 294.

279 Tony Blair, *A Journey* (London: Hutchinson, 2010), p. 110.

280 *Daily Politics*, BBC Two, 9 September 2015.

Chapter 12: Punch and Judy Politics

281 Tony Blair, *A Journey* (London: Hutchinson, 2010), p. 109.

282 David Cameron, speech on winning the Conservative Party leadership, 6 December 2005, available at https://www.theguardian.com/politics/2005/dec/06/toryleadership2005.conservatives3 (accessed 9 March 2018).

283 David Cameron, 'How Do the Conservatives Win This Time?', speech to Independent News & Media Fringe, Conservative Party conference, 4 October 2004.

284 Dominic Lawson, 'News Review interview: David Cameron', *Sunday Times*, 23 November 2008, https://www.thetimes.co.uk/article/news-review-interview-david-cameron-2b23v0508wt (accessed 9 March 2018).

285 Peter Riddell, *In Defence of Politicians (In Spite of Themselves)* (London: Biteback, 2011), p. 33.

286 Hansard, HC Deb, 2 February 2011, vol. 522, col. 853.

287 Francis Elliott and James Hanning, *Cameron: Practically a Conservative* (London: Fourth Estate, 2012), p. 225.

288 *Tuned In or Turned Off? Public Attitudes to Prime Minister's Questions*, Hansard Society, 2014, p. 5, available at https://assets.contentful.com/u1rlvvbs33ri/46hBiI2AYo6OmicoOCW2cS/791191941cacaa140a87ab31935d3382/Publication__Tuned-In-or-Turned-Off-Public-Attitudes-to-Prime-Ministers-Questions.pdf (accessed 9 March 2018).

289 *Tuned In or Turned Off?*, p. 31.

290 Hansard, HC Deb, 11 September 2013, vol. 567, col. 971.

291 David Cameron, Sky News, 9 January 2012.

292 *Tuned In or Turned Off?*, p. 6.

293 *Tuned In or Turned Off?*, p. 23.

294 *Tuned In or Turned Off?*, p. 15.

295 *Tuned In or Turned Off?*, p. 31.

296 Hansard, HC Deb, 16 September 2015, vol. 599, col. 1037.

297 David Cameron, 'Taking on No. 10', *The Guardian*, 2 May 2002, https://www.theguardian.com/politics/2002/may/02/davidcameron.politicalcolumnists (accessed 7 March 2018).

298 Blair, *A Journey*, p. 393.

INDEX

Baker, Kenneth 19
Balls, Ed 62, 190, 197, 219–20, 225–6,
    292–3
Beckett, Margaret 257
Benn, Hilary 293, 294
Bercow, John
    on questions of Leader of the
        Opposition 25
    on Neil Kinnock at PMQs 26
    on John Smith at PMQs 27
    on length of PMQs 36–7
    and David Cameron at PMQs
        118–19, 160
    and Gordon Brown at PMQs 129
    on Tony Blair's first PMQs 141
    on noise levels at PMQs 204–5
    support for backbenchers at
        PMQs 228–9
    and small parties at PMQs 247
    and televising of PMQs 275–6
    defence of PMQs 325
Bertin, Gabby 23, 259, 260, 262, 263,
    264, 265, 266, 269
Bertram, Theo
    on preparation for PMQs 15–16, 140
    preparing Gordon Brown for
        PMQs 140–41, 157, 158
    on Tony Blair's preparation for
        PMQs 151–2
    on jokes during PMQs 190
    on David Cameron's self-control
        during PMQs 218–19
    on Gordon Brown's authenticity
        221–2
    and coup attempt against Gordon
        Brown 252
    on stand-ins for PMQs 284
Biffen, John 297
Blair, Tony
    on importance of PMQs xvii, 330,
        331–2
    on American interest in PMQs
        xviii

changes to PMQs 2, 10, 30–3
and engagement questions 10
and Prime Minister's office 15
wears make-up for PMQs 21–2
questions as Leader of the
    Opposition 27–8
and blocks of questions from
    William Hague 35
choosing questions for PMQs 40
questioning style of 44
and William Hague's questioning
    style 45–9
strategies for PMQs 52
ambush questions from William
    Hague 61
humorous questions from
    William Hague 62–4
detailed questions from Iain
    Duncan Smith 64–5
asking detailed questions 65–7
preparations for PMQs 78, 84, 87,
    88, 136–7, 141, 147, 151–3, 155–6
attitude to Iain Duncan Smith
    90–91
mimicked by George Osborne
    97, 98
answers at PMQs 121, 130–31, 134
Conservative difficulties with 132
question to Margaret Thatcher 142
glasses needed for PMQs 148
exchanges at PMQs 165, 175–80,
    182–3, 185
on noise levels at PMQs 195
and front bench during PMQs 198
and Alun Michael's resignation
    199
effectiveness at PMQs 223
on questions from backbenchers
    229–30
'teaser' questions 233
planted questions to 241–2
question from Menzies Campbell
    249

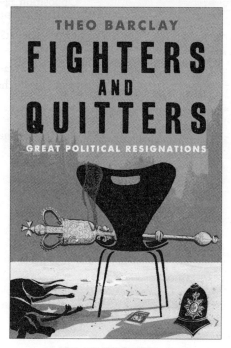

336PP HARDBACK, £20

They say the first rule of politics is never to resign. It seems, however, that Britain's leaders have all too often failed — or refused — to heed this sage advice.

Fighters and Quitters charts the scandals, controversies and cock-ups that obliterated dreams of high office: from the ex-minister who faked his death in the 1970s, to Geoffrey Howe's plot to topple Margaret Thatcher in the 1990s, Chris Huhne's journey from dispatch box to jail cell in 2013 and up to Damian Green's demise in the 'Pestminster' furore of 2017. Then there are the sex and spy scandals that heralded doom, from peers busted in bed with prostitutes, to MPs caught cavorting in public parks and, of course, the infamous Profumo affair.

Who jumped and who was pushed? Who battled to keep their job and who collapsed at the first hint of pressure? Who returned, Lazarus-like, for a second act? From humiliating surrenders to principled departures, *Fighters and Quitters* lifts the lid on the lives of the politicians who fell on their swords.

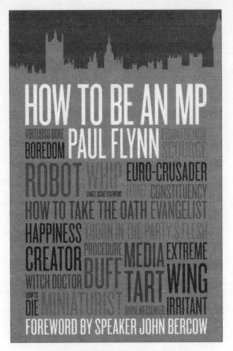